NEW POLITICAL ECONOMY

Edited by
Stephen Resnick
University of Massachusetts

A ROUTLEDGE SERIES

NEW POLITICAL ECONOMY

STEPHEN RESNICK, *General Editor*

POLITICAL ECONOMY FROM BELOW
*Economic Thought in Communitarian
Anarchism, 1840–1914*
Rob Knowles

STRUCTURALISM AND INDIVIDUALISM IN
ECONOMIC ANALYSIS
*The "Contractionary Devaluation
Debate" in Development Economics*
S. Charusheela

STRUCTURALISM AND INDIVIDUALISM IN ECONOMIC ANALYSIS

The "Contractionary Devaluation Debate" in Development Economics

S. Charusheela

Routledge
Taylor & Francis Group

NEW YORK AND LONDON

Published in 2005 by
Routledge
711 Third Avenue, New York, NY 10017

Published in Great Britain by
Routledge
2 Park Square, Milton Park, Abingdon, Oxfordshire OX14 4RN

Routledge is an imprint of the Taylor & Francis Group.

First issued in paperback 2012

Library of Congress Cataloging-In-Publication Data

Charusheela, S., 1964–
    Structuralism and individualism in economic analysis : the "contractionary devaluation debate" in development economics / S. Charusheela.
        p. cm. -- (New political economy)
    Includes bibliographical references and index
    ISBN 0-415-94927-0
    1. Developing countries--Economic policy. 2. Economic development. I. Title. II. Series.

HC59.7.C3484 2005
332.4'142--dc22   2005012915

ISBN 13: 978-0-415-94927-9 (hbk)
ISBN 13: 978-0-415-65204-9 (pbk)

For
Amma and Appa

Contents

Acknowledgments

This project would not have been completed without the support of a very large group of people. My single largest debt is owed to Colin Danby, who provided extensive and critical discussion, comments and reflection at every step of the project. Stephen Resnick and the members of my dissertation committee provided sharp critique and careful reading that went far beyond their professorial duties. Members of the Association for Economic and Social Analysis provided the intellectual sustenance necessary for this project to reach fruition. I would also like to thank those in various institutional spaces who have helped me throughout this project. I am indebted to faculty and fellow graduate students in the Department of Economics at the University of Massachusetts-Amherst who provided the personal and administrative support needed for the thesis to develop. The Social Thought and Political Economy Program (STPEC) at the University of Massachusetts-Amherst provided material and intellectual sustenance over the long gestation period for the thesis. Antonio Callari and Eiman Zein-Elabdin at Franklin and Marshall and Kathy Ferguson at the University of Hawai'i at Mānoa provided the on-going support needed for me to finally convert the thesis into a book. And finally, I would not have made it through these years without the personal support and encouragement of my parents and siblings, Colin, my nephews and nieces, and my friends—thanks for all your support.

Preface

The dissertation this book is based on emerged from my exposure to debates over development discourse in the late 1980s as a graduate student at the University of Massachusetts, Amherst. My concern then, as now, was to work systematically through questions of ontology in economic analysis.

I defended my dissertation in 1997. As an examination of the contractionary devaluation debate and the development literature, therefore, it covers the period from the 1940s to the mid-1990s, and I have resisted the temptation to update my treatment of these literatures. In any case, the dissertation uses these literatures as case studies, as examples of the way in which, while ostensibly opposites, the structuralist and individualist ontologies share a subterranean link, a layer of fundamental assumptions that I believe needs to be challenged. Adding a few more years of case studies would not change my argument. More exciting has been the growth in recent years of scholarly literatures in the social sciences and humanities that either critique economics directly or provide more advanced tools for such a critique, and if I were writing the dissertation today I would position its critique and analysis with respect to recent work on race, postcoloniality, gender, and culture. The reader interested in this scholarship is referred to Zein-Elabdin and Charusheela 2004.

What this dissertation does that remains missing from the current literature is that it provides a close reading and examination of economic theory, a reading that takes the internal logic of that theory very seriously while also employing the insights of postcolonial theory and poststructuralist Marxism. Rather than treating orthodox economics as a self-contained unit, I show that it may be thought of in terms of two linked-but-opposed ontologies, both of which arise from a modernist base whose "Cartesian" properties the dissertation examines. Economic thought contains powerful ways of understanding the world and reshaping it, and a truly critical project needs to dismantle it carefully and examine its workings. I hope this book is a small contribution toward that larger project.

Thus, with the encouragement of Stephen Resnick and Colin Danby, I here present most of the 1997 dissertation—the parts devoted to a close reading of the discourses and models of development economics and economics policy—as a separate book. I have left out portions of the original dissertation that do not add to this close reading. I hope the reader will find it as useful to explore the history of the contours of ontology in the field of development economics, and the effects of this on economic policy discourses, as I have.

S. Charusheela
University of Hawai`i at Mānoa

Chapter One
Introduction

ECONOMIC THOUGHT, ECONOMIC POLICY AND THE *CONTRACTIONARY DEVALUATION* DEBATE

Economists not only *think* about the economy and society, but also influence and shape it by participating in policy-making. Thus, the nature of their theories has direct consequences for large numbers of people. Many of the theories discussed in the history of economic thought and economic philosophy arose from policy debates. For example, David Ricardo formulated his theory of Comparative Advantage while debating the repeal of England's restrictive trade laws, to argue that free trade would lead to growth for the British economy.

As debates take place and accrete over time, the participants often lose sight of the implicit assumptions underlying their policy recommendations. This is especially true as policy-making becomes institutionalized, and economists as a profession view themselves not as products of historically specific theoretical and philosophical debates, but as possessors of universal "tool kits," which can be deployed to find the appropriate policy for a given situation. They ignore the extent to which specific theoretical and philosophical assumptions affect policy-making.

This book makes explicit the relationship between philosophical assumptions about economic agency and policy outcomes. I do this by examining the philosophical assumptions about economic agency used in one specific policy debate, the "contractionary devaluation" debate (referred to in the text as the CDD) in the field of development economics. This debate emerged as part of a larger debate about the impact of the IMF's (and until recent years, the World Bank's) policies of Structural Adjustment in Less Developed Countries (LDCs), undertaken against the backdrop of the debt crises of the 1980s.[1] More specifically, the CDD focuses on the impact of exchange rate devaluations in LDCs.

1

Here, I show that this is not just a debate about which foreign exchange policy option an LDC should follow. It is a debate about the appropriate way to understand economic agency, a fight over different ontological assumptions used by economists to understand the economies of third world countries. Here, I modify the initial framework for examining the role of ontology in economic debates developed by Cullenberg (1989), who examined the Marxian debate over the falling rate of profit in capitalist economies.[2] In such a modified framework, I demonstrate that the IMF perspective in this debate is based on a particular type of individualist view of the economy. Opposing it are those who typically hold a structuralist view.[3] These two different and contending approaches to understanding third world economies produce radically different policies.

Before I proceed to the next chapter (where I provide a detailed discussion of ontology, and of individualism and structuralism), it might be useful to understand the policy context of the CDD, and to see what the contributions of an ontological reading of that debate would be. The next section will provide a brief introduction to the CDD (taken up in greater detail in chapter five), and the following section will explain why examining the CDD from an ontological perspective is useful.

WHAT IS THE "CONTRACTIONARY DEVALUATION DEBATE" ABOUT?

The International Monetary Fund (IMF) helps provide interim financing to countries facing balance of payments problems. It can do this by allowing member countries to draw on Special Drawing Rights (SDRs), helping to negotiate a loan agreement with private banks, or itself providing loans. When it provides this assistance, the IMF analyzes the causes of imbalance in a debtor country's foreign exchange markets and recommends a series of policies aimed at correcting the imbalance. Such policy packages are generally called "structural adjustment policies."

Many LDCs have had to undertake some form of structural adjustment policy in the decade following the Third World debt crisis.[4] These policies primarily call for domestic credit constraints, public deficit reduction, *and exchange rate devaluation*.[5] In addition, they frequently call for producer price increases, trade liberalization, and elimination of subsidies, support prices, and wage controls[6] (see Balassa and McCarthy 1984; Balssa and Williamson 1987; Choksi and Papageorgiou 1986; Corbo, Goldstein and Khan 1987; International Monetary Fund 1987; Khan and Knight 1981). The goal of these policy packages is to restore a viable balance of payments position, contain inflation, remove price distortions, and thus promote efficiency and growth in these countries (see Guitian 1981; International Monetary Fund 1987; Khan and Montiel 1989). As will be shown, the basic idea behind such policies is to correct certain interventions or imperfections in the economy in order to permit individuals to react properly to true market incentives. Such a view will conform to what will be discussed below as individualism.

Not surprisingly, these policies are highly controversial. Opposed to these policies are those whose approach has been informed more by what will be discussed below as structuralism. These critics have argued that at best the policies did not help, and at worst, they inflicted enormous damage to the countries to which they have been applied. The damage is assessed in terms of output contractions, unemployment, exacerbated distributional problems, and further foreign exchange and savings and investments constraints draining growth possibilities (See Dell 1982; Díaz-Alejandro 1981, 1984a, and 1984b; Killick 1984; Krugman and Taylor 1978; Taylor 1981).

Devaluing the local currency has been, and to remains, one of the key policies of such structural adjustment packages (as part of the stabilization phase of these policies, devaluation is often the first policy required by the IMF in creating a structural adjustment package). As a key policy, devaluation has been the terrain for very strong debate and dissension. The issue is summed up in the "contractionary devaluation" debate: Do devaluations cause stagflation? Do they really attract foreign exchange or improve the Balance of Payments? If so, to what extent, and at what cost?

Individualists tend to be proponents of exchange rate devaluations (the IMF uses individualist theories for its policy analysis) for countries facing a payments deficit. Reducing the value of domestic currency is expected to reduce imports, increase exports, and thus eliminate the foreign exchange imbalance in the deficit country. The IMF also hopes that reducing the cost of domestic currency will make it cheaper to invest in the country in question, causing direct foreign investment to increase. Inflows of foreign capital would help promote employment and growth.

Structuralists tend to be critics of devaluation. They argue that through a variety of structural mechanisms devaluations cause inflation, economic contractions, and worsening income distribution. In an already weakened economy, they contend, these effects are devastating, and the human, economic, and social costs of such a program are unacceptable. Since the 1980s, this view has become associated with the "New Structuralists," particularly with the theoretical position refined by Lance Taylor (1979, 1981, 1983, 1988, 1989, and 1991; see also Hamilton 1988 for a review of the structuralist literature on contractionary devaluation).

A series of empirical studies have attempted to settle the dispute between these contending views[7]. The evidence, however, remains ambiguous and spotty. For example, Edwards (1986) finds that though devaluations were followed by contractions in the initial one to two years, they were followed by recoveries in the years after. And, as the repeated studies and continuous efforts to adjudicate this debate accrete, it becomes clearer that to a large extent, the specific empirical results one gets depend heavily on the various "control variables" and specific underlying models one uses in the econometric tests. Thus there has been no empirical resolution of this debate.

WHY AN ONTOLOGICAL READING OF THIS DEBATE?

As noted above, the CDD is one of the unsettled theoretical debates within the field. While it is associated with the debates surrounding devaluation experiences in recent years, the book will show that both theoretically, and in terms of concrete policy experiences, it is not a new debate in developing countries. Empirical attempts to adjudicate the debate have not helped, despite both the age of the debate, and the availability of many "case studies and data points" with which to undertake empirical analysis. An ontological reading of this debate can help to break the current impasse in the literature by showing how the assumptions about agency used by each side produce their policy results. This would help us see why this debate has not been resolved for so long.

First, by showing how the debate is at root about the nature of economic agency, we can show why the debate is unresolvable. Since both structuralists and individualists have different assumptions about the nature of economic behavior, they have *different definitions* for terms like "payments imbalance" or "appropriate price level." Thus each side in the debate conceptualizes the basic categories of analysis differently. In addition, because they have different assumptions about the nature of economic behavior, they have very *different criteria* by which to assess the impact of a policy. Thus, each side measures and assesses the causes and effects of devaluations very differently. These fundamental differences between the participants of the CDD leave the debate *unresolvable* in empirical terms.

But going further, by exploring how the ontological assumptions constitute the discourse of development, we can examine how a discourse has concrete policy consequences. Thus, this book makes explicit the inherently ideological nature of economic theory and policy formulation: *ideological* because each theory is based on what are ultimately unprovable ideological assertions about the meaning and nature of human activity. But while the book emphasizes the ideological bases for each theoretical position, it does not suggest that we lapse into relativism, or that since ideology is inescapable, any ideology is acceptable. This is because of the material impact of ideological formulations.

In the case of development policies, both structuralism and individualism have taken their turn in shaping policy. As structuralist theories were first seen as the "hope" for developing countries and were ascendant in the discipline in the 50s, 60s, and early 70s, their policies were adopted by LDC governments. When structuralism's promises of development and growth with mass prosperity at little economic and political cost to the better-off groups in the country failed to bear fruit, the theory lost its luster. Economic crises and political dissent were on the rise. At this point the alternative theory comes into its own. Individualism is in its turn lauded and adopted. These pendulum swings from one pole of the structure-agent dichotomy to the other come at wrenching costs for the poor masses in LDCs. As the profession swung from structuralist to individualist views in the period between the mid-sixties and mid-to-late-eighties, development policies shifted, affecting the lives of millions.

The hope that lies behind this project is to make the space for an alternative approach to both structuralist and individualist perspectives, by noting how both these perspectives are defined by their shared commitments to Cartesian forms of analysis that mask their shared comprehension of the non-West through the lens of deviance. Since the project for constituting an alternative cannot be undertaken by a lone scholar, the hope is that this book, by making the case for taking ontology seriously, opens the door for promoting on-going projects for generating alternate approaches to economics (see Zein-Elabdin and Charusheela 2004 for further discussion of the need for alternatives, and suggestions about the shape that such alternate approaches may take).

BOOK OUTLINE

The rest of the book focuses on providing a close reading of development economics and the CDD, with a focus on ontology. Chapter two defines ontology and provides the necessary background on the two key ontologies that have shaped development economics and have emerged as the key opposing perspectives in the CDD, structuralism and individualism. Chapter three provides a history of development economics, exploring the roles of specific perspectives and theories in shaping first the import-substituting industrialization (ISI) phase of development projects after WW2, and the inbuilt tensions that lead to swing from that to the neoliberal perspectives that marked—and continue to dominate—mainstream development projects and perspectives since the Third World debt crisis. Chapter four provides background in international finance, with a focus on excavating the ontological assumptions that lie behind the often-daunting theories and accounts that constitute the field of international economics. Chapter five pulls this material together to provide a discussion of the CDD, while chapter six concludes the book.

Chapter Two
Ontology and Economic Analysis

This chapter lays out the theoretical basis for an ontological reading of development discourse and the contractionary devaluation debate. Here, I define the ontological terms used in the book, and examine the inner logic of the various theoretical positions based on their ontological perspective.

ONTOLOGY

When analyzing the social totality and the social processes comprising it, the analyst takes a position, or has a world view: What is the totality? Is it an agglomeration of individuals, or a set of relationships among them? Does it exist as something more than or somehow beyond these individuals? Is the totality an entity with its own rules and life? Is it (either as an aggregation of individuals or as an entity independent of them) moving to some greater end or goal, or does it have no destination? Ontology is the term describing the position taken by the theorist about the "nature of the world," or "object of analysis," or "subject under consideration."

I examine two contending ways of understanding the social totality—individualist and structuralist.[1] There are of course other ways of understanding the social totality, and other taxonomies one can use to examine the theoretical terrain. There is, for example, the Hegelian totality versus the Cartesian totality as described by Cullenberg (1989, 1995), in his analysis of the debate over the falling rate of profit in Marxian economics. Or, there are essentialist versus non-essentialist approaches to analyzing society, as used by Resnick and Wolff (1987a and 1987b).[2]

The particular mode of organizing theories I use here extends the approach developed by Stephen Cullenberg (1989). While Cullenberg, in his examination of the debate over the falling rate of profit in Marxian economics, develops a taxonomy that distinguishes between the two broad

7

categories of Hegelian and Cartesian approaches, I focus here on two approaches *within* Cartesianism, structuralism and individualism.[3] The category of Cartesianism can illuminate some of the striking differences between structuralism and individualism, while pointing out the similarities that a shared Cartesianism provides. It also shows the ideological underpinnings of each argument, pulling apart the analyses of human nature and the conception of social order used by each theory.

Both individualist and structuralist approaches in economics attempt to answer the following question: What is the appropriate way to set about understanding social interaction? If the social whole (here the economy) is thought of as having parts (here, human agents), should one proceed to analyze the whole in terms of the nature of its constitutive parts? *Or*, should one look for the logic of the whole, which will then in turn define the parts? Individualists and structuralists provide radically different answers to this question.

Individualists conceive of the social totality (the economy, the social whole, etc.) as comprised of autonomous individuals. They start from the underlying nature and motivations of individuals, and deduce from their aggregated actions the regularities in the whole.[4] Structuralists see the whole as having certain underlying structural regularities which cannot be adduced from the nature or motivations of autonomous individuals. Such structural regularities or laws are specified prior to, and are independent of, the actions of individual agents. Individualist approaches adduce the structure of a society from the behavior of atomistic individual agents, while structuralist approaches propose that it is the structures in society that govern individual response.

The following two sections examine individualism and structuralism, respectively. Here, I highlight the differences, and internal workings of these ontologies. Given the different ways the term "structuralism" is used in the economics profession, that section is a fairly lengthy explication of the core structuralist ideas. The section "Similarities between Individualism and Structuralism" discusses the dialectical relationship between the two ontologies, and the shared Cartesianism of these two positions, to draw out the important similarities between the two positions. "Politics and Entry Points: A Glimpse Ahead" discusses some of the policy implications of these ontological positions.

The goal of this chapter is to bring to light not only the differences between these two ontological stances, but also the dialectical link between them. Structure and agent are two dialectically linked poles: both positions start by positing a distinction between structure and agent, and then try and derive one end of the opposition from the other. Thus, the two positions are linked in opposition, each drawing on its opposite for intellectual coherence. I would thus stress that though I present my arguments as first demonstrating the differences/opposition between the two positions, and then turn to the similarities/contradictions that link them, this order of presentation is dictated by expositional ease. The differences between the two positions do not make them independent of each other, nor do their similarities indicate an end to their opposition—instead, they are participants in an intricate intellectual dance, each one both rejecting its opposite and depending on it for intellectual coherence. This dialectical dependence of each position on its opposite is key to understanding the contractionary devaluation debate as a site where this tension is played out.

INDIVIDUALISM

Economics has a particularly strong tradition of methodological individualism. In this section, I first present the logic of methodological individualism, and then describe the deployment of individualism in economic analysis.

Individualist Ontology

In this mode of analysis, the object of knowledge can be completely captured and understood by looking at its constituent parts (here, *independent* human beings). Structures (like demand and supply schedules, and final market outcomes) are more appropriately seen as aggregate expressions of the parts that make up the whole. These parts are assumed to be logically prior to the whole. Thus the regularities of the whole can be understood only and completely by understanding the individual parts. Put simply, the assumption is that the parts cause the whole.

Individualism, then, is not simply a *recognition* of individuals. It is a view that they must completely determine the whole. Further, these individuals are "atomistic"—they add up to the whole in much the same way that all matter is understood as the addition of basic, underlying building blocks in some kinds of atomistic physics. *Any regularities in the whole (the economy) can be understood only through the regularities in the individuals themselves.*

Individualism in Economic Analysis

There is a strong tradition of individualist analysis within economics. Individualism as a mode of analysis has its roots in liberal thought's attempt to locate all social and political activities within an underlying, universal, pre-specified human nature. Starting with at least Adam Smith's *The*

Wealth of Nations, one finds explanations for economic outcomes based on the rationales and motivations of atomistic economic agents.[5] Individualism is based on efforts to pin down human subjectivity, and to locate all explanations for economic outcomes in the underlying human agent. Thus individualism is *humanist,* since it locates all aspects of the social totality as being ultimate expressions of that which is *internal* or *intrinsic* to the human agent.

All microeconomic general equilibrium reasoning is individualist. This is because one can deduce the nature of the entire economy from the underlying nature of the human agent. The nature of the agent is specified prior to and independently of the economy in which she lives. Any regularities in the economy's behavior can be understood as resulting from regularities in agent behavior. The behavior of the economy mirrors the behavior of its individual agents.

The purpose of most microeconomics is to describe the meshing of decisions by individuals in input and output markets. In doing this, one arrives at explanations of how the market decides what, how, and for whom to produce (the regularities of the market that have to be explained by recourse to the pre-specified characteristics of human agents). I will describe how one example of individualism in economics explains how the market decides what, how, and for whom to produce, by reducing the totality to a reflection of the underlying human agent: Walrasian general equilibrium.[6]

In the Walrasian model, one starts by postulating agents with *given* preference orderings, and an innate desire to maximize. This underlying agent, with priorly specified desires, and a priorly specified motive, is not explained as arising from the exchange process, or her position (or role) in the market. Rather, for any given economic decision (to produce, consume, exchange), the outcomes in markets are all explained by (or already contained in) her mapping of desires, across all states of existence, and all future possibilities.

Next, technology (production functions) and property distribution are specified. Each agent is assumed to possess both knowledge (skill, technology in the narrower sense of knowledge, knowledge of self, that is, of desire and interaction, in the broader sense), and ownership (given endowment of resources in the narrower sense of ownership, ownership of actions, of options, choices, decisions, in the broader sense). In this environment, the already-constituted agent is set loose in the market. Note that technology and distribution (knowledge and ownership) in no way affect the prior specification of the agent. The demand and supply framework provides the mechanism from which the economy's behavior (the social whole/structures/outcomes) is adduced. But the demand and supply schedules are themselves reflections of the atomistic agent.

Thus all economic outcomes are traced back to the independent maximizing agent, defined by axioms of choice, resources, and an inherent ability to produce (i.e., a fully pre-specified subject or self, that logically creates the world). Because the complexity of the economy is reduced to the individual, and individual self is in turn reduced to preferences, technology, and resources (desire, knowledge, and ownership respectively), microeconomic theory becomes an essentialist theory—a complexity of economic and social interaction reduced to an essential, underlying simplicity, through a preformed and centered subject or self. This is the type of analysis found in almost any introductory economics text (see Samuelson 1980, for example). Figure 2.1 at the end of the next section (which provides a discussion of structuralism) provides a brief outline of this mode of thought.

As the next few chapters will show, the proponents of IMF and World Bank-sponsored policies for stabilization, liberalization, and privatization, particularly their policies for exchange rate devaluation, use an individualist ontology to understand LDC economies. Their arguments are based on two strands of individualist theory: a marginalist-Walrasian model that focuses on the real sector of the economy (the Walrasian theory described above), and a marginalist-monetarist model that provides individualist analyses of the role of money in the macroeconomy (an extension of the Walrasian model to a monetary economy).

STRUCTURALISM

Structuralism has also had an important role in economic analysis, especially in macroeconomics, in much of the Marxist tradition, and in the works of world-systems analysts and dependency theorists.[7] Since structuralism as an approach has such a diverse following, it will take some careful unpacking to show up its ontological underpinnings. I will provide a brief note on terminology, in the first section below, and then provide a very brief discussion of the works of various key structuralists in a broad range of disciplines in the section after that. Only then will I define the basic ontological foundations of a structuralist analysis (to parallel the first section of the discussion of individualism above) and discuss the use of structuralism within economic analysis (to parallel the second section of the discussion of individualism above). This mode of exposition has the advantage of pulling together the key aspects of an otherwise diverse body of analysis.

Structuralist Economics and the Structuralist Tradition

The term "structuralism" has multiple usages within and outside economics. Within economics, there is one school of thought explicitly termed "Structuralist economics." This is the work of the Latin American ECLA school, whose theories emerged in the 1950s, out of debates about the source of inflation in LDC economies (a debate often referred to as the "Monetarist-Structuralist debate"). The term "structuralist" was actually never used by any of the economists from this school of thought to characterize their work in the 1950s. Instead, Campos (1963), a key monetarist dissenter, takes credit for having coined the term in Campos 1961. The term stuck, and this particular group of economists has been called "Structuralists" ever since.

A group of economists, most prominently Lance Taylor, have recently revived the arguments of the ECLA school in the context of the 1980s debates over IMF-World Bank policies of structural adjustment. These economists call themselves "New Structuralists" as a way to acknowledge their debt to the older Structuralist economists of ECLA. The CDD of the 80s is an extension of the older structuralist-monetarist debates of the 50s and 60s, and thus both the "Structuralists" and the "New Structuralists" are key participants of this debate.

Outside economics, structuralism denotes a specific ontological approach associated with the works of analysts across a broad spectrum of disciplines. That is, it defines a *specific approach to the object of analysis*. In this book, I use the term structuralism in this broader ontological sense.

The terminology can thus create confusion, since it turns out that the Structuralists and New Structuralists of economic terminology are also structuralists in the ontological sense of the word. But as noted above, they are by no means the *only* ontological structuralists in the field. Many other economic analysts are also structuralists in the ontological sense. Throughout the text, I will use the terms Structuralist economics and New Structuralist economics when referring to the specific schools of economic thought (with a capital "S"), while I will use the words structuralism, structuralist method, or structuralist analysis, when using the term in the ontological sense.

The Broad Structuralist Tradition

Most analyses of human interaction concern themselves with the regularities, or structures, of social life. But structuralism, as a mode of inquiry in the social sciences and humanities, does not simply refer to all attempts to explain such regularities. It is a specific approach to social explanation which has taken root in a broad range of disciplines, most notably in Linguistics, Social Anthropology, some branches of Psychology, Literary Criticism, History, Semiology, and Philosophy. In these traditions, theorists who explicitly term themselves as "structuralists" have deployed a "structuralist method," characterized by a specific ontological assumption about the nature of social wholes. As a broad movement, structuralism is hard to pin down, since it emerged through the cross-fertilization of theorists across a broad range of disciplines. This section discusses the two thinkers most identified with the development of structuralism as an intellectual tradition, Saussure and Lévi-Strauss.[8] The next section summarizes the core propositions of structuralist ontology.

Ferdinand de Saussure

Most analysts date the origins of structuralism to Saussure's *Course in General Linguistics* (1966).[9] Saussure's discussion of Language provides a good synopsis of the key elements of structuralist thought, and is worth presenting briefly.

Saussure argued that in analyzing the totality of a language system, it is a mistake to proceed by looking for the intrinsic quality of the words/sounds made in speech. Words or signs, Saussure argued, were *arbitrary.* There was no intrinsic or necessary property of the sound or sign that linked it to the things it referred to. For example, there is no necessary correlation between the symbol "brown," and the concept of the color brown that is associated with that symbol.[10] Since the word or sign was arbitrary, its logic or meaning must lie not within itself, but in its relationship to other words within the language system of a society as a whole. This relationship was what, in fact, gave meaning to the word or sign.

If one were to understand *"Langue"* or *Language,* as the totality of its elements (words) and all the rules for their usage and combinations, then Language is a social possession. This is to be distinguished from *"parole"* or *speech,* which is the specific use any one person makes of this available Language. To study Language was to study the total system, and the logic governing the operation of the system as a whole. Thus Language, and the production of meaning, are social possessions, and should not be confused with the activities of any one individual.

This concept of Language is based on Saussure's careful distinction between *synchronic* and *diachronic* systems. A synchronic system or a synchronic analysis examines the internal relationships between aspects of a Language at a given time, as it exists in the collective consciousness of a given society. A diachronic system relates parts of two *different* Language systems that exist at different historical times, and exist for different collective consciousnesses. Language is above all synchronic, since it is a system of words and rules for their combination that exists "at a given time," as a whole in the collective consciousness of "society."

Saussure's system posited that words are part of synchronic systems of language, where each word is associated with a "referent" in the external world. But, there is no necessary correlation between the words and the objects they refer to. In fact, the logic of words in Language comes from their relationships to each other, within a systematic structure of rules which govern their operation. These rules are rules of *differentiation:* What makes a sign like the sign for the color "brown" have meaning? It is the *difference* of that sign's physical, phonetic and conceptual attributes from other signs. We know "brown" by knowing what it is *not*.

Each word consists of two parts: the *signifier* and the *signified*. The signifier is the symbol or sound that denotes a word. The signified is the concept or meaning associated with the word. Any word always contains both signifier and signified at the same time. (Signified denotes the mental conceptions or ideas associated with the word, and is not to be confused with the "referent," or object in the external world that a word may refer to.) The logic of this system is in the rules governing the relationships of these signifiers and signified: for each word, its signifier is linked to other signifiers through a system of similarities and differences (we distinguish between the signifier "brown" and the signifier "blown" by the difference between "r" and "l"); and similarly, its signified is linked to the signifieds of other words in a system of similarities and differences (the signified "brown" is distinguished from the signified "red"). Thus one gets a "chain of linkages" between words spreading through Language.

This chain of linkages between signifieds and signifiers, and links of differentiation between the signifieds, and between the signifiers, denotes the "value" of a word for Saussure (the value of a word is the way in which by a process of linkages to other words, this particular word takes on its specific connotations and distinction from other words). An important aspect of Saussure's concept of linguistic value is that the signifier and signified are dialectically linked: the concepts do not precede the symbols, the symbols themselves can shape the concepts. If this were not the case, then Language would simply be a catalogue of sounds for pre-existing concepts, and all Languages would be the same: they would not convey any difference in meaning, and translation between languages would be perfect. But it turns out that this is not the case. Take for example, the terms "river" and "stream" in the English language.[11] Translated into French, the closest equivalents we get are the signs "rivière" and "fleuve." But these signs do not translate: "river" and "stream" exist within the Language English, and are quite distinct from the "rivière" and "fleuve" of French. It is not just that the signifiers are different; in this example, the signifieds are quite distinct. The concept "river" is distinguished from the concept "stream" in the English language by the size of the moving body of water, while in French there is no equivalent for such a distinction between large and small moving bodies of water: instead the French distinguish between bodies of water that flow into the sea (rivière), and those that do not (fleuve). Thus the conceptual plane is as arbitrary as the phonetic or symbolic one.

Thus, the structure identified by Saussure is a system of linkages between words that gives meaning to a specific word. This is a system of differences and similarities, in both the signifier (sounds/symbols) and signified (concepts/meanings). Language is this entire system, and words derive their meaning from the relationships they have with the signifiers and signifieds of other words. The "value" of a word, and its relationship to other words, is to be found precisely in the ways in which it is shaped by the laws governing the differences and similarities between words, both in their signifier and signified aspects.[12]

Thus, there is a key implication of Saussure's structuralism that should be highlighted. The human speech act becomes a product of the structure of Language in society, instead of societal meaning being a product of the acts of isolated individuals (because each individual practices speech acts, but Language is a systemic possession of society as a whole that 'decodes' the speech act). This means that in society, it is the social sphere that creates or determines the possibilities and limits of the individual speaker, rather than the individual speaker/participant creating the whole. This idea is picked up by Lévi-Strauss and is, I think, a key aspect of structuralist ontologies.[13]

Claude Lévi-Strauss

Lévi-Strauss (1963, 1983, 1991) is the key figure associated with Structuralism in the Social Sciences. He is one of the few structuralist writers who explicitly saw himself as developing a structuralist tradition, and views it as the primary form of analysis to be used in all theorization. He brought over structuralism from linguistics[14] and analyzed culture as a synchronic system, whose meanings and rules are part of the collective system of Culture (as with Language) in a given society. The elements of a culture's meanings emerge as the relationship between a series of dualities or opposites whose meaning exists primarily in their relationships to each other. Thus, as with Saussure, Lévi-Strauss points to structural laws. These structural laws are the laws that govern the *relationships* between elements of a structure. This idea of the relationships between parts is of a system of *differences*—for example, male and female only have meaning in the relationship that exists between them, a relationship that *differentiates* between these two categories. Lévi-Strauss used this mode of analysis to describe the structure and meaning of a host of cultural practices, most famously to analyze the practices of marriage, linking them to the underlying system of the incest-taboo in kinship systems. This linkage takes the form, again, of a series of oppositions and differences—who is and who is not kin, who is and who is not part of a the group of people one can marry reflecting underlying laws governing who is and who is not part of the enate (linked by relationships on the maternal side) relations of a person. In addition, Lévi-Strauss examined myths, similarly arguing that the meaning of a myth is to be found in the linkages and relationships between various "mythemes" within the system of mythology: again, the system of linkages being one of oppositions and divisions (sorrow/happiness, courage/fear) linking different themes within a myth.

The main aspect of Lévi-Straussian structuralism is that the meaning of social interactions and cultural practices is to be found not in the intrinsic qualities of the individuals of a society, but in the relationships that the social structure creates between various aspects of culture and meaning. The individual grasps the world, and participates in society as a locus of these cultural systems. *The social whole creates the human agent, and not vice versa.*

Core Aspects of Structuralist Ontology

Since structuralism itself is a tradition that spans many works, there is of course some disagreement across authors about what constitutes structuralism. For example, Piaget (1971) excludes Husserl and areas of inquiry in the Humanities from his description of Structuralist thought. Sturrock (1986), by contrast, views the tradition much more broadly, and thus includes Husserl, and areas of inquiry such as literary criticism that Piaget excludes. Here, I focus on structuralism as an ontological tradition in the social sciences, and so will develop my definition with this focus in mind. I will adapt this description from Piaget's (1971) work—since this is one of the few works that has attempted to not just *present* the writings of various structuralists, but to rigorously distill from these works the set of underlying principles on which structuralism is based—though I diverge from his description in some key ways, which I return to in the next section.[15]

I identify the following two aspects that must necessarily be present for an ontology to be viewed as structuralist:

The Object of Knowledge is the Whole

The whole will consist of "parts" (usually dualities, or a series of differentiated parts). But the key to understanding the whole does not lie in the "intrinsic" characteristics of the parts. The parts gain their meaning only in their relationships to each other in the whole. Hence, the key lies in grasping *the rules that relate each part to the other, to form a systemic whole.* The structuralist makes a clear distinction between a *structure* and an *aggregate.* As Piaget (1971, p.7) emphasizes, " . . . the former being wholes, the latter composites formed of elements that are independent of the complexes into which they enter."

No part exists autonomously or independently of the whole, nor can one grasp the meaning of any part except in terms of its location within the structure of relationships and rules governing the whole. Structuralism does not simply claim that the "whole" somehow prefigures the parts, or emerges simply as a totality: its method is to examine *how* the whole constitutes the parts, and is constituted *as a whole.* This emphasis involves examining the *relationships* between parts. Again, to cite from Piaget (1971, p. 9, emphasis added): " . . . the *logical procedures* or *natural processes by which the whole is formed* are primary, not the whole, which is consequent on the system's laws of composition . . ." Thus structural *rules* in the whole are prior to their constitutive elements, and are by nature *structuring* of the constitutive elements. Any regularities found in the whole are part of the way these laws will govern the constitutive elements (here, human agents), and not a result of the innate characteristics of the constitutive elements.

Piaget takes the issue of structural rules further, and postulates that they must be "transformational laws": laws that are "deep structures," and whose presence is detected by the way they govern transformations within a system. Transformations can be understood temporally, that is, transformations taking place in time through history. Piaget insists that any thoroughgoing structuralist ontology has to have such a temporal "law of motion," in order to explain a system *both* synchronously and diachronously. But a transformational rule or (using the term coined by Chomsky) "transformational grammar" need not be temporal. It simply involves a mechanism by which some elements of a structure are logically "transformed" or linked via the laws of the structure. Thus, within economics, one could look for the transformation of values to prices, in Marxist Structuralism, or the transformation of savings into investment in macroeconomics. These are *logical* transformations, not temporal ones.

The key aspect of a transformational rule is that it creates the order and logic of the whole. But there are ontological gaps or fissures that arise when one considers either the meaning of transformational rules *through time,* or the process by which transformations are met within a synchronous system, which I will take up in section 2.4 (where I describe the collapses of structuralism into individualism, and vice versa). The specific issues that emerge around transformational laws are issues of "equilibration," the process by which the transformation is accomplished within the system and the structuring properties of the law are sustained through the process of change. For now, I simply argue that any ontology that postulates structural laws that govern or determine the logic of the whole follow structuralism. I do not follow Piaget's insistence on a *temporal* transformational law as a necessary part of a structuralist ontology, though there are some theories in economics that use such a temporal transformational law.[16]

The Structure is Self-Reproducing and Self-Regulating

Any structure must be closed and capable of recreating itself or being recreated. This is key, since if any part has value or meaning only by virtue of its linkages to other parts, then the links must be repetitive, or found in the relationships between many parts, in order for them to have meaning as a structure (or else we would just have an arbitrary series of "events" with no systemic or structural formulation). A "law" that applies to a single relationship between two parts, and which is never repeated, is not structural—it is isolated. But if this linkage is repeated over and over, either in the way a whole host of parts are linked, or in the way two specific parts consistently interact within the whole, then it is structural. For example, a single event would describe how a single man and a single woman interact at a given moment. For this to reflect something structural, these linkages need to be repeated over and over in the relationships of men in general and women in general. Let me take each element of this in turn.

> *Closure:* The structure must be "closed." This means that any transformation (say of expenditures into income) generates a result that is internal to the system (the new income creates expenditures that conform to the transformational laws of the system). If this were not the case, it would imply that the transformations or laws governing a system had left some aspect of the logic governing the parts within the system untheorized. Thus closure is necessary if the totality is fully to determine the logic of the parts. Without closure, the totality will start to disintegrate, since the relationships between the parts may not hold when "extra-systemic" elements impinge on the system.

> *Self-Regulation:* The system must be self-regulating. In mathematical or logical systems, there is no distinction between the laws themselves and

the process of regulation: the laws *are* what regulates the system. But when one is describing a *social* whole, there is a possibility of non-reversible error on the part of individuals. The system must thus have internal mechanisms which regulate and reproduce it. This is the point made earlier about the importance of a system being fully articulated: articulation requires a mechanism by which the agent grasps and internalizes (however unconsciously) the laws that govern the structure. Lacking this, the agent is not fully articulated, and may thus act in ways that will not reproduce the structure.

The combination of full closure and full articulation would lead to a completely closed self-reproducing system: that is, a synchronic system which is in "equilibrium," in which the structuring laws are obeyed and reproduced. Structuralist ontologies thus postulate within their framework some notion of closure, and of self-regulation. Within economics, the postulates of closure and self-regulation are usually not discussed explicitly.

Finally, before moving from our general discussion of structuralist ontology to a discussion of structuralism in economics, note that for an ontology to be structuralist, it must postulate that the social whole possesses *both* the attributes of holism and self-regulation. Thus, postulating a self-reproducing state that depends on the innate properties of pre-specified parts for its existence or stability is not structuralist ontology. Similarly, postulating some element of structural rules without ensuring that the ensuing analysis is both closed and self-regulating causes the analysis to disintegrate.

Structuralism in Economic Analysis

Economists are rarely self-conscious about the ontological underpinnings of their arguments (though heterodox economists tend to be more self-conscious about ontology than mainstream economists), and macroeconomists in general, including those who are called Structuralist or New Structuralist, rarely refer to ontological sources when making their arguments. However, I argue that though there may not have been any *overt* or *conscious* attempt by these economists to model their work on the structuralist tradition in the social sciences, their analyses use an ontology that can be called structuralist in precisely such a sense.

Many theories within the economics profession use structuralist ontology. Each different structuralist analysis identifies different types of relationships or rules governing the interaction of human agents. Examples can be found within Keynesianism, Marxism, dependency and world systems approaches, feminist economics, Institutionalism, neo-Ricardian and Sraffian approaches, in addition to Structuralist and New Structuralist economics.

These theories are often in sharp disagreement with each other about the specific types of structural rules that govern economic behavior and types of analyses that should be used to comprehend economic phenomena.

However, all these theories share a disagreement with the ascendant individualist vision, and provide a causal role for economic structures in their descriptions of human subjects. Almost all challenges to the microeconomic general-equilibrium vision (the individualist theory described in section 2.2) have come from some recognition of the causal role of structure on the human agent. Here I will examine just one of the many structural traditions in economics, macroeconomics of the IS-LM variety (also called the neoclassical-Keynesian synthesis), to show how structuralist thought is used in economic analysis.[17] IS-LM macroeconomic theory has gained canonical status within the discipline, and is the most widely used form of structuralist ontology in economics. Almost all the assumptions and structural rules defined by this theory are retained by the Structuralist and New Structuralist dissenters within the CDD.

The IS-LM vision of macroeconomics is structuralist because it understands the outcomes or regularities in the economy as manifesting the underlying structural rules governing the labor market, goods market, and financial market. One deduces the nature of each economic agent or part based on these rules. The parts conform to the inner rules of the structure of the economy.

The behavior or regularity being explained in macroeconomics is, as in microeconomics, the behavior of agents interacting in markets. But here, "agents interacting in markets" does not imply *logically prior* agents as they did in microeconomics. They simply denote that the agents participate in markets *governed by the structural relationships* of the economy. The regularities of what, how, and for whom to produce are then explained through the operation of these structural rules that govern market interactions.

The Whole Governs the Parts

IS-LM analysis assumes that economic aggregates are the appropriate place to start analysis. In this vision, social aggregates are not simply the addition of the behaviors of pre-specified individuals. Instead, the aggregates under consideration (Income, Consumption, Investment, Monetary demand and supply) shape—define—agent behavior. Thus, the emphasis is on the systemic nature of the whole.

One starts by dividing up the economy into macroeconomic "sectors" or segments—labor, goods, and money markets. Each of these markets or sectors corresponds to a *different* aspect of economic behavior: behavior of agents as the hirers of workers, or as people looking for work, in the labor market; the behavior of agents as buyers and sellers of commodities in goods market; and the behavior of agents in deciding how to hold wealth/assets in the money market. None of these markets exists "independently" of the others, since none of these behaviors is independent of the whole. The role of macroeconomic theorists is to a) uncover the rules governing each of these parts of economic behavior; and b) show the relationship of these parts of economic behavior to each other.

An extended discussion of the structural rules deployed in IS-LM analysis can be found in the original dissertation (Charusheela 1997). To summarize:

1) In the labor market, institutional structures lead to downwardly inflexible wages, usually explained through the institutionalized behavior of workers. Agent behavior as an employee of workers is left untheorized by IS-LM Keynesians, and they are often attacked for this. In terms of the economic *totality*, the implicit rule relates hiring decisions in labor markets to demand decisions in the goods market, as capitalists hire workers based on the amount of output to be produced.

2) In the goods markets, final consumers demand goods based on their income. The underlying relationship between income and consumption is governed by the marginal propensity to consume. The rule for investment demand is not as well specified, and individualists often attack the lack of adequate specification of investment behavior by IS-LM Keynesians.[18] Investment is usually adduced from a semi-individualist investment function, with level of investment demand dependent on the interest rate emerging from money markets. Suppliers of goods simply supply goods based on the total demand for output, at given prices.

3) In the money market, institutional forces control the supply of money, and liquidity preference governs the demand for it.[19] Liquidity preference is a social behavior that arises because so much of economic decision-making is dependent on the relationships between different agents and different aspects of economic behavior, which makes economic decisions risky. The supply of money is governed by institutions of the banking system, and the policies of the government.

The three markets are not independent of each other: Consumption behavior is linked to incomes earned, decisions to hire are linked to output demanded, decisions to invest are linked to the money market via the interest rate, liquidity preferences are linked to the general relationships and risks that govern economic interaction. The final outcome in the economy will depend on the joint impact of all these behavioral rules that govern economic interaction.

Note that agents are not "missing" from this story. They are deduced from, or "determined by" the roles they play as workers, consumers, investors, and bankers *through* the behavioral rules described above. Thus all economic outcomes can be explained in terms of the underlying behavioral rules governing how different aspects of agent behavior in the economy relate to each other.

Self-Regulation and Closure

IS-LM analysis, by using an equilibrium framework, posits closure. The underlying relationship that governs closure for IS-LM analysis comes from two relationships: a) The parts respond according to the structural rules specified. b) The underlying rule for any economy is that everything produced must be distributed across the various agents/sectors of the economy so as to ensure that the system can repeat the cycle in the next period. "Equilibrium" is simply a state in which both a) and b) are met, so that the system keeps reproducing itself: the amount produced is distributed across agents whose demand behaviors will then consume/invest exactly what is produced, and so on. If production is not fully absorbed by consumption and investment, then production will be lowered in the next period, until total production and total incomes exactly match total expenditures *while all the rules governing agent behaviors are met.* Thus all the rules governing agent behavior within the system "mesh," to give a neat, closed, and self-regulating system (Branson 1989). Figure 2.2 provides an outline of this mode of thought.

Section Summary

To recapitulate the main points of this section on structuralism: a structuralist ontology is one which argues that the social whole is prior to the parts. The whole consists of transformational laws and linkages which are structuring of the parts. This whole is self-regulating and closed.

Structuralism, like individualism, is reductionist. The complexities of economic interaction, of agent decisions, of change, and of articulation, within the economy, are simply ignored. Instead, this complexity is reduced to a series of neatly meshing, fully specified structural laws that completely and coherently describe all interaction without any contradictions. All aspects of the economy are reduced here to simple rules that govern decisions

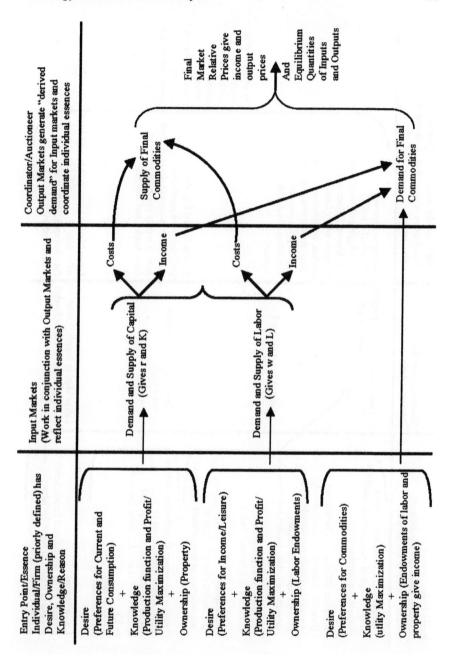

Figure 2.1 The Logic of Individualism in Economics: Walrasian General Equilibrium

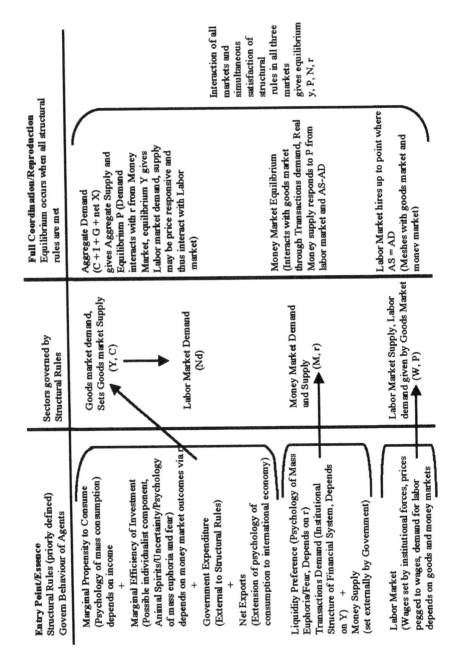

Figure 2.2 The Logic of Structuralism in Economics: IS-LM Neoclassical-Keynesian Analysis

to work, to buy, and to own (in the labor, goods, and money markets respectively). Further, these rules themselves fit coherently with each other, and there is no contradiction between the rules governing one set of decisions (to work, say), and those governing other aspects of economic life (like buying goods, say). Thus the rules governing labor markets neatly mesh in with rules governing output demand, and rules governing investment fit in with the rules governing the money market. This reductionism provides an easy policy solution for the state (since policy makers can depend on agents following through on these structural rules to attain the right outcome).

SIMILARITIES BETWEEN INDIVIDUALISM AND STRUCTURALISM

So far, I have carefully described the differences between individualist and structuralist ontologies. However, these two modes of analysis are not watertight categories. In economics they have been locked in a clumsy embrace, neither able to escape the other. They share some similarities in their analysis and logic, and the boundary between them is often blurred and sometimes crossed. These similarities are key to understanding the confusion that marks the "cross-paradigm" conversations that mark the CDD. The first section on these similarities will examine the blurred boundaries of structuralism and individualism, by showing how and why individualists collapse into structuralism, and vice versa. The second section on the similarities between the two paradigms examines the shared reductive logic deployed by structuralism and individualism through their use of the Cartesian framework.[20]

Collapsing Determinism within Individualism and Structuralism

Mainstream economists do not tend to be ontologically self-conscious, and most economists view the theories available to them as "toolkits" which can be deployed as and when suitable. The same economist will often shift between structuralist and individualist ontologies. For example, Krugman takes a structuralist approach in his 1978 article "Contractionary effects of a Devaluation," (with Taylor), but uses individualist models in his work on strategic trade theory (Krugman 1986). Similarly, within the CDD, one will often find a theorist deploying both ontologies in different contexts, without any sense that this is contradictory.

But in addition to the shifting positions of theorists in the field, there are internal tensions and contradictions within each of the ontologies, which lead individualists to rely on structural arguments to shore up their analyses, and structuralists to fall back on individualism to justify their structural rules. Thus, in economics, each ontology falls into its opposite, and the carefully separated determinism of agent and structure starts to collapse.

Some analysts, like Bardhan (1988) see the collapses and blurred boundaries as a sign of true scientism within the field: the blurred boundaries, for them, are a sign of convergence between different economic theories toward "truth." However, as I point out here, there are strong reasons for such blurring and seeming convergences that have little to do with arriving at a "true" theory. Rather, these collapses and convergences are the product of contradictory intellectual projects that cannot resolve the tensions in their approaches.

Individualism's Collapse into Structuralism

To show how individualist theories come to rely on structuralism, let me now return to a point made earlier. Saussure claimed in his *Course in General Linguistics* (1966 p.79) that he got the concept of "system"[21] or structure from economics. More specifically, the idea of synchronicity is taken by Saussure from economics. In order to see what that implies, it is worth citing from the *Course* at this point:

> On the contrary, that duality [between a synchronic approach and a diachronic/historical approach] is already forcing itself upon the economic sciences. Here, in contrast to the other sciences, political economy and economic history constitute two clearly separated disciplines within a single science; the works that have recently appeared on these subjects point up the distinction. Proceeding as they have, economists are—without being well aware of it—obeying an inner necessity. A similar necessity obliges us to divide linguistics into two parts, each with its own principle. Here as in political economy we are confronted with the notion of *value*; both sciences are concerned with *a system for equating things of different orders*—labor and wages in one and a signified and signifier in the other. (Saussure, 1966, p. 79)

Saussure goes on to argue that any social science needs to distinguish between the relationships between variables or parts in a system at a given time, which is what confers meaning to each part in that system; and the origin and development of that system over time, which is more properly seen as the narrative of the evolution of a system. The former he describes as *synchronic* linguistics, the study of the relationships between words in a given Language system. The latter he terms *diachronic* or evolutionary linguistics, which is the study of the relationships between different Language systems, and the shifts from one Language system to another. This is made parallel to political economy, the study of the relationships between values in a given system of exchange, and economic history, the study of the relationship between past economic systems and present ones, and the evolution of the latter from the former.

Saussure presents a structuralist theory of the word or sign, where he develops the concept of the *value* of the linguistic sign, which is determined by its *commonalities and differences* from other signs (see Saussure, 1966, Part II, Chapter IV, "Linguistic Value"). The use of the term *value* seems quite deliberate here, evoking the concept of the *economic value* of a commodity. Saussure develops the conception of similarity and difference as crafting the value of the sign, by evoking the metaphor of exchange:

> To resolve the issue, let us observe from the outset that even outside language all values are apparently governed by the same paradoxical principle. They are always composed:
>
> > (1) of a *dissimilar* thing that can be *exchanged* for the thing of which the value is to be determined, and
> >
> > (2) of *similar* things that can be *compared* with the thing of which the value is to be determined.
>
> Both factors are necessary for the existence of a value. To determine what a five-franc piece is worth one must therefore know: (1) that it can be exchanged for a fixed quantity of a different thing, e.g. bread; and (2) that it can be compared with a similar value of the same system, e.g. a one-franc piece, or with coins of another system (a dollar, etc.). In the same way a word can be exchanged for something dissimilar, an idea; besides, it can be compared with something of the same nature, another word. Its value is therefore not fixed so long as one simply states that it can be "exchanged" for a given concept, i.e. that it has this or that signification: one must also compare it with similar values, with other words that stand in opposition to it. Its content is really fixed only by the concurrence of everything that exists outside it. Being part of a system, it is endowed not only with a signification but also and especially with a value, and this is something quite different. (Saussure, p. 115)

Thus Saussure draws from economics (i) the division of the field into a synchronic and a diachronic mode, and (ii) the concept of value. What economic theory did he have in mind?

Appendix A in the original dissertation (Charusheela 1997) and Charusheela (2003) explore the textual evidence on this question. The conclusions that emerge are (a) that Saussure does not provide adequate evidence to let us pin down the economic theory that was his model for synchronic linguistics, and (b) what little evidence there is points more obviously to the labor theories of value deployed by most 19th century political economists than to the newer utility-based approaches of Jevons, Menger, Walras and Pareto.

It is therefore fascinating that the most prominent secondary literature in the history of economic thought has awarded Walras that status of being Saussure's inspiration. Both Piaget (1971), the pre-eminent codifier of structuralism, and Donald McCloskey (1994), a skilled rhetorician, analyst of language, and neoclassical economist, state this opinion. What is the relationship that these sophisticated theorists see between Walrasian *individualism* and Saussurean *structuralism?*

The relation is the inescapable reliance of individualist analyses on a structuralist notion of *coordination,* in order to achieve closure. To see what that moment of closure is, let us examine Piaget's description of Saussurean synchronic structures:

> Saussure, in elaborating on this point [the independence of the laws of equilibrium that regulate and govern relationships between parts of a structure, and ensure self-regulation; and the laws of the development of a structure over time], drew his inspiration partly from economics, which in his day chiefly stressed the former (Walras' and Pareto's "general theory of equilibrium"); and it is of course true that economic crises may lead to radical shifts of value quite independent of antecedent price history—the price of tobacco in 1968 depends, not on its price in 1939 or 1914, but on the interaction of current market conditions. (Piaget, 1971, p. 77)

Thus, here we find Piaget arguing that the main point where Saussurean structuralism is based on Walras and Pareto is *not their behavioral theory of economic subjects, but their postulation of equilibrium.*

If we follow Piaget, and assume that Saussure, when referring to "value," is really referring to the Walrasian (equilibrium) price, then, the price is not an inherent property of the commodity (just as value is not an intrinsic property of the sign or word). Instead, the Walrasian price is, ultimately, a relative price. Thus, in the Walrasian price system, the price of a good has no intrinsic meaning. One can only discuss the system of prices for a series of commodities, since the meaning of a price is ultimately relational. Thus, one could argue that value is a system of differences. These prices only have meaning in the context of a general equilibrium framework, linking the prices of different commodities *at a point in time across a system.* Thus Piaget's point: in a general equilibrium framework, the price of an apple is found in a synchronic system, in that its meaning and determination are not historic (i.e., the price of an apple depends not on the past prices of an apple), but on its relationship to other prices at the same time.

McCloskey (1994) too, points out the "eerily similar" parallels between Walrasian general equilibrium and Saussurean structuralism. Commenting on the section on the value of a sign quoted at length above, McCloskey says, "Saussurean language is economistic throughout, eerily similar to Walrasian language. In a chapter called 'Linguistic Value' Saussure arrives at a view of the 'value' of a word similar to opportunity cost (a notion becoming clear to economists at about the same time) . . ." At the end of this foray into structural linguistics, McCloskey makes a key point that indicates the moment of structuralist collapse, and how such a collapse occurs (McCloskey 1994, p. 368-69). Looking at the parallel to Saussure, he realizes,[22] that just as the lingual "part" for Saussure is not the *speaker,* but the *word,* so too in the aspect of value theory that Saussure has identified as structuralist, the economic equivalent of the word is not the *subject,* but the *price/value* of the commodity.[23]

Let us examine this notion of the Walrasian system, where prices are the words used by the economic agents to speak to each other. As Saussure pointed out, then, any single exchange or any single agent's acts of exchange are to be seen as individual speech acts, or *parole.* The entire system of prices which bring into equilibrium all agent decisions, that is, the whole price mechanism, is not the possession of any one individual. That is a social possession, which is the language, or *Langue,* of the whole. How does any individual learn or come to know/internalize this system of communication? This, as we noted before, is the question of articulation, or internalization, that Saussure left untheorized. The Walrasian vision of equilibrium leaves this question unasked too. Instead, it posits the following:

a) The relationship between the signifier and the signified may be arbitrary for Saussure, but it is *not* arbitrary for the Walrasians. The information contained in the price has a very well defined, non-arbitrary relationship to the "referent" in the external world: the underlying essence of desire and reason in the pre-specified agent. Thus, while in the Saussurean system the meaning or knowledge contained in the sign (the signified), and the representation through sound or symbol (signifier) mutually determine each other,[24] the communication via prices in the Walrasian system gives primacy to the signified over the signifier. The unfulfilled desire that is signified as excess demand is the primary, singular, and complete determinant of the signifying price level in the market. Thus, the mutuality and dialectical interplay found in the internal constitution of the Saussurean structure is absent here.[25]

b) While the signifier of price may contain unambiguous and complete meaning/information, and be reduced to the underlying signified of desire and ownership within the Walrasian system, the
problem that confronts this system is the disarticulation between
parole and *Langue*.[26] How does one ensure that all the speech
acts are not only in accordance with the system, but also that the
ensuing dialogues/exchanges, are coordinated so that they emerge
as harmony, and not as cacophony? Faced with the possibility of
breakdown, and constrained by their desire to posit closure, the
individualist ontology collapses into structuralism. The equilibrium system assumes an *Auctioneer*, some force that is external to
the agents, that exists as a social or systemic mechanism that coordinates and regulates the whole "as if by an invisible hand."
The auctioneer metaphor is ultimately the equivalent of a structural law in the whole,[27] that is not in any of the agents, but that
like *Langue*, is the underlying rule that is a *social* possession and
regulates the whole. This structure in the whole is fully articulated, since all agents use the price mechanism to fully communi-
cate their desires without any fissures or gaps. What emerges is a
closed and self-regulating system.

Thus, the individualist general equilibrium framework assumes a synchronic, fully articulated structure that coordinates agent behavior! Why
does this happen? I think that this occurs because the neoclassical tradition
has two historical aims. The first, based on the roots of such analysis in the
liberal tradition of John Locke, is a desire to show that civil society, property ownership, and capitalism, are the logical product of freely interacting
pre-specified human nature. In the original formulation of civil society as the
product of underlying human nature, Locke, in his *Second Treatise on
Government*, is quite explicit in creating individuals who *choose* the structure of society. Here, fully formed, atomistic, universal human beings possessed of reason, knowledge, and work, entered civil society. The civil
society itself is the conscious product of consenting reasoning beings who
see that such a form of interaction is superior to a pre-civil state. This consciousness extends both to ownership, and to the sanctity of the contract,
and the agent has carefully determined to enter into the system after having
given all options full consideration. Thus, the systemic nature of society and
social structure is itself the product of human reason for Locke. Here we
have a fully formed individualism, where the agent in all his aspects literally
creates the social whole.

But liberal theory now faces a problem: Can one seriously claim that there is something *within* the atomistic subjects of liberal thought that assures the full ability of the system as a whole to function and reproduce itself? After all, one can hardly posit that each agent chooses the capitalist system of exchange in a conscious manner, with a view to social harmony, when engaging in individual acts of exchange: it is rarely the practice of a consumer, for example, to ponder the logic of the system, and to consciously decide to uphold it, when buying milk. Similarly, one is hard pressed to argue that capitalists are consciously attempting to work for the social good as an active component of their decision to hire or fire workers, or in their efforts to set the wage and make a profit. One can no longer argue, as did the older individualist approaches stemming from Locke, that the individual consciously creates the structure: reasoning beings craft a structure of civil society precisely because they know what is needed for social harmony, but do reasoning beings similarly ponder and craft the market or the capitalist economy?

So, starting with Smith, economics emerges as the field that addresses this challenge. Here, as with Locke, the task was to show that freely interacting beings would find social harmony in the economic whole. But in modern economics, following Smith's invisible hand (but without Smith's social-moral subjects), the aim becomes to show how the innate capacities of pre-specified human atoms would create order *even when the pre-specified human actor was not specified as consciously working for such order.* Thus, the general equilibrium vision sought to reproduce the liberal results, but abjured the fully individualist moment where the structure itself is the product of conscious human agency. This leads to the collapse into structuralism in the face of an inherent contradiction: at this point, after having specified prior agents, but not having specified them as actively and consciously creating social harmony, the general equilibrium vision conjures up a structure for social harmony: the auctioneer.

An additional point that individualists take for granted is pre-specified property rights. Just as the pre-specified structure of the auctioneer coordinates individual activity, an external structure, the state, either enforces and maintains "pre-specified" property rights, or intervenes to enforce new property rights (through land reform, for example), and upholds the sanctity of the contract. In the original liberal formulation by Locke, the civil state enforces and maintains property rights because that is the carefully reasoned basis on which consciously choosing agents decide to leave the "state of nature." In Locke's formulation, this is the *raison d'être* for the state. But again, having eschewed carefully-deciding conscious actors who cogitate on the type of structure they will put in place, neoclassical economists must either view the state as a structure outside the economy, or admit that their theory applies only to those that have, in fact, opted for a liberal civil state, and where citizenship and nationality are freely chosen rather than pre-specified by birth. But in individualist thought within economics today, the state is not usually explained in terms of the behaviors of underlying agents, and is left unspecified as an external structure not governed by the activities of underlying human nature.[28] The structures of citizenship and nationality that 'assign' individuals and activities to particular states are also not specified, but taken as 'given' when we discuss the nation as a pre-performed economic unit (see Danby 2004).

Therefore, though the Walrasian paradigm has within it the "invisible hand" of structure, it should still be considered as primarily individualist. This is because the structural law is one of coordination, but it is carefully specified in a manner that leaves agents untouched. A useful distinction can be drawn between the equilibrium requirements of the paradigm—which are structuralist—and the notion of economic subjectivity—which is individualist.[29] While Walrasian theory has fissures and gaps, its overall commitment to pre-specified human agents leads me to argue that it is still most usefully viewed as individualist. It only calls on structuralist ideas to fill its unavoidable gaps, and does so in an uncomfortable way and at an ill-defined ontological level—nobody believes the auctioneer really exists.[30]

Structuralism's Collapse into Individualism

Just as individualists collapse into structuralism when faced with fissures and gaps in their analysis, so too do structuralists collapse into individualism when confronted with gaps in their framework. Responding to challenges to their framework, they posit closure by referring to *innate,* or *pre-structural* universal human traits like rationality to justify their analysis.[31]

To see why structuralism collapses into individualism, let us start by recapitulating the fissures faced by structuralism that I pointed to in the previous section. As I noted before, structuralist thought postulates that: a) that the rules that govern the parts are prior to the parts, and must completely determine the parts, and b) that the rules must govern the logic of the parts in such a way as to ensure a closed, self-regulating structure that reproduces itself. In contrast to individualists, equilibrium poses no problem for structuralists. In the IS-LM framework described above, equilibrium emerges from the law $Y = C + I + G + (X - M)$, in the goods market, with $Ms = Md$ in the money market, and so on. These equations are the structuring laws of the whole, and equilibrium is simply the outcome in the whole when the structural laws are *all* met, so that the system can reproduce itself.

Coordination and relational transformation are the heart of structural laws, and equilibrium is simply a statement that this coordination has taken place.

But structuralists in the social sciences have to describe not only equilibrium, but also change. In positing their structures, the structuralists need to explain a) The origin of the structural laws, and b) Their evolution and change from one synchronic structure to another. The need to explain change within a synchronic structure is key for structuralists. As Piaget points out:

> The question of transformation makes the question of origin, that is, of the relation between transformation and formation, inevitable. Certainly, the elements of a structure must be differentiated from the transformation laws which apply to them. Because it is the former which undergo transformation or change, it is easy to think of the latter as immutable. (Piaget, 1971, p. 12)

He then goes on to say:

> Now the implicit hope of anti-historical or anti-genetic structuralist theories is that structure might in the end be given a non-temporal mathematical or logical foundation . . . But if what is wanted is a general theory of structure, such as must meet the requirements of an interdisciplinary epistemology [interdisciplinary, so as to meet the needs not only of structuralism in the hard sciences, or the workings of anti-historical, immutable, structures, but also the needs of a discipline like anthropology, sociology, economics, and especially development economics where the whole point of the discipline is the possibility of temporal, historical change in the developing economy's structure], then one can hardly avoid asking, when presented with such non-temporal systems as a mathematical group or a set of subsets, how the systems were obtained—unless, of course, one is willing to stay put in the heavens of transcendentalism. (Piaget, 1971, p. 12–13)

What this implies is that for any structuralist inquiry, unless one is ready to assert that structural laws are immutable and trans-historical, one needs to explain how they were formed. However, there are two factors that constrain the ability of structuralist ontologies in economics to explain the origin of and change in structures: the first constraint has to do with the historical origins of the field, the second is theoretical.

In its own historical origins, the discipline of economics, especially in its liberal-mainstream aspects, has an uneasy relationship with historical explanations of structures in the economy. Too close an examination of the historical origins of structures opens up a Pandora's Box of politics and ethics.

The IS-LM Keynesian synthesis, for example, posited structures of the economy in consumption, investment, and labor market behavior. But theorists in this tradition avoided looking too closely at the sources of, say, the consumption habits and the marginal propensities of workers to consume. Nor did they want to open to historical inspection the origins of the current wage rate, the existing distribution of property, and relationships between workers and capitalists. Thus, liberal structuralists in economics have tended to simply nod toward history, but have not taken up the question of origins in much detail.[32] This constraint applies less strongly in the works of radical structuralists, like the Institutionalists, Marxists and dependency theorists, who take up the question of the historical origins of structures much more actively.

The second, theoretical problem, which constrains structuralist analysts' ability to examine the origins of structures has to do with the articulation and closure needed to formulate a self-reproducing synchronic whole. Structuralism tends to be empiricist and inductive, looking for empirical patterns in a social whole to identify the rules that govern the whole. Unless one posits a single, universal rule that structures all societies in the same way, or argues that the rules we see in society are immutable and eternal, structuralism needs to explain the origin and evolution of structural laws.

The first possible solution to the origin of structural laws is history. As noted above, the liberal roots of the field of economics constrain the ability of economists to use such a reference point. But additionally, the logic of structuralism also limits the ability of structuralists to utilize history as a source for the origin and change of structural laws. If one argued that the structural rules emerged from the changes in society through history, one would have to examine a system *diachronically* to see where the rules came from. But structuralism is eminently *synchronic*. While it *claims* (starting with Saussure) the need for a diachronic study, all that diachronic studies do is to *compare* the rules of one system with the rules of another system. This is the essence of the comparative static method, where one simply postulates a law, looks at the equilibrium, and then assumes that somehow, the structural laws function to move a reproducing whole from one outcome to the next without having to re-describe how the agents' change behavior as the outcomes change. We still need some analysis of *how* the rules change: we need a theory of the evolution of a system.[33]

But now structuralist thought faces an additional problem: how can one posit that in the diachronic sphere the rules *change*, when in the synchronic sphere they *reproduce* themselves? What would cause them to change? One mode of positing change, as I noted, is to assume that the change comes from external stimuli, as Lévi-Strauss suggests. But this implies that there is no internal history to a people, only a history that comes from external forces—a position that reflects modernist conceptions of non-modern cultures, and has very negative connotations in the area of development.

Another mode is to posit an underlying structural rule governing diachronic as well as synchronic axes, so that all structures are contained in the originary point of history. But then the neat meshing of closed synchronic structures that keep reproducing themselves is lost: these synchronic structures cannot reproduce themselves, since they have to give way to the new emerging structures of the future. If the system is closed, synchronic, *and* self-regulating, then it lacks inner drives pushing the laws to change: it is eminently static.

In economics, despite the fact that development and the project of changing LDC economies is ultimately one of structural change, Structuralist economists do not squarely address the disjuncture between the synchronic equilibria they posit, and the diachronic process of change. The laws are identified empirically, history is referred to in some broad sense as the origin of these laws, and then they are deployed to analyze a closed synchronic system. The external stimuli which will change the structural rules will come from the *state* (which is also posited as external to the overall economic structure). Thus, as with individualism, structuralism too leaves out an analysis of the state from the *logic* of the structure. In individualist analysis the state is simply assumed to enforce property laws, and do no more, with no assessment of motivations and constraints on the state. In structuralism within economics, the traditions I study similarly posit that the state will simply follow policies which will in turn move the system to a new equilibrium, but the state itself is not analyzed structurally. There are no structural rules governing the meaning, nature, and behavior of government agents or government policy. It is, perforce, external to the system, since it is from the state that one will get the external stimulus which is the only possible source of change in a self-reproducing, fully articulated structure.

Even if one simply assumes that we can somehow look to history for the origins of structural laws, without addressing the issues raised above, structuralists face an additional theoretical problem. Individualists in economics question structural behavioral rules. They not only question the origin and formation of the rules, they question their reproduction. Why, they ask, would agents conform to the rules? How does the agent internalize these rules? Structuralists rarely respond, "because the rules are structuring" (something a structuralist like Lévi-Strauss would have no hesitation in doing). Such is the influence of individualism and the humanist liberal tradition in economics, that they either reduce the rules to underlying human nature (as in the effort to explain the marginal propensity to consume by reference to the underlying, universal, human life-cycle in savings), or they concede that they know of no reason in the long run why the agents would not conform to the atomistic description. Thus, they eschew structural laws for the long run, but claim that in the short run they are valid.

Finally, structuralists face a problem when positing evolution of the structure: while they have a way to describe the impact of external things on the structural outcomes, they need a theory of the systemic evolution of the economy, to be able to formulate a policy for change. But if the system is fully articulated and synchronic, by what means will the agents internalize or reproduce new structural laws? And if the agents are capable of learning and reproducing new structural laws, they were not fully articulated with the original structure, so why does the current structure reproduce itself? In the face of this dual desire, they close the fissure by falling back on individualism: the agent will, in the long run, with just a little help from the state, act in a manner that promotes development, because *underneath* the structure, humans are rational beings.

Thus, structuralists face a gap: a desire to posit closure, reproduction, and full articulation, for their synchronic analysis, combined with a desire to explain change, openness, and the possibility of non-reproduction for the goal of positing policies (this is especially true for debates about LDCs). Faced with such incompatible dual needs, they shift terrain, and two aspects of the theory emerge: their lapse into individualism when asked to explain the origins of behavioral structures (this requires a discussion of how articulation emerged), and their lapse into individualism when asked to explain change (this requires a positing of mutability in the diachronic sphere even as one posits reproduction in the synchronic sphere).

Consequences of Fissures and Collapses for Policy Debates

Thus, while *equilibrium* is a point of fissure for the individualists, *change* is a point of fissure for structuralists. The consequence for policy debates is that precisely those points where such "collapse" takes place become focal points for attacks by those who espouse the opposing ontology (even as they draw on each other to shore up their analyses). Thus, within development economics, structuralists attack the "auctioneer," full employment equilibrium, and pre-given property rights of the individualists as pointing to the logical incoherence of individualist analysis. And the individualists attack the "mis-specification of individuals" or the "short run" nature of structuralist analysis as evidence that structuralist theories lack intellectual substance.

The main point to note in these collapses is that there is a tension, or contradiction in the relationships of these theories. Each draws on the other for logical coherence (individualist drawing on the auctioneer, structuralists falling back on individualist justifications when pressed to describe how structural change will take place, or to justify their structural rules). But each is undermined by the presence of the other theory.[34] This tension leads to constant swings between structuralism and individualism: within each theory, in the writings of any given theorist, and in the intellectual shifts within the profession as a whole. This continual swinging has been one of the hallmarks of the CDD, and in debates about policies for LDCs.

Cartesianism in Individualism and Structuralism

Structuralism and individualism have a contradictory relationship. As shown above, given the project set out for the economics profession, each one collapses into the other, and depends on the other for logical coherence. The project set up by both structuralists and individualists is to provide a reductive discussion of economic activity: in one case a reduction to agents, and in another case a reduction to structural rules. In addition, they seek to present the economic outcomes in the economy as closed, non-contradictory and self-reproducing.[35] The combination of reduction, closure, and self-regulation in both leads them to use a very similar method of analysis: Cartesianism. Cartesian analysis is the mode of reasoning that is eminently suitable for breaking up the whole into reductive elements, and then analyzing the whole as constituted by these essential underlying ingredients. Cartesianism, then, is a shared language, since it expresses a shared commitment to reductionism with self-regulation and closure. It is also a language that crafts a shared logic of analysis: a shared commitment to the appropriate method to describe the economy: building from the first principles, or essences, to the whole, in a step-by-step manner. Here, I examine the shared Cartesianism of individualism and structuralism. This examination helps pinpoint very clearly the logic of determinism, moment of collapse, attempt at closure, and need to maintain the essence that I have described in the these ontologies so far. I use Cullenberg's description of a Cartesian totality to make my argument (Cullenberg 1989).

The Cartesian totality is specified as a space or plane, where the aspects that make up the space/plane completely determine it. The Cartesian method of analysis is "mechanistic" in its reductionism. This mechanism is drawn from the analogy of studying machines, where each part can be removed from the totality and studied, and then reinserted. This study of the different parts is the same thing as the study of the machine, since by understanding

these parts, one can understand the whole machine. Both structuralist and individualist ontologies as described above share a Cartesian conception of the
social totality, as defined by Cullenberg (1989).[36]

Individualism is clearly Cartesian, since one comprehends and captures the whole through the complete study and appropriation of the logic
of the parts (individuals). One can study each individual in isolation from
society to pinpoint the underlying, universal nature of the agent: thus one
can start with the story of Robinson Crusoe, and from this parable, describe
the operation of the economy at large. At first glance, structuralism does not
seem to lend itself to this method of isolation and description. But structuralism is *also* Cartesian. In structuralism, the "parts" are not individuals, but
rather, each structural law or "segment" of the analysis. Thus here too, one
comprehends the whole by examining each of the parts that make up the
whole (here, the structural laws). Lévi-Strauss makes this point in his study
of myths, when he argues that it does not matter which structural law one
starts with, or which myth one studies. One can unravel one law, study it
carefully, then move on to the next, then study the relationships between
these laws, and so on. Similarly, in the structuralist IS-LM analysis, the axes
of the plane, that is, the parts or descriptors of the economy are: wages and
labor in one graph/segment of the economy, the interest rate and investment
behavior in another, money demand and the interest rate in another, and
consumption and investment in the last. These various "planes" or "structural levels" together comprise the social totality. The analyst can begin with
any one of them and work through to the others.

Each particular structural law can be *understood* and analyzed independently of the others. This does not mean that these parts are not related
to each other structurally. But it implies that each specific set of structural
laws can be studied independently of the rest, and has some autonomy from
the rest of the economy. Thus one can comprehend and describe consumption behavior, a "part" of the social totality, independently of money market behavior, of investment decisions, of labor market conventions. The
marginal propensity to consume, for example, does not depend on liquidity
preference, or decisions governing the labor market. It is a law based on the
mass psychology of consumers, and resides in the collectivity of individuals
who consume. Similarly, the investment decision, based on the marginal efficiency of investment, is independent of the money market behavioral rules.
Thus the total level of investment may depend on the interest rate, set in the
money market, but the underlying rule relating investment decisions to the
interest rate is independent of rules governing liquidity preference. Instead,
it resides in the mass psychology of investors, in the collectivity of those who

invest. These parts are studied independently from each other, and then "put together" in the classic four-quadrant diagrams, where the complete economic space (the relationship between income and interest rate shown in the IS-LM graphs being the first step or first level of analysis, and the AS-AD graphs being the final total space) is comprehended as the sum of these parts.

The shared Cartesianism between individualism and structuralism shows up in the analysis undertaken by economists in two ways:[37]

i) in the exogenous/endogenous distinctions used by both modes of reasoning, which describes both the totality under consideration and the parts from which such a totality is constructed, which will describe the behavioral essences of the ontology; and

ii) the process of "reassembling" the parts in markets used by both analyses, which provides the equilibrium framework for closure and reproduction for both systems.

The next two subsections will examine each of these analytical commonalities in turn.

The Exogenous/Endogenous Distinction and Behavioral Essences

Under Cartesianism, the analyst can proceed by identifying the parts of the space, and study each part separately. This procedure requires the analyst to specify the plane or space under consideration. Thus the analyst has to decide what aspects of social life are to be identified as part of the subject matter under consideration. In the example of studying a car given earlier, the analyst must decide what is to be considered part of studying the functions and workings of the car, and what is not. Thus, though traffic patterns or the bad driving habits of others can also affect one's actual experience in driving, the Cartesian analyst here limits analysis to the mechanical operation of the car. The other factors are "exogenous."

Thus, in some kinds of economics, for example, a storm may affect the economy, but is external to the economy proper, just as buses on the road may affect the functioning of a car on the road, but are exogenous to the study of the mechanisms and parts of a car. While most analysts share a Cartesian framework, they disagree on what should be properly considered "exogenous," however. Policy variables are usually understood as exogenous in this sense, since they can affect the specific outcomes of the social totality, but are operated from outside the totality, and do not affect the logic of the totality The state, as the primary operator of policy variables, is thus external to the logic of the theories, as I pointed out earlier.

Neither individualists nor structuralists posit a theory of the state. (This has been the case for much of mainstream economics, especially in policy debates: thus this point is the hallmark of an economics geared to prescribe policy. But in other analyses that do not have such an aim, as with the New Political Economy of Buchanan for individualism, or the Marxist theories of the state for structuralism, this is not true).

Having determined the scope of the subject matter, the Cartesian analyst must now proceed to examine the workings of the parts identified. In doing this, the parts must be capable of being analyzed independently of the whole. This leads to another type of exogeneity in Cartesian analysis. This consists of aspects or parts of the economy which are seen as internal to the economy (thus they are not "outside" the economy, the way that say storms and viral infections are). However, they are *explanatory or causal* variables (or essences) in the analysis. *This set of variables consists of the priorly determined variables from an ontological standpoint: the essences described above.* Thus, for example, the causal role given to individuals in individualism implies that analytically, preferences are exogenous: they cannot be changed, since they are the basis for explaining everything else. Similarly, within the structuralist analyses, the rules governing consumption as shown in the marginal propensity to consume, governing liquidity preference as shown in the money market demand curve, and investment as shown in the marginal efficiency of investment schedule, are exogenous. These rules are the causal factors in structuralist analysis. They have to be exogenous. Since this set of exogenous variables is crucially important to the logical operation of causality, any question of their instability cannot arise without seriously threatening the analysis.

Thus both structuralism and individualism share a conception of exogenous variables that can be used like policy variables: external to the economy's operation, but whose actions can change economic outcomes. Both sides often agree on what these variables are (for example, both agree that taxes are exogenous in this sense). This gives a spurious sense of commonality to their discussions. But they also have another set of exogenous variables (different in each case), which cannot be touched without destabilizing their analysis. These variables are their essences: and it is by identifying these variables that one can identify whether a particular model is individualist or structuralist. This is the set of variables that take on a causal role in the analysis of each ontology. For individualists, any attempt to have endogenously generated changes in agent preferences, or knowledge, or property rights causes their system to collapse. Similarly, any effort to endogenize the marginal propensity to consume would lead to a breakdown of the IS-LM system. It is often in these areas where causal factors can be disturbed that each side draws on the other to shore up its own analysis, since any disturbance of the essence would lead to analytical breakdown. Thus structuralists draw on individualism any time their structural rules are questioned, and individualists draw on structuralism any time that agent coordination or property rights are called into question.

Equilibrium

Both modes of argument adhere to an equilibrium formation of the social totality (equilibrium in both ontologies being understood as a state when the logic of all the parts is satisfied simultaneously). "Equilibration," or change from one equilibrium to another, is one process that creates the most potential for collapse in these approaches. Equilibration is the process of bringing together all the parts of the social totality, and ensuring that their various specifications "mesh" with one another, *without changing any of the independently specified logic of each part.*

For equilibration to be met within these frameworks, the process of fitting together these parts must be seamless and timeless; "seamless" in the sense that *no* interaction or relationship between economic parts can be left loose or unresolved in the equilibrium. Timeless because given the absence of history and change in *both* ontologies (note that the structuralism here is the synchronic structuralism of Cartesianism, not the through time structures of say, Hegelianism), the point when all rules are met must also be the point where there can be no more change. This is because if there are specific ways in which the irreversibility of time can affect the outcomes, then time modifies and changes the logically-prior parts. This renders the process by which the analyst fits the parts together in equilibrium meaningless. For example, if the process of reaching equilibrium involved undertaking new trades that changed the underlying property distributions, or changed agent's preferences for individualism, then their analysis will break down. Thus the only way for them to move from equilibrium to equilibrium is to call on an auctioneer: a structure that can move the priorly specified agent safely from equilibrium point to equilibrium point.

The same problem does not seem to emerge as acutely for structuralists. Given the nature of their analysis, there is nothing to prevent them from specifying a structural rule by which the agent can move unchanged from the old equilibrium to the new one. Equilibrium for structuralists simply requires that all the rules be met. It does not have the additional requirements that this be done so with all agents being satisfied, since structuralist agents are simply products of the structural rules governing economic behavior. But if one looks a bit more closely, we find that structuralists too face a problem. Given their assumptions about the agent's articulation with a given structure, how is the same agent to suddenly articulate to a new structure? Thus, how is one to explain, for example, sudden changes in liquidity preference or investment behavior? Where does this change come from? As long as structuralist "changes" involve parametric changes that leave the overall structure of the economy unchanged (so let us say taxes rise), they have no problem, since the rules governing agent behavior are the same. But if the changes involve any change in rules (like a change in the investment decision or liquidity preference, or a change in labor market behavior), they cannot explain how the agent moved from the old set of structural rules to the new ones. Unfortunately, most policy debates on growth and development focus on how to increase investment to spur growth: a change that requires changes in the structural rules governing investment. This focus leaves structuralists particularly vulnerable in theoretical debates within the field of development. They too then fall back on individualist assumptions about human nature and rationality to explain how agents adopt the new structural rules.

The two forms of analysis share not only a similar concept of equilibrium but also similar notions of change (comparative statics). The actual move from one logically-determined moment to the other is usually fuzzy or left unspecified in most analyses. The place where both structuralists and individualists describe the process of change through time is growth theory: a key source of ideas in development economics, since economic growth should presumably lead to national well-being and better standards of living for the LDC poor.

In the case of growth theory, each approach has to specify *additional* laws and relationships to explain change over time (thus each side develops its own form of growth theory, where additional assumptions about how resources or demand grows are added to the analysis). All that has happened here is a redefinition of the Cartesian space, adding one more dimension (time) and one more causal law (law governing the rates of change of resources, technology, labor, or investment) explaining its operation. Thus the weaknesses and gaps identified in each ontological position are left unresolved, and the debates between the two theoretical traditions continue in this area. (I discuss the literature on development in detail in the next chapter.)

POLITICS AND ENTRY POINTS: A GLIMPSE AHEAD

The analysis of structuralist and individualist ontologies presented above brings into sharp focus two issues—what can be called the entry point of analysis and the logic of the analysis.[38] The entry points of analysis for the participants in this debate are either conceptions of individuals or of broad behavioral structures identified in the economy. The particular entry point chosen shapes the political agenda set by the analysts (and vice versa). In the following chapters, I show that the entry points used in the CDD implicitly set the agenda for a struggle over whether the LDCs need to focus on growth and distribution (the New Structuralist position) or on growth and efficiency (the IMF position). This struggle emerges because each entry point sets up its own evaluative criteria to define development and to measure the policy's success or failure. They are using different "yardsticks" to measure the impact of a devaluation.

But though the differing entry points set up "incommensurable terrains" in terms of the evaluative criteria and goals for economic policy that they define, the logic of analysis used by both theoretical traditions is Cartesian. The complete reduction of the social totality (the LDC economy in world markets) to the parts identified by each leaves very little room for a discussion of the ways in which contradictions in the social totality could simultaneously reinforce and disrupt processes set off by a devaluation. Thus the participants in this debate have different ontologies, but share a common reductive method of analysis. This shared method is in part the result of their shared epistemological adherence to rationalist and empiricist analyses (see Resnick and Wolff 1987a and 1987b for a discussion of epistemology in economics). In the next few chapters, I examine the development literature (chapter three), the literature on balance of payments and exchange rates (chapter four) and the CDD (chapter five) in detail. I show how the use of such reductive analyses affected policies, as the profession swung from one pole of the structure/agent reductionism to the other.

Chapter Three
Structuralism and Individualism in Development Economics

INTRODUCTION

The CDD has focused on the impact of devaluations in developing economies, and has therefore been strongly marked by the direction that Development Economics took in its formative years. This chapter will show that in its early decades, Development Economics rested on a peculiar combination of structuralist and individualist ontologies, in a complementary relation that excluded other ontologies. Neoliberal critics in the 1980s and 90s have rejected this dialectic and sought to expunge all but the most minimal structural assumptions required for the operation of a neoclassical economy from the analyses of LDC economies.[1] This chapter traces that history, using ontology as a frame of reference. The next chapter will examine the ontological legacy of the field of international finance and exchange rate theory, and chapter five will draw these two discussions together to take up the CDD.

Since the literature in the field of development economics is vast, this chapter will limit discussion to the two over-arching theoretical visions that mark this shift from structuralist to individualist ontologies within development economics:

a) The structuralist ontologies of the import-substituting, state-led development project, with industrial development as its unifying goal (referred to as ISI); and

b) The individualist ontologies of the neoclassical counter-revolution, or the neoliberal response to ISI, which has the project of dismantling the state, and replacing it with private property and free markets as its unifying goal (referred to as NL).[2]

I will take up the structuralist analyses first, and then discuss the individualist analyses. This sequence is based on the historical sequence in which each rose to prominence.[3]

"Structuralist Analyses in Development Economics" takes up the structuralist ontologies of ISI. Here, I examine the intellectual origins of ISI, and track the ways in which structuralism was deployed to support it. I show that:

a) The development project understood the LDCs primarily in terms of their distance from the West, and not in terms of the historical legacy of colonialism and subsequent decolonization.

b) Classical Economics was an important source of ideas. This resulted in a peculiar inversion of historically Western concerns and worries onto the non-West.

c) Ontology played a key role in this vision of development, with individualism being seen as the hallmark of the developed economy, and structuralism deployed to describe the source of the difference between the DC and LDC; and

d) The structuralist ontology as deployed in ISI had the consequence (whether intended or not), of eliding class and producing a harmonious vision of national weal.

After that, "Individualism in Development Economics: The Neoliberal Counter-Revolution" will take up the NL counter-revolution. Here, I argue that:

a) The individualist paradigm was already voicing dissent, especially in the arena of trade policy, from the very beginning of the development project. The current NL strategies draw on these early dissensions.

b) The dissension was marked not by an assertion of difference from the West (which structuralism provided), but by "sameness," which came from individualism, especially the type of individualism deployed in economics.

c) Again, the re-organization of the field had the consequence (whether intended or not), of eliding class and producing a harmonious vision of national weal.

The "Conclusion" wraps up the chapter.

STRUCTURALIST ANALYSES IN DEVELOPMENT ECONOMICS

"Development economics," in the general sense of examining the historical development of an economy, has long existed. For example, Marx's (1977) discussion in *Capital Vol. 1* of the enclosure movement and the transition from feudalism to capitalism is the story of the economic development of capitalist relations within Britain. But usually this kind of study has been designated as economic history, rather than part of the field of economic development. *Development* economics refers to the specific set of theories that emerged in the 1950s and 60s, and identified the economies of the decolonized Third World as their object of analysis. It had as its agenda not merely *description*, but *prescription* as well. Its *raison d'être* was the elaboration of policy to change contemporary LDC national economies, with such explicitly stated goals as poverty eradication, growth, and industrialization.

Development Economics as a field emerged after World War II. Arndt (1987) argues that the question of the economic problems of underdeveloped nations became central during World War II, and crystallized into a project for the betterment of the LDC soon after the war ended. Escobar (1995) provides discussion of the social context of the rise of development economics in the post-World War II period, and the various ways in which it functioned to cement the West's global power.

Here, instead of examining how and why the field emerged when it did, I discuss its ontological contours and intellectual history. In the first section, I examine the overall shape and nature of development economics that emerged in the late 40s, 1950s and 60s. In the next section, I analyze the theories and models identified in that first section to show how they are mainly structuralist, and when and why they draw on individualism. The last section discusses the anomalous aspects of the field's turn to structuralism, and examines some of the consequences of adopting structuralist ontology in development economics.

What was Development Economics?

In order to trace the contours of the development field in the period leading to the rise of ISI, I examine the general literature emerging in the 40s, 50s and 60s. I start with two texts that claimed to be compendiums, or surveys of Development Economics as a coherent *field:* Meier and Baldwin's (1957) text *Economic Development: Theory, History, Policy,* and Okun and Richardson's 1961 *Studies in Economic Development: A Book of Readings.*[4]

The key points that emerge (each taken up in the following sub-sections) are summarized in Table 3.1. The topics in the table are organized in the order in which they will be taken up below. The table presents the topics covered in each sub-section (column 1), the assumptions about LDC ontology deployed by the theories examined in each sub-section (column 2), and the consequences of these assumptions for policy and for the historical development of the field (column 3). The sequence of rows, by contrast, depicts the logic that these authors and editors imposed on the field.

The West as the Reference Point: Underdevelopment as "Difference"

Both the Meier-Baldwin text and the Okun-Richardson reader start by describing the poverty of the LDC. Meier and Baldwin focus on the disparity in income levels between developed and underdeveloped nations, and define development as " . . . a process whereby an economy's real national income increases over a long period of time" (p. 2). The distinction between first and third world is made by drawing heavily on the work of Kuznets: he is referred to in the section on measuring national income (p. 4); in arguing for theories that look at the forces behind growth in national income and growth in population, rather than looking at per capita GDP as a measure of development directly (p. 6); to argue that both in absolute and relative terms the gap between developed and underdeveloped nations has widened in the past century (p. 10); and to present data on the differences between developed and underdeveloped nations (pp. 10-11). The Okun-Richardson reader's opening article (the only article in their section called "Introduction") is by Kuznets: his 1950 "International Differences in Income Levels."

What makes Kuznets important? Kuznets (along with Colin Clark, Louis Bean, and other economists) had

> a) attempted to pin down the descriptive contours of the developed world, in his *Modern Economic Growth,* and

> b) systematized the distance between first and third world, in terms of a series of markers—income, patterns of occupation, proportion of employment and production in agriculture and industry, standards of living.

This approach becomes the backdrop for development economics, since it leads to two questions:

> a) What accounted for the high standards of living, and the material progress of the developed nations in the past century (and possibly more)? They too had once been low income, agrarian economies, so how did they transform? What happened to produce the contours of the developed economies identified by Kuznets and others?

> b) What accounts for the failure of the third world nations to replicate this pattern of progress? What prevents them from entering the ranks of the developed and how can one prescribe policy to overcome these barriers?

Table 3.1 Historical Origins of the ISI paradigm

Topics	Content and Assumptions	Consequence of Assumptions
First subsection: Definition of Underdevelopment	a) LDC as Distance from DC: location of LDC difference from DC. b) LDC as historically following in footsteps of DC, and goal of development set up as the convergence between LDC and current DC economy: location of possible sameness of DC and LDC.	a) Elision of colonial history and class. b) Hunt for internal structures in LDC that explain difference between LDC and DC. c) Definition of LDC aspirations as a achievement of sameness with DC d) Hunt for policies that accelerate anticipated convergence of LDC and DC e) Ontological tension between sameness and difference in the origins of the field.
Second subsection: The Role of the Classicals	a) Classicals as a source for History of DC success: mapped onto LDC as a source for strategies. b) Classicals as a source for possible worries about DC failure: mapped onto LDC as source for LDC failure.	a) LDC failure viewed as a reflection of internal problems in the LDC. b) Fabrication of collective national interest in growth. c) Classicals' worries about DC stagnation "mapped on" to LDCs' as the source of their "difference" and failure to reproduce DC success.
Third subsection: DC Growth Theory	a) DC growth theory as a source for possible mechanisms in the DC that overcame Classicals' fears of DC stagnation. b) Mapped onto LDC as the source of structural parameters that mark LDC difference.	a) LDC failure viewed as inability of LDC to overcome the factors identified by DCs as possible constraints to their own growth by Classicals. b) DC success provides a policy-hope for the ability to replicate DC structures that proved Classical anxieties wrong. c) Strategies prohibitively expensive, field still unsure about ability to convert LDC difference into LDC-DC sameness.
Fourth subsection: ISI	a) Three key areas of difference picked out for policy: values, population and investment/growth from the DC theories about DC success (third section above). b) Deployment of "sameness/difference" tension generates both identification of barriers to growth, and strategies to overcome the barriers and produce sameness.	a) ISI Theory and policy elides class and colonial history. b) Tension between identified difference and hoped-for sameness between LDC and DC left unresolved. c) Tension between sameness and difference shows up as a tension between structuralism and individualism. This leaves the field vulnerable to pendulum swings from one ontology to the other. d) Individualist dissenters who wish to emphasize sameness gather forces for the NL counter-revolution.

What I wish to emphasize here (since it will become key to understanding how development economics used selective individualism in the section below), is that from the outset, the field took the developed world to be the norm against which the underdeveloped world was known to be underdeveloped. Meier-Baldwin and Okun-Richardson set up the question of underdevelopment from the outset as an interrogation of how and why the developing world *deviated* from the developed world. The developing world was *different*, its difference was known by its *deviation*, and in its deviation lay the *causes* of its poverty. The goal follows automatically—the elimination of difference, and the reproduction of the West in the non-West.[5]

Further, as this difference was located in markers like industrialization, patterns of occupation, income levels and standards of living, the question asked, "what accounts for LDC failure/deviation," looked at these specific issues and patterns, and not to colonialism or history. The way in which the question was posed as *deviation*, rather than as historical mechanisms by which the LDC ended up as different, led to an elision of colonial history, and instead a focus on extant (ahistorical timeless) "structures" found in the developing world. As will be shown below, the focus on "national" poverty drawn from Kuznets also elided class.

And finally, since the task of development became the *elimination* of difference, the field had to simultaneously postulate the possibility of sameness-to-come. What emerged, as I will show, was a tension between sameness and difference, with difference marked by structuralist ontologies, and sameness marked by individualist ontologies.

The Classicals as a Source of Answers

The next sections of Meier-Baldwin's text and the Okun-Richardson reader start with a systematic presentation of ideas from Smith and Classical economics. Both locate Smith, Ricardo, and Marx as key classical sources for the field (Meier-Baldwin put Marx in a separate section, while Okun-Richardson include Malthus). Thus, development economics in its origins saw the Classicals as a key source for analyses about the process of development. Theories about the process of development in the *West* become the source for the theory of underdevelopment in the *non-West*. This interest in the Classicals is not surprising: if the issue at stake is why and how did the First World manage to become prosperous, then the Classicals are an obvious choice.

The Classicals posed their analysis in terms of two questions (at least as picked up by the analysis, articles and excerpts chosen for presentation by both Meier-Baldwin and Okun-Richardson):

a) *What accounted for the phenomenal growth of material well-being under capitalism in western societies? How did the set of relationships that allowed this growth emerge?* This question was taken up particularly by Smith and Marx. Smith saw specialization and the division of labor due to the emergence of markets as the providing the impetus for the dynamic growth of the West. Marx saw the enclosure movement and the rise of merchants as providing the dynamic which then allowed primitive accumulation and the transition from feudalism to capitalism in a variety of ways.[6]

b) *Would this process continue indefinitely? What was the "fuel" which would keep the economy growing? Would the economy inevitably run out of steam?* Ricardo, Malthus and Marx took up this question. Malthus saw population growth as ultimately leading to a dampening of the engines of growth, with the economy converging to a steady state. Ricardo saw diminishing returns in agriculture and lagging agrarian productivity as a possible limit to growth. But he thought that trade, and distribution of value away from landlords and towards capitalists, could provide the necessary fuel to keep this process in motion. Marx saw the limits to accumulation and growth in social terms: accumulation was uneven, crisis prone, and based on exploitation. Eventually, the demise of the system would come not from any issue of *physically* running out of fuel for growth, but due to a change in social relationships, just as the end of feudalism and the move to capitalism was not merely due to the physical constraints to growth in feudal societies, but because of a change in social relationships marked by struggle.

Three consequences were picked up by development theorists:

a) *The Classicals saw the forces leading to the development of capitalism in the West as primarily internal:* Whether they saw the development of capitalism as benevolent or exploitative, they saw it as a product of internal changes in western society. Absent from this story is the question of whether the pools of resources that financed primitive accumulation, and the changed social dynamics of relationships within the West, were at least partly derived from the colonial encounter and imperialism.[7]

The classicals did talk about the non-west. In Ricardo, one finds not the word "colonialism," but the much more benevolent and benign word "trade." Trade becomes an exchange of equals, benefiting all, and is thus an engine of growth. Ricardo spends little time on discussing the *origins* of the system of exchange and capitalist production. For Marx (or rather, the version of Marx found in the mainstream literature), one sees the issue of colonies emerge in terms of how the colonies are transformed by contact with capitalism, and how changes in the colonies can create crises in an already extant capitalism. Colonialism follows capitalism—capitalism may even necessitate colonialism, as in Leninist theories of imperialism—but colonialism has little to do with the story of the *emergence* of capitalism.[8]

This is an important omission, since it has implications for how development theory perceives the process of development. If the *origins* of dynamic growth are rooted in colonialism, then the ability to follow the same path to capitalist development is probably closed for the newly decolonized nations.[9] But since the development project drew on a notion of a completely internal engine of growth, drawing on internal resources, development as a project from the very start assumed that development in the LDCs would also be a primarily internal matter, which could replicate the experience of the West. All that was needed was to find out what prevented the pool of resources from accumulating for unleashing growth. Once identified, these could be changed via policy.

b) *Development Economists, following the Classicals, used poverty as a national marker, and the nation-state as the unit of analysis:* The Classicals, discussing growth in the context of civil society and established nation states, looked at material well-being in *national* terms, and looked for the causes of material well-being in dynamics internal to the pre-formed unit of the "nation." The definition of development described above maintained this tradition of examining the pre-given and closed nation.

Similarly, Kuznets' definition of the LDC stresses *national* deviation of a host of countries all marked in exactly the same way by this deviation, as the marker of underdevelopment. The poverty described by the theories that emerged (Kuznets, Rostow, Harrod-Domar, discussed below) was not *individual* poverty, but *National* poverty. What marked developing societies, and created a role for the state, was not merely that these were economies that had large numbers of poor individuals, but that in some other sense, some fundamental sense, these economies were *themselves* poor.

Thus, poverty in an LDC for Kuznets, Rostow, Rosenstein-Rodan, Nurkse, and the panoply of development economists in the 40s, 50s and 60s, is not to be mistaken with the poverty found among those who live below the poverty line in the developed world. Individually poor people may draw on a welfare state, but when the nation is itself poor, when poverty is a collective marker of the nation, then creating a welfare state is not a viable option—the resources for handling such *collective* poverty simply do not exist in such a society. This focus on the causes of collective poverty was a precondition for debates about national growth, to be taken up in the next section. It also allowed development to be easily identified as in the collective and harmonious interest of all participants in the LDC nation-state. High GDP per capita and growth become the solutions to collective poverty, while redistribution or political struggle, which might be a response to the poverty of groups *within* the nation, could be set aside.

c) *The Classicals looked for constraints or limits to capitalist growth.* As noted above, many classical economists (and some later economists like Keynes and Schumpeter) were worried about the ability of capitalism to continue to grow, and identified a variety of factors that could produce stagnation. These concerns receded among economists as DCs continued to grow, but were revived in analyses of barriers to LDC growth. Thus, to answer the question of what creates the "collective poverty" in the non-west, development economists took the Classicals' worries about limits to capitalist growth in DCs as their starting point (overpopulation in Malthus, lagging agrarian productivity in Ricardo, lack of markets in the version of Marx picked up by the mainstream, insufficient demand and inadequate investment in Keynes, and lack of entrepreneurship in Schumpeter).

Hans Singer (1964) notes this curious set of parallels between the worries of the Classicals about the prospects for continued DC growth, and the worries about the barriers to growth and development in LDCs found in the development economics literature of the 40s and 50s. In his *International Development: Growth and Change* (1964), Singer examines the parallel between the concerns of the Classicals and the concerns of development economics. He says (D stands for developed, U stands for underdeveloped, D-pessimism is pessimism about DC growth prospects, U-pessimism is pessimism about LDC development prospects):

> It is more important, however, to look at the reasons which make the great economists D-pessimists and to realize why this list sounds so familiar now to us who worry about the underdeveloped countries. Worries about lagging productivity in agriculture (Ricardo)—worries about population growth (Malthus)—worries about lack of markets and purchasing power (Marx)—worries about the failures of, or interference with, entrepreneurship (Schumpeter)—worries about the absence of exhaustion of productive investment opportunities (Keynes): why has this list such a familiar ring about it? Of course! These are precisely the things that we are worrying about now when we think of the underdeveloped countries! It is an instructive, and perhaps chastening thought to realize that all the things that we are worried about in relation to the underdeveloped countries, and that have made so many economists into U-pessimists, were far from unknown to the great economists of earlier days. Quite the contrary: these things were in the forefront of their minds. But they were worried about these things, not in relation to the poor or underdeveloped countries, but rather in relation to the conditions created by economic progress. This is certainly one of the most curious and dramatic reversals of thinking. (Singer 1964, p. 5)

Singer's book, written in 1964, came at the height of optimism about the prospects for LDC development through ISI. Singer's purpose here is to use the optimism about DC growth, and the fact that these obstacles did not materialize or hinder growth, to argue that if we can just create the right conditions, LDC growth will emerge too—just as we are now D-optimists, we need to become LDC-optimists. Whatever worked to overcome these limits in DCs is the key—it is these things that will also shatter the barriers to growth and progress in the LDC. Here, in a series of very revealing arguments, Singer has identified DC progress as goal for LDC, analyses of DC problems as source for the problems and limits identified in LDCs, and DC success as the source for solutions to the problems. Goal, problem, solution, all seem to be curiously reflective of the DC.[10]

Having a) identified the dynamics of development as primarily internal, b) posed the issue of what the central problem is in terms of collective poverty of a region *per se* and not in terms of the poverty of specific groups of people within the region, and c) located the causes of this collective poverty by drawing on Classical and later theories about limits to DC growth, development economists sought to identify the sources of these blockages to LDC growth, so as to develop policies that could overcome them.

It is at this point that development economics turned to growth theory. Growth theory was first formulated in the context of DCs. These theories were formulated by Rostow, Harrod-Domar and Schumpeter, among others, to counter the Classical argument that DC stagnation was inevitable. They explained the continuing growth of DCs and showed that when certain conditions were achieved in the DCs, growth would continue without limit and ensure perpetual prosperity. These were answers to the problems posed by the Classicals, and since development economists took the Classicals as their starting point, they turned to those theorists who had effectively responded to the challenge of stagnation posed by the Classicals.

Growth Controversies

Since growth was to be the solution to collective poverty, growth theory became the arena for debate about the best policies for LDCs to follow. The struggle to define the best strategy for growth came to be known as the "growth controversy." It is worth examining since aspects of this controversy resurface in the NL counter-revolution.

Earlier theories about the possibilities of growth and self-sustaining development in the LDC were pessimistic about the possibility of any quick solution to the problems of LDCs, and predicted a long period of difficult transformation before the LDCs saw much growth. The later theories (which originated as dissensions from the earlier ones) were optimistic, and predicted that once a few key barriers that created difference from the West were identified and removed, the process of change would proceed apace in a self-feeding mechanism of dynamic growth.

The debate proceeded along three interlinked lines of thought:

a) Growth Theory, which examined how DCs overcame the Classicals' dire predictions of inevitable stagnation,

b) Linear Stages of Growth and Balanced Growth, which extended this work theoretically and by examination of DC history, to prescribe what was needed for an LDC economy to do likewise (the set of prescriptions being onerously long and difficult), and

c) Unbalanced Growth, which argued that the set of actions needed to tip an economy into self-sustained development and allowed the LDC to replicate the DCs were not difficult to put in place via policy.

I take up each one of these below.

Growth Theory in the DC

In their section on "Theory of Economic Development," Meier-Baldwin present a discussion of the mechanisms by which one can have an endogenously generated steady state in an economy where Savings and Investment automatically equilibrate at full employment, and resources are allocated efficiently via the market. The question is primarily one of the relationships between efficiency, full employment, and growth in a modern capitalist economy. Here, the limits to growth are overcome by a process of accumulation and efficient resource allocation, under harmonious relationships, with investment for growth guided by the entrepreneur.

They have three sub-sections: "Neo-classical analysis," "Schumpeterian Analysis," and "Post-Keynesian Analysis." The section on "Neo-Classical" analysis makes no mention of the Solow-Swan growth model. They primarily refer to Clark, Marshall, Pigou, Hicks, Cassel, Wicksell and Edgeworth. None of these writers is particularly known for their analysis of the conditions in LDCs. Instead, the focus is on efficient resource allocation as a prerequisite for the growth of productive resources. Schumpeterian analysis primarily focuses on the role of entrepreneurship in overcoming limits to growth (again in DCs). Here, the focus is on the ability of the market to generate growth via the dynamic opportunities created for innovation, entrepreneurship, and progress.

The sub-section on "Post-Keynesian analysis" is not about "Post Keynesianism" in the modern sense of the word, but simply describes authors who follow Keynes' lead in assessing the possible limits to capitalist accumulation because of insufficient demand in the growth context. Therefore, this section is an exposition of the Harrod-Domar model, which discusses the conditions needed to ensure that limits to DC growth are overcome automatically as each period's savings provides the investment for the next period. For this to happen, growth in production generated by investment has to match the growth in demand generated by investment. In addition, Meier and Baldwin have a section on the historical analysis of growth in Britain (separated out from the theoretical analyses), where one finds discussions of the emergence of industrialization. The categories they choose to examine in this section reflect their theoretical emphases: innovation, entrepreneurship and capital accumulation, and changing norms and social values.[11]

The Okun-Richardson reader similarly includes readings one would not find in any text on economic development today. In the section on "The Advanced Countries: Theories and Models of Growth," one finds (after Smith, Ricardo, Malthus, J. S. Mill and Marx) a discussion of Marshallian growth by Youngson (a reflection of what Meier and Baldwin refer to as Neo-Classical analysis); Schumpeter on entrepreneurship; Domar on the Harrod-Domar model; and Hansen on how declining population growth overcomes the Malthusian population trap. This closely reflects Meier and Baldwin's three categories in their "theory" section, with an article which explicitly addresses population and Malthusian worries added to the list.

Thus, the first set of growth theories that are examined address the ability of the DCs to overcome the limits to growth identified by the Classicals. The savings-investment linkage overcomes the worry about inadequate resources, the demographic transitions and changes in population growth address overpopulation as a source of stagnation, efficient resource allocation addresses worries about poor growth due to bad resource utilization, and Schumpeterian innovation addresses worries about inadequate investment opportunities or falling productivity over time.

Linear-Stages of Growth and Balanced Growth

Growth theory had argued that one need not worry about DC stagnation. But what would it take to get LDCs to the point where they too can overcome limits to growth? Here, the key theories identified are "Linear Stages of Growth," (Rostow, Kuznets, Colin Clark), and "balanced growth" (Nurkse, Rosenstein-Rodan).

Meier-Baldwin discuss the theories of the stages of growth in their section on the "Historical Outlines of Economic Development," especially in the chapters on "Emergence of the Center."[12] They present the theories of linear stages of growth developed by Hegel, Marx, Rostow, Clark and others. They argue that while useful, these approaches do not allow for the possibility that nations can develop by "jumping" over some stages, so that a classification of "subsistence economy" (peripheral/underdeveloped) versus "market economy" (developed/central) may be more useful. Okun-Richardson follow their discussion of DC growth theories with a section on "The Underdeveloped Countries: Modern Approaches to Development." Here, the opening articles are by Rosenstein-Rodan, Nurkse, Fleming, Viner and Singer. The next section ("Characteristics of Growing Economies") has articles by Rostow, Kuznets, and Bauer and Yamey.

The question of "stages of growth," and the possibility of accelerating development by "by-passing" some stages, became the heart of the growth controversy. The "stages of growth" models were first propounded by Rostow in his *Stages of Economic Growth*, and developed in various directions by Kuznets, Rosenstein-Rodan, and Clark to form the "big-push" theories of sustained economic growth in LDCs.

In this theory, the historical path to sustained growth by DCs is seen as the culmination of a series of historical stages (Kuznets, Rostow, Clark). This set of historical steps is the mechanism by which all countries will grow, and is the historical sequence of events to unfold in all societies. The LDCs are at various stages of development depending on how close they are to the developed country template. Since the full ability to "take off" into self-sustaining growth requires that all the pre-conditions for this historical state be in place, development required a "big push," to put all these factors into place.[13] This required both an enormous outlay of resources (beyond the reach of the poor LDC economies), and the readiness to be resigned to a long period of continued poverty and low growth as each of these factors was painstakingly put in place. The proponents of this view of development came to be called the proponents of "balanced growth."

The balanced growth proponents (Nurkse, Rosenstein-Rodan) felt that all the factors identified as key to sustained DC growth were important, and the absence of any one of them could prevent self-sustained growth from occurring. This placed a rather formidable barrier before LDCs. The key snag identified by balanced growth proponents was the simultaneous development of a variety of markets, so that supply and demand grew in tandem, and as one sector started to slack others took their place.

What accounts for this rather grim vision about LDC's prospects? Although this pessimism about LDC growth drew on the Classical pessimism about DC growth, LDC pessimists like Nurkse and Rosenstein-Rodan were nonetheless optimistic about DC growth. This DC-LDC difference they explained through a set of theories with a historical story about the rise of human creativity, technological advancement, thrift, socio-cultural change, and institutional change in the DCs. These changes generated the institutions and practices of free markets, with agents capable of acting with reason and forethought in these free markets, and provided the minimal structures of modernity which then unleashed self-sustaining growth.

But these development economists defined LDCs in terms of their *difference* from DCs. LDC stagnation was attributed to a variety of structures (traditional culture, overpopulation, lack of entrepreneurial spirit, inadequately developed markets) that created a *divergence* from the conditions and institutions found in DCs as identified in the theories above. If the reason for LDC poverty was the *absence* of these qualities and institutions, then the hope for LDC take-off is very poor indeed.[14]

These initial theories of growth did not argue that growth was *impossible,* or that take-off into development would *never* occur. But they did seem to indicate that this required an enormous expenditure of will, social change, institutional change, and investment. The LDC had to address the Ricardian worry about agrarian productivity, the Malthusian worry about population growth, and the Schumpeterian worry about values and norms and entrepreneurial spirit.

The neoclassical, Schumpeterian, and Harrod-Domar growth theories outlined above focused on the ability to sustain growth in the DCs by undertaking efficient resource allocation, using entrepreneurial technological innovation, and creating a self-sustained cycle of savings-financed investment respectively. Linear Stages and Balanced Growth had added to this a historical, teleological story about DC entry into the type of society described by the neoclassicals, Schumpeter and Harrod-Domar. They identified the freeing of humans from tradition, the move to enlightenment and reason and a culture of hard work and thrift, along with the development of markets, the rise of production in manufacturing sectors through the industrial revolution, and a shift to high rates of capital accumulation, as key preconditions for DC success.

Policy Optimism and Unbalanced Growth

Linear Stages and Balanced growth did not promise quick solutions. While these theories identified the various structural bottlenecks and characteristics that prevented LDC growth, they could not provide any well-defined solutions to the problem of LDC poverty. The extent of structural difference postulated was so complete that it doomed any prospect of rapid convergence to the West.

Suppose that *all* the structures identified by the Linear Stages and Balanced Growth proponents were not required for change, but only one or two key structures were needed? In other words, if those one or two structures were changed, they would set off a dynamic process which would pull down all the remaining barriers to growth. Development was attainable and perhaps inevitable, though it might take a little time to attain as the dynamic changes worked their way through the economy. It is this optimism that one sees in Meier-Baldwin's rejection of the "linear stages of growth," and their insistence that one can "by-pass" some of the stages and emerge from peripheral status. In the Okun-Richardson reader, the articles that encompass this vision are those by Fleming, Lewis, and Hirschman.

Hirschman's theory of unbalanced growth was crucial in arguing for an optimistic vision of accelerated development. Drawing on a variety of theories about industrial organization, innovation, and entrepreneurship (see Hirschman 1993 for a discussion of the sources for his theory), Hirschman (1957, 1958, 1965, 1971) argued that LDCs could grow without all the preconditions identified by the Linear Stages and Balanced Growth theorists. If one could identify a few key sectors with many backward and forward linkages, they would provide the demand and create new markets for other industries and markets, create dynamic shifts in still other industries and markets, and tip the LDC economy over into development.

This response to the pessimistic position of the balanced growth theorists was a key story in the nexus of theories that form the heart of ISI. This set of theories came to dominate the field: the answer to the problem of converting LDC difference to LDC sameness lay in selectively focusing on capital accumulation, and on identifying the key arenas in which to create growth. A series of models by Lewis, Hirschman, and Prebisch-Singer formalized this hopeful approach and laid the theoretical foundations of ISI.[15]

Development Optimism: Growth and ISI

Let us look at how this optimism is reflected in the two development texts we are examining. They were written at what seems to be the cusp of the debate between pessimists and optimists. But they still reflect the emergence of a general consensus that development was not impossibly formidable. Here, I provide a condensed version of the key factors identified by both texts.

Both Okun-Richardson and Meier-Baldwin discuss three key areas for development intervention in the LDC (woven through their chapters and readings, and found in different sections of their texts): Population, Norms and Values, and Growth. These three areas became targets for development policy from the outset, and changing patterns of population growth, reshaping norms and values, and accelerating growth became the three prongs of development strategy. Here, I focus on the emergence of growth and ISI, since this is the set of theories that became the center of controversy in the NL counter-revolution and in the CDD.[16]

In the theories identified by these books as key for the vision of development and industrial growth, three theorists appear as crucial—Lewis, Hirschman, and Prebisch-Singer. The combination of their approaches created a coherent vision of development and industrial growth that crystallized into ISI. I discuss the emergence of a coherent vision of ISI in three sub–sub-sections: I first take up Lewis and Hirschman, and then examine Prebisch-Singer. The ultimate emergence of ISI as the overarching vision of the field of development economics has some tricky aspects to it, as the section on Prebisch-Singer makes clear. The contradictions that emerge in the triumph of ISI are taken up in final sub-subsection.

The Room for Development: Lewis and Hirschman

The first barrier placed before LDCs was the level of capital needed, and the question of how one was to create the urban industrial labor force without jeopardizing food security. The Western story had seen the enclosures, and the mass exodus of workers to the urban centers to become the industrial labor force. But in a country facing a growing population and thus needing larger levels of agricultural production, would not a mass exodus of people to the industrial labor force create a food shortage? The Lewis Labor-Surplus model showed that the availability of labor and the supply of food were not problems, since LDC economies could move labor from agriculture to industry without any problem. In fact, the very unproductiveness of agriculture which differentiates the LDC from the DC creates the opportunity for the LDC to find the labor for industrialization at no cost, and with no pain. The LDC difference—agricultural backwardness—itself provided the door for possible LDC success.

Since growth did not seem to be limited by the availability of labor, then capital must be the key problem. Capital investment required three things: a) financing, b) opportunities for investment, and c) ready entrepreneurs who will undertake the investment.

The financing of capital investment required two things: either endogenous financing via savings, or external financing via aid and loans. Second, the LDC would need technical assistance in developing the skills and new technologies which would unleash growth quickly. Thus, the state would have to find ways to generate internal resources via forced savings or deficit spending, and the international organizations could help with the external financing.

What of opportunities for investment? The earlier balanced growth advocates had argued that investment, to be able to generate adequate linkages and demand for the output produced, would have to take place along a number of lines simultaneously. Drawing on Schumpeterian notions of a dynamic process, Hirschman argued for an unbalanced growth path which, if strategically chosen, would itself create the dynamic linkages and markets needed for further growth, in a self-sustaining process. All that was needed was to find the industry and finance the investment.

Trade, Protection, and Development: Prebisch-Singer

And so the final question left concerned the type of growth strategy to pursue, and the kind of industries to target. Clearly one had to target Hirschmanian high-linkage industries, and provide the initial capital which would set the development process and the transition from a backward, tradition bound, stagnant agrarian-subsistence economy to a dynamic, industrial, modern one. But where was the entrepreneur? What prevented the LDC entrepreneurs and capitalists from taking the helm and setting off this process on their own?

The internal structures preventing development had been identified, and the possibility of turning the economy around and eliminating these barriers had been posited by Lewis and Hirschman. What of the external structures, and relationship of the LDC economy to the rest of the world? Were they benign, or were they, too, acting as barriers to the unleashing of growth and entrepreneurial spirit and capital accumulation in the LDCs? The debate centered on the role of trade in the process of unleashing growth and transforming the LDC economy.

A series of economists (Jacob Viner, Gottfried Haberler, R. E. Caves, Harry G. Johnson), drawing both on Ricardian comparative advantage and on Adam Smith's formulation of trade as a "vent for surplus," [17] argued that state policy should encourage exports and open trade. This group of economists still saw a strong role for the state in providing the infrastructure, institutional development and creation of adequately large pools of savings needed for capital accumulation and growth.[18] But they saw growth as inextricably linked to trade, and argued for a more open economy. They lost the policy battle in the 50s and 60s, and repositioned themselves in the 70s, with their theories becoming the basis for the NL counter-revolution in the field (the next sub-section examines how this group of theories came to play a key role in the subsequent development of the field, and why they lost the policy debate of the 50s and 60s).

Theoreticians who deprecated the role of trade laid the basis for ISI. The most important theories here were those of Prebisch-Singer, and Chenery. Prebisch and Singer argued that because of their focus on primary production, LDCs faced a secular decline in terms of trade. This meant that openness eroded both the ability to generate adequate pools of foreign exchange to finance imports of technology and thus hurt investment, and also resulted in deteriorating profits in these sectors, leading to lower investment opportunities. If LDCs were to develop, they would need to radically change their production composition and move from the primary products to manufactures. But this meant competing with well established DC industries, and so some form of protection would have to be put in place if the LDC entrepreneur was to move into these sectors.[19]

Added to the Prebisch-Singer view in later developments of the ISI vision of development was the question of foreign exchange and the role of aid in the development process. The most famous presentation of the link between development and foreign exchange was Chenery's two-gap model. If development was about reproducing the industrial technologies of the west in the LDC, Chenery argued, the LDCs needed not just savings (which financed investment), but also foreign exchange (which financed the purchase of technology and imported inputs).

Thus, based on the vision of industrial development and promotion of entrepreneurship under protectionist barriers (coming from Lewis, Hirschman, and Prebisch-Singer), ISI became a policy agenda, with the state actively protecting domestic capitalists, promoting industrial production via a series of subsidies and technological assistance programs, supporting food security via the green revolution, and using borrowing and aid along with deficit financing and taxation to finance industrialization.

Trade Debates and Ontology in Development Economics

Why did the structuralist position of Prebisch-Singer and Chenery prevail? Since the debate between the pro-trade economists (Viner, Haberler, Caves, Johnson) and protectionists (Prebisch-Singer, Chenery) is replayed in the CDD, and these early theories are the source for the NL and New

Structuralist theories respectively, the question is worth examining in some detail. I will discuss the relationship between structuralism and individualism as they emerged in the field here, and present a glimpse of how this set the stage *both* for the triumph of ISI in the 40s, 50s and 60s, and the subsequent rise of NL in the late-70s and 80s.

The pro-trade camp drew its theories in support for free trade from the individualist, neoclassical vision of comparative advantage. Using a Walrasian equilibrium framework, the free-trade group argued that free trade provides income gains and efficient resource use. These gains can be used to finance increased levels of growth and production. This vision was based on a theory that used individualism, and did not identify any *difference* between DC and LDC except in resource base. There was no aspect of the story that provided any reason to believe that there was much that could be done if the resource base was the cause for poor LDC growth, or that there was any role for the state to accelerate development.[20] The protectionist story told by Prebisch-Singer and Chenery instead drew on structures— structural bottlenecks and structural relationships between DC and LDC that explained LDC *difference*. In doing so, they provided a theory of how that difference could be overcome. Since the pro-traders could not explain the source of LDC difference, or provide a story of how to erase difference, their theory did not fit easily into the development project as it emerged in the 40s and 50s.

In the debates as they played out in the 50s, the focus was on locating the sources of difference between DC and LDC, which is why the policy battles were won by the structuralist vision of protectionism. What emerged was a state-led effort to induce the entrepreneur to invest under ISI as the key strategy for growth and investment. Thus, population control, education and skill development (at least on paper this was always included!), and ISI and infrastructure development for developing resources and increasing investment, became the over-arching vision of development economics in this period.

But the tension generated between structural difference and individualist sameness was not resolved. The question of *how* one moves from difference to sameness remained murky, since the field used the equilibrium formulation of structure in its models (as noted in chapter two, the use of equilibrium creates problems for structuralists positing structural change, and causes a collapse into individualism). The result was that in a variety of arenas, especially in discussing the investor who would lead the economy into modernity by investing in industrialization, development economics had to fall back on individualism.[21]

The Structuralist Ontology in Development Economics

In this section, I examine the theories identified as crucial to the constitution of development economics in the previous section on the history of the field, and show how they are structuralist.

A Brief Recapitulation of Structuralist Ontologies

Before I proceed, it will be useful to briefly remind the reader of the key aspects of structuralist ontology from chapter two. For an ontology to be structuralist, it must have two aspects:

a) Structural laws govern or determine the logic of the whole. These laws are not deduced from underlying human nature, but instead constitute the rules which determine or structure the behavior of the parts. As noted in chapter two, one can locate the key ontological assumptions of the model by seeing whether any effort to endogenize the variable causes the structuralism to collapse.

b) The whole is self-reproducing and closed. This aspect of the ontology poses problems for development economics, since the whole point of the agenda is to find ways to break this self-reproduced and closed low growth economy, and transform it to a dynamic and growing one. As noted in chapter two, this tension causes structuralism to collapse into individualism at some key points.

Theories Examined

Here, I examine a subset of the theories described above as important to the development of the ISI vision: Kuznets as an important figure who identified the sources of LDC underdevelopment and argued for a "big-push" with a large number of pre-conditions to development in the first sub-section; the Harrod-Domar model as a key theoretical expression of growth theory and the need for savings to finance investment in the next sub-section; Lewis' Labor Surplus model in the sub-section following that; Hirschman's vision of unbalanced growth after that; and the Prebisch-Singer hypothesis of secularly declining terms of trade along with Chenery's two gap model in the last sub-section. Each of these theories will be examined to see whether and how they deploy structuralist ontological assumptions about LDC economies.

Kuznets

As noted earlier, Kuznets was instrumental in the development of the indices of what constituted development. In his *Modern Economic Growth* (1950; hereafter MEG), as well as in his "International Differences in Income Levels," (1966; hereafter IDIL) Kuznets identified a series of main indicators which both identified the key characteristics of a developed country (MEG), and contrasted these with the lack of such characteristics in LDCs (IDIL). Here I examine his assessment of what causes these differences as laid out in IDIL.

He starts by providing a statistical picture of the differences between LDC and DC. These differences define development (and automatically, by their absence, define underdevelopment). He starts with per capita GDP (the LDC nation is poor, since using per capita GDP measures the collective poverty of a group as compared to the collective wealth of another group). Kuznets notes that differences in income levels are associated with:

i) Higher population growth in the LDCs: He notes that the problem of increasing the per capita GDP of the LDC is aggravated by the high population growth rate. In the same section as population growth rate, he notes that low income countries have low literacy levels.

ii) Differences in industrial structure: DCs are industrialized and LDCs are agrarian, and DCs engage in higher levels of investment in industry per worker than LDCs. The low incomes in LDCs are clearly linked to the preponderance of agriculture in the economic structure, low levels of productivity in agriculture, low rates of industrial investment, low consumption of energy, and underdeveloped transportation systems.

Having identified the key areas where LDC and DC diverge, Kuznets asks: which factor causes which? His answer is most revealing. On page 9 of IDIL, he concludes:

> Two conclusions can, I believe, be safely drawn from the discussion so far. (1) Factors such as population growth pattern, literacy, industrial structure, and capital investment are of *some* importance in determining international differences in levels of income . . . (2) these characteristics are associated with income levels, both as causes and consequences, and together, with many others not specifically indicated in the table, form an interrelated complex.

And later, on page 17: "First, the range of international differences in income levels must be much wider today than it was say 150 to 200 years ago." And, continuing on this point, on page 18:

> Therefore, from a starting point of more equal levels, marked inequalities in per capita income have developed . . . What factors induced and permitted some countries to attain a high rate of growth in per capita income, and why were the same or similar factors not operative in other countries? . . . history suggests that the factors that operated in some countries and not in others are those associated with

the "industrial system" . . . combined with certain social and political concomitants, that is the basis of the rapid growth of per capita income in some countries.

And on page 19, asking whether the industrial revolution can be reproduced in the LDCs:

The feasibility of using the results of modern science and empirical knowledge in economic production is not merely a matter of availability of a stock of discoveries contributed by original workers or practical-minded adapters. Let us disregard for a moment the importance of social and economic organization as a precondition for adoption on a wide scale of the contributions of science to economic technology. A minimum of cultural adaptation is still required . . . in a society whose general outlook has not been sufficiently secularized to place a high value on rational calculation and material welfare.

Kuznets is in effect arguing that:

a) The structure of the LDC economy is a self-reproducing and closed whole, with social structures and political structures reinforcing each other. Particularly, poverty is both a product of and a cause of low productivity, low industrialization, low investment, and high population growth. This is a set of rules that do not emerge from the intrinsic and underlying human beings, nor are they deduced from underlying agents. Instead, agents are created as people who cannot break free of these closed structures,

b) The heart of this structural whole is the attitude and culture which shapes human subjects. In particular, he argues (without asking how or why the change in structure could emerge), that vast structural shifts in the rules governing agent behavior in effect produced the agent of the West. The western market society can be analyzed using individualist analyses because the social rules governing agent behavior have *created* individuals. The rules governing the individuals of the non-west have not produced such subjects, and so they are trapped in a 'cycle of poverty.'

Harrod-Domar and the Need for Savings

For most development economists, the main reason for industrialization was the promise of rapid economic growth. The Harrod-Domar model (Harrod 1939, Domar 1946) provided the first basic growth theory for development economics. It examined the relationship between growth and capital requirements—a necessary component for any project of state-led development. If capital is a key constraint to growth, state-led development can find out what causes the constraint and work to overcome it.

The Harrod-Domar model as presented within development economics is implicitly structuralist in that it makes some key assumptions about the nature of a) capital-output relationships, and b) subjective behaviors that "close" the model. These locate the structural parameters that make the LDC unlike the DC. If one can see what is required for growth, then the absence, or low parametric value of these factors, is what marks the LDC economy as different from the DC economy.

The original model was developed to examine the growth prospects of DCs. The model was unique in that unlike the earlier classical theories that looked at the productivity enhancing role of investment on the supply side alone, it also examined the demand side, to ask whether demand would grow in tandem with supply growth to ensure full employment over time. In effect, the question asked is: what is the rate at which investment must grow if the increase in demand and income is to match the rate of growth of productive capacity?

In its simplest formulation, the Harrod-Domar model postulates the following:

i) Output is a function of capital stock (K) and the capital-output ratio (k):

$$Y = K/k$$

k, the capital-output ratio, is constant. At first glance, this may seem like a simple technical assumption,[22] but implicit here are a series of assumptions about the nature of social relationships by which a capital stock is converted into a given output level. Ultimately, k is a "relational rule," which relates the level of Y to the level of K—it assumes for example that, there is full capacity utilization, social relationships between labor and capital operate in a well-defined and clearly set pattern, and institutions function to ensure this transformation of potential technical capacity into actual output produced.

From the above equation, it follows that

$$\Delta Y = \Delta K/k$$

Note that k does not change. But what does it mean to say that k does not change? Here, we can draw on the discussion of exogenous and endogenous variables raised in the previous chapter. The parameter k is exogenous, but there are two types of exogenous variables—those whose instability or endogenization will explode the analysis, and those which are exogenous, but whose changes do not destabilize the analysis. If k is to change randomly, it is not merely an "external shock." If k changes, as we will see, the growth rate "g" becomes unstable and indeterminate. Any effort to acknowledge changes in k has to be done very carefully—it has to be changing by some clearly defined *rules* (such as via a reconceptualization of k into the marginal productivity of capital determined by technology, and depending on the underlying, well-defined mechanisms of cost-minimizing investment behavior, as in the Solow [1956] revision of the Harrod-Domar model[23]). k functions here, then, as an implicit structural rule. Its instability will explode any effort to capture the rules that determine growth.

That said, let us manipulate this equation (since this is a set of synchronic structures governed by well-defined relationships which fully mesh within the equilibrium, equation manipulation is allowed, since it does not change the underlying relationships one is describing).

Dividing by Y, we get:

$\Delta Y/Y = (\Delta K/Y).(1/k)$

Or,

$g = (I/Y).(1/k)$

where g is the growth rate and I is investment. This is the relationship between growth in productive capacity and investment.

ii)   We now add two more relationships:

$S/Y = s$

which means there is a stable, underlying behavioral relationship found between income and savings. This is a clear structural rule that governs agent behavior in the economy, and again, any effort to endogenize or destabilize s will explode the model. ("s" too can be reformulated, but only with great care. Here, I have used the simplest version of "s," where the marginal propensity to save is equal to the average propensity to save. One can reformulate this to be the marginal propensity to save alone, but no matter what the formulation, one needs an underlying structural rule linking savings to income for the model to work.)

iii)   And:

$S = I$

This is the "coherence" or equilibrium condition for a self-regulating structural whole. If for some reason S and I do not equate, then one is "out of equilibrium" and the simultaneous satisfaction of all the rules will not emerge. There are assumed to be internal mechanisms in the system that ensure coherence and drive the economy to equilibrium. Implicit here is the idea that S determines I— this is a savings driven model, where I automatically adapts to S. Since there is no discussion here of the determinants of I, and since Y is endogenous (after all, it is the growth rate that is being sought as the solution or outcome, rather than being "pre-given") then this implies that there must be some implicit endogenous mechanism that will ensure that I keeps pace with S.[24]

iv) This becomes clearer in the next step of the model:

Substituting S/Y for I/Y above, we get

$g = s/k$

The original model was deployed to show that if for some reason the rate of growth of demand from investment did not match the rate of growth of productive capacity due to investment, then the economy would not have a stable full-employment equilibrium over time. If investment were not savings driven, the neat reduction of growth into the relationship between the two key structural parameters s and k would not obtain. The steady-state growth path above implicitly assumes that investment will adapt, particularly because there is no discussion or description of what drives investment behavior, or behavioral rules or structural parameters governing investment here. Implicit is the idea of coherence—that there needs to be some internal mechanism in the economy that will in fact ensure that all savings will go into investment, so that the growth in demand matches the growth in productive capacity. This was the Harrod-Domar "knife edge," where unless I absorbed S exactly, and the growth in demand exactly matched the growth in productive capacity, one could spiral out of equilibrium.

But in development economics, what was picked up was the link between the rate of savings and the steady-state growth path that an economy could aim for. Instead of discussing the nature of investment decisions within this model, the focus became the levels of k and s, and the ability of the state to manipulate them and thus generate growth. k was seen as technologically fixed, while s could be raised more easily via state efforts. Though in the long run, presumably, the state could try and push k up via infrastructure building and technological change,[25] the quickest way to have growth was to create a higher level of savings—in effect, the key constraint to growth was the ability to finance investment. The demand side of the problem, as we will see, was set aside by both the implications of the Lewis model and the Hirschman model, leaving the focus on the supply side, and the need for savings to enhance productive capacity.

Thus, one key preoccupation for the development state was finding ways to intensify financing, and overcome the savings constraint. Taxation, mechanisms of creating forced savings, deficit financing (not to generate demand, but to finance growth in productive capacity), and borrowing from abroad to overcome the domestic savings constraint, became key parts of the ISI model of development.

The Harrod-Domar model was unsatisfactory both for the way it looked at a single sectored economy, and because of the lack of any clear description of investment. A variety of adaptations emerged to handle these issues, many of them drawing on individualism in selected assumptions (for example, in the determinants of k, but not of S in the Solow [1956] model). It is beyond the scope of this chapter to discuss this rich literature here, but for all the adaptations and mathematical reformulations, the issue of financing development remained (and remains) a central preoccupation of development economics.

Sectoral Issues: The Lewis Surplus-Labor Model

While the growth model above was seen as useful in locating some of the key constraints to growth, it was not very useful in capturing the main dimensions of the development project. Within the vision of development was not merely a vision of growth, but a vision of a sectoral transformation, a radical shift in the nature of production, from agricultural to industrial production. Needed then was a model that could take up the sectoral changes that the ISI state envisioned as its policy goal.

Lewis' two-sector Labor-surplus model was probably the most influential of the models that discussed the mechanisms of transition from an agrarian to an industrial society (Lewis 1954). Following Lewis, a variety of such two-sector models emerged, the most famous being Fei and Ranis' (1964) adaptation of Lewis' model of Labor Surplus.[26] But while there are some distinctions between the models, the key set of assumptions about behavior remain remarkably similar. The models, in their exposition, straddle individualist and structuralist assumptions and language, and it takes some work to pull apart their structural assumptions, and see how/why they incorporate some individualist assumptions. So let me proceed by showing the implicit structuralism in the general class of surplus-labor models, and discuss how they selectively use individualist notions in some arenas.

The simplest exposition of the Lewis model has the following features:

i)   In agriculture, the wage is fixed.

Wa = fixed

where Wa is the agricultural wage.
Where does the fixed wage come from? It is variously described as the aver-age product of labor, the constant institutional wage, or the subsistence wage. But no matter what formulation one uses, implicitly, agricultural so-cieties do not structure their behaviors according to the norms that govern micro-rational behavior. Further, the wage is not the reflection of any under-lying aspect of innate individual behavior. Indeed, it turns out to be the re-flection of structural/societal behavior regardless of which of the above formulations one adopts, though the first one (Average Product of Labor) seems to be individualist, in drawing on some individualist language. But in all cases, the key to the argument that wages are set differently in agriculture is that agricultural societies follow a different set of behavioral norms when it comes to determining the social process of allocating work and output. The wage is rooted in conventional practices and relationships, and does not emerge from an individual calculus based on pre-formed beings.

ii) This structuralist notion of agricultural wages is seen from the sec-ond, additional piece of the model's description of the agrarian sector:

MPLA = 0

where MPLA is the Marginal product of labor in agriculture.
Why is the MPLA seen as being zero? Again, this assumption needs to be linked to the general structural characteristics that the Labor-Surplus mod-els identified in describing the LDC. LDCs were agricultural, and their agrarian sectors were governed by structural rules of reciprocal behavior. In such a society, everyone shared in the process of work, and in the outputs. Thus, people may be working at low or sub-optimal levels of productivity, which is reflected in the low MPLA. The subject contained within these so-cial/structural relationships is not the individual of neoclassical theory. The existence of this sub-optimally utilized labor force was the mark of a labor-surplus in agriculture—more people were there in the agrarian sector than were needed or could be optimally utilized, and so this excess was denoted the surplus labor.

Note that the individualist assumptions are implicitly here—they mark the norm of full utilization, and are implicitly the basis of the standard used to identify the deviation from the norm (the existence of surplus labor and the constant institutional wage marks the LDC deviation). The reasons for the deviation, however, are structural, and reflect the structural rules governing economic behavior in the agrarian sector of the LDC.[27] Thus we see a pattern that marks much of the emerging theories of developing countries—individualist assumptions are deployed in those sectors, and those aspects of the theory that examine what constitutes developed societies, or the goal of development. The structuralist assumptions are deployed to explain why the LDC economy does not reach the goal. Thus, structural assumptions mark the deviation of the LDC from the DC, and individualist assumptions allow one to measure the extent of deviation and become the marker by which the LDC's underdevelopment is known.

The above two rules (constant institutional wages and zero MPLA) are the parametric expressions of the structural rules governing agrarian behavior in LDCs.[28] The existence of a labor surplus now gives one a path to industrialization. Primarily it shows us that industrialization could proceed by drawing on agrarian labor without harming agricultural output. As the government promoted such industrialization, growth would increase as the foundations for a modern economy were laid down.

Mathematically, this shows up with the following key aspects of the model:

iii) If the urban wage is slightly higher than the rural wage, then the surplus labor will move to the industrial sector, and do so without harming agrarian production as long as MPLA = 0. Thus,

$Wi > Wa$

where Wi is the industrial wage, and Wa is the agrarian wage.

iv) Industry will hire labor up to the point where it is profitable:

$MPLI = Wi$

where MPLI is the marginal productivity of labor in industry. As industrialization proceeds, the existence of surplus labor ensures that wages do not rise. Instead, profits stay high and are reinvested, generating more employment, more output, and more profits. This cycle continues until the excess labor is absorbed.[29]

While the discussion of the agrarian sector is clearly structuralist, the last two assumptions—that wage differentials will cause people to move out of agriculture and into industry, and that industrialists make hiring decisions based on marginal calculations, are clearly neoclassical individualist assumptions. The response to wage differentials is based on maximizing individuals' calculations of higher wages on the margin in industry. The hiring decision comes from the micro-rational profit-maximizing firm.

This is a call on individualism in order to handle one of the problems that structuralists face when closing their models. As I noted in the previous chapter, a properly specified, well-articulated structuralist model has a hard time handling change. The Labor-surplus models, however, are attempting to demonstrate change from an agrarian to an industrial structure. So a sudden change in economic subjectivity is postulated—from being governed by convention, institution, tradition, to becoming a rationally calculating, maximizing individual. Again, the laws governing the goal (industrial sector's expansion) are marked by individualism, while those governing backwardness (agrarian sector) are marked by structuralism.[30]

There is actually some trouble in this abrupt transition, which raises a question. If in fact industrialists are profit-maximizing, then why did the transition not take place already? Why did they not already go ahead and pay a wage faintly higher than the agrarian wage, and hire up to the margin? Who needs a state? More curiously, what is the process by which the agricultural laborers, steeped in the norms and institutions that govern economic life so that they work under the structural rules, suddenly stop using such norms and become maximizers?

Since presumably the hold of convention was mainly because there were no alternatives, since movement to the city is itself a subject-changing activity, and since the new industries would not have any norms governing work relations set in place, this latter issue was not seen as a serious one. The worker, on leaving the tradition-bound village and entering the city, would be freed from the shackles of tradition. But the former is a serious concern. The Lewis model was widely seen as providing the answer to the question of what happens to agriculture if industrialization proceeds. But it left untheorized the issue of why the *state* was necessary.

To answer this question, additional theories were needed.

Investment and the Absent Entrepreneur:
Hirschman's Theory of Unbalanced Growth

Having identified the possibility of a sectoral transition, then, the issue was what prevented industry from taking up this opportunity to industrialize. Already, the Harrod-Domar model presented one possible reason—inadequate savings with which to finance the investment. The key constraint was capital, not labor. The second possible reason for the absent entrepreneur was the lack of technical knowledge. Further, one saw theories that examined inadequate institutional knowledge of risks and hence a disincentive to invest (Aubrey 1955), poor infrastructure that prevented profitable investment (Kuznets, Rostow). Thus, there emerged a set of theories about what was needed to get the reluctant entrepreneur to invest in industry—providing better infrastructure, resources, or technical assistance. One additional thing was needed for the reluctant entrepreneur to start the process of industrial development—markets and avenues for profitable investment.

The "big-push theories" had identified inadequately developed markets and hence insufficient demand to sustain profitable production in a variety of industries as a key constraint to development (Nurkse, Rosenstein-Rodan). Here, I examine Hirschman's discussion of how, if one key industry is chosen and the industrial process is set in motion by the state there, the rest of the economy would follow as markets opened up and opportunities for the entrepreneur emerged.

Hirschman's advocacy of unbalanced growth was based on a two-pronged strategy: firstly, balanced growth spread resources thin, and in savings or capital constrained economies, resources were scarce. A "big push" in a multiplicity of sectors required a lot of resources. Instead, Hirschman preferred to identify a few key sectors, and invest heavily in them. The spill-over effects would create a larger impact on the economy using a smaller amount of resources. This effect would arise from the interlinkages in production—activities that provided inputs to the sector would be stimulated since a market for their services had emerged (backward linkages). Additionally, the emergence of this key industry could also provide a stimulus for then entering into new industries that utilized the output of this industry as inputs and could now get them locally (forward linkages). Finally, the emergence of a consuming class in the area surrounding the industry would spark ancillary industries to arise which catered to the needs of these consumers. Thus, Hirschman's strategy relied on a notion of a series of sequential linkages connecting different aspects of economic activity.

What makes this structuralist? Here, one sees again the fascinating mix of individualism and structuralism that marks development theory. The reasons for a lack of investment are structural—bottlenecks, resource shortages, poor markets. The response then has to work with these structural impediments, and use them creatively. Here, one sees individualism, primarily the innate drive for profit, mark the creative responses of an industry in its organization, and sequence of investment decisions as development proceeds. Difference (absences, shortages, bottlenecks) mark the distance from development, sameness (universally creative humans, profit motives, innovation) marks the responses to this difference which let loose development. All one needs is the trigger—the right industry, selected for maximal linkages and possible sequences of entrepreneurial investment to set the process in motion. In Hirschman's story, the individualist entrepreneur waits in the wings, listening for his cue.

Trade, Aid, and Development: Prebisch-Singer and Chenery

As seen above, Harrod-Domar showed the way to savings-financed industrial development, Lewis provided the assurance that both the labor resources and the profit-financed resources for capital accumulation were in place, and Hirschman identified some key strategies by which the entrepreneur could emerge from the shadows. Finally, Prebisch-Singer and Chenery provided the rationale for sweetening the pot for domestic capital and bringing the reluctant investor onto the field via protection, and looking to import-substituting manufacturing industries as the key ones with maximum linkages as envisaged in Hirschman's story.

Raúl Prebisch (1950, 1959) and Hans Singer (1950, 1964) both argued that there were a number of reasons for the inability of LDC economies to use trade and exports as their vehicle for industrial development. Hence, LDCs would need to find ways to delink their economies from exports and rely on aid for foreign exchange during the development process. Their arguments hinged on two key structural observations:

a) The structure of LDC production for trade was concentrated in primary product exports, and the domestic manufacturing sector was not able to compete with DC manufactures, leading to a high import of industrial goods from the DCs.

b) The structure of demand in DCs leads to low income elasticity for primary products, while the demand for imported manufactures from DCs was high. Thus, LDCs faced a secular decrease in their terms-of-trade.

The secular decrease in the terms of trade implied that sooner or later, the LDCs would be unable to finance imports, and that the resources available for financing industrialization were instead being used to finance ever more expensive imports. Further, the continued decline in terms-of-trade leads to a redistribution in the gains from trade, and hence of income, away from the LDCs and towards the DCs. This created a continued loss of income and hence a loss of investable resources for growth and industrialization in LDCs. Thus, LDCs would have to change their structure of production, and to do so would have to protect their import competing industries.

What makes the above analysis structuralist? Let us look at the two sides of the argument. On the supply side, it is the structure of production, and the concentration of production in some sectors that would need to be changed. This structure of production is not theorized as the outcome of rational, individual investors deciding to invest, but is seen as the outcome of the historical mechanisms of colonialism, and the use of peripheral economies as sources of cheap raw materials and labor for the developed economies.[31] The demand side constraint—lack of adequate absorption, comes from the structure of demand. It draws on the empirically observed structure of demand as a function of income (along Keynesian lines), and does not derive from any deployment of micro-rational behavior of consumers responding to relative-price signals (thus, the decline in the relative price of primary products does not generate a shift in consumer spending away from manufactures and towards primary products).

Again, structural bottlenecks in production and consumption mark the divergence between DC and LDC. A policy of protection will eliminate the bottleneck, and via changes in production and internal growth, replicate the DC in the LDC. But why will the policy of protection ensure that investment will take place? Implicit here is the assumption that if we just ensure that the bottlenecks are removed, industrialists *will* exhibit microrational behavior and engage in investment. Implicit individualism provides the mechanism by which the structure can change.

Finally Chenery's two-gap model (Chenery and Adelman 1966, Chenery and Bruno 1962, Chenery and Strout 1966) discussed the case for foreign aid in ISI in terms of financial needs, and not in terms of trade. The basic argument is that in order to transform the underdeveloped economy and move from a stagnant low-growth economy to a high growth one, as with Harrod-Domar, the key is to find ways to finance investment. However, investment financing requires two types of finances: savings to finance domestic investment, and foreign exchange to finance imported capital inputs. A shortage of either of these resources can prevent a take-off into growth. The key assumption in the model is that the domestic and foreign resources are not substitutable—that is, each is fixed by its own structural parameters, and the structure of production does not allow one to be substituted for the other. If the foreign exchange gap is binding the economy needs to have access to foreign exchange in order to grow.

Algebraically, Chenery's model can be shown as follows:

i) Savings Gap:

$I \leq F + sY$

Where I is investment, F is foreign capital inflows which add to domestic resources, and s is the marginal (and average) propensity to save, so that sY is savings.

Here, we see that Investment behavior is left untheorized as in the Harrod-Domar formulation above, and that resources are the binding constraint. F is externally given, and savings is based on a structurally determined behavioral parameter.

ii) The foreign exchange Gap:

(m1) I + (m2) Y - E ≤ F

where m1 is the marginal import share of investment, and m2 is the marginal propensity to import for consumption. I is investment, E is exports, and F is again foreign capital inflows. Note that m1 and m2 are structural parameters. m1 denotes the required import content of investment, and is determined by production structure—it is not determined by the internal resource allocation behavior of cost minimizing investors. m2 similarly is a behavioral parameter that reflects consumer behavior—like the marginal propensity to consume, it reflects social behavior, and does not emerge from a rational calculus of individual consumers deciding to maximize at the margin between domestic and foreign consumption. E is exogenously determined (presumably by the combination of current export structure and foreign demand), as is F. For a given Y, E and F, clearly one of the two above equations will become binding on investment and hence on growth. As with Harrod-Domar, one sees that Investment absorbs all resources up to the point where a constraint prevents further investment—there is no theory of what determines investment here, and this is a resource constrained, rather than demand constrained model.

So, there is a role for foreign aid and technological help added to ISI, which will further help the state-led strategy of generating market-oriented industrial capitalism in LDCs. Again, however, just as with Prebisch-Singer, Lewis, and Hirschman, Chenery is making some assumptions about investment behavior. While investment has structural constraints in financing, investment itself is forthcoming up to the constraint. By some mechanism, just as with the Harrod-Domar model, investment absorbs all of the available resources. Again, the entrepreneur who undertakes investment is simply postulated. He is ready and waiting to apply rationality and foresight and to undertake investment according to principles of efficient technology and rational calculation once the bottleneck is overcome.

ISI takes shape as a strategy for development—Lewis provides the assurance of labor-resources, and the Fei-Ranis reformulation assures agrarian surpluses to finance industrial development and prevent rising food prices as well. Hirschman assures us that the entrepreneur will come if we just set the stage, and Prebisch-Singer and Chenery tell us what the needed cue is for the domestic industrialist to find ways to finance investment and compete in manufacturing industries. In all the ISI models described above, the investor is simply proclaimed, and investment behavior is not adequately theorized. Since the investor is the subject who promises transformation of the LDC economy, and the vehicle by which structural difference is translated into modernist sameness, he is left unstated. Implicitly, the investor is acting along individualist lines of a rational calculus of profit maximization. To fix him in structure would preclude the possibility of change.

Consequences of the Use of Structuralist Ontologies in Development

Above, I traced the origins of the field of development economics, and argued that it turned to structuralism in order to explain LDC difference. I examined the key models deployed in arguing for ISI and showed how and why they were structuralist. What is striking about the emergence of structuralism at this point, and the way in which it came to dominate the field, was that this period saw the rise of individualism everywhere else in economics—it was the time that Arrow and Debreu were developing the mathematical foundations of general equilibrium theory, that Samuelson, Solow and others were developing the mathematical models for general equilibrium, that saw the nascent attempts to microfound Keynes in the neoclassical tradition, and saw the development of game-theoretic models in microeconomics. At a time when the rest of the field was digging microeconomic foundations, and when the majority of economic theory was turning to individualism, Development economics turned to structuralism.

While I do not think that one can fully explain why this happened, I suspect that in the very origins of the field, with its effort to locate the *difference* that marked LDCs, there was a tension that required, at least in economics, a turn to structuralism. The type of individualism found in economics and in the Walrasian vision could not explain difference or prescribe policy for a move to sameness. Walrasian individuals are inherently the same—they have the same type of maximizing behavior in all contexts. If there is any difference that emerges, it will be because of differences in tastes or resources. Neither of these are reasons for policy intervention.[32] Difference required structure.

Of course, that still leaves open the question of which structures were chosen for attention. Development economics, as shown above, chose to examine only *certain* structures. The focus on these specific structures rather than others had certain consequences:

a) *The elision of Class:* While this is not inherent to structuralist ontologies *per se,* structuralism leaves open the question of which
structural rules will be identified as key to the social totality. What
emerges in all the rules described above is the extent to which they
identify structures that elide class. Whatever marks the LDC, it is
not class—instead, a variety of markers, especially industrial
structure, investment structure, subsistence production, are identified as the key structures in these economies. The two key areas
where structural constraints were identified were a) Demand and
markets, and b) Production and growth.

b) *The erasure of history:* Again, with the possible exception of
Prebisch-Singer, the theories do not look to locate the specific
structures identified in LDCs within the context of LDC history.
LDC history was seen primarily as an absence—a failure to follow in the steps of the DCs—and not as a presence—an actual
history of the dynamic interaction between internal class conflict
and colonialism/imperialism that shaped the structures found in
LDCs today.

c) *The fabrication of the harmonious national interest:* The elision of
class and the concentration on the nation as the unit of analysis,
and as the unit whose development and well-being would become
the focus of policy, led to the singular focus on the needs of one
group of people (the absent LDC entrepreneurs), and in effect postulated the structuralist equivalent of "trickle down" economics—
the benefits granted to the LDC import-substituting industrial
capitalist would trickle down as employment and growth, and
hence higher living standards, for everyone in the nation.

d) *The erasure of LDC subjectivities:* One consequence of the use of
structuralist ontologies was that it upheld colonialist attitudes towards LDC subjects. Structuralism as we have seen, postulated
two types of agencies: the individualist agency marks the DC, and
marks the developed sector of the economy. Structuralist ontologies are deployed whenever the *distance* between the LDC and DC
have to be explained. Thus, the structuralist ontologies, especially
since they were postulated sans history or context, postulated not
LDC subjects but LDC deviants who were trapped by structures,
incapable of either acting reasonably within them or moving to
change them. The LDC subject is known primarily as the "distance" from the DC, and not as an embedded subject making decisions and voicing resistance in his or her own right.

e) *Proclivity for Swings between Structuralism and Individualism:*
And finally, one consequence of the way in which structuralism
was deployed was to create a tension between structuralist ontologies (marking difference) and individualist ontologies (marking
sameness, or the possibility of sameness). Unlike other types of
structuralist ontologies, which can generate their own telos, contradictions, and possibilities for change, development economics
used a Cartesian equilibrium structuralism. As noted in chapter
two, the deployment of such structuralism creates problems for
theorists of change—closed self-reproducing structures in equilibrium do not change except in response to external shocks. But development economics was about change, it had at the heart of its
vision of LDC difference a vision of possible LDC sameness in the
future—it needed change. The theoretical inability to create stories
of change left large areas of the field untheorized—the key area
being investment and production decisions.

Further, development economics had already taken a particular vision
of individualism—efficient and dynamic DC markets driven by efficient and
maximizing individuals—as its goal. This meant that when it did draw on
individualism, it tended to draw on individualism that reflected that goal—
the individualism of neoclassical economics. This set the stage for a vision
based on precisely this type of individualism to become the source of the new
theories that replaced ISI.

INDIVIDUALISM IN DEVELOPMENT ECONOMICS:
THE NEOLIBERAL COUNTER-REVOLUTION

As noted in the section on structuralism in development economics above,
the watertight distinction between the structuralist ontologies of ISI and the
individualist ontologies of the neoliberal counter-revolution is misleading. In
development economics both have been used together: structuralism is deployed when difference is defined, and individualism is deployed in appeals
to sameness.

But while the development discourse was structured by the tense interplay of the structure-agent dichotomy, the two ontologies themselves, as
deployed in economic theory in the *West,* had emerged not as complementary, but as *competing* visions of economic agency. Within the economic
theory of the West, individualism was about a vision of economic agency
unfettered, with none but the most minimal of structures called on (the

auctioneer) to close the model. Structuralism was about a very different vision of economic agents—agents who failed to optimize properly and instead acted on convention.

This was an intellectual battle about the "right" form of theory. The period when structuralism flourished in development economics was also the period in which most economic theory shifted to individualist analyses, and neoclassical theories were being developed.[33] The struggle of neoclassical economics against structuralism was not, I think, solely a matter of politics, but also a battle to define the ontological parameters of the discipline.[34] Economics, rather than being about the *economy,* became a pure, rationalist *science,* built on utility-theoretic rational individualism and equilibrium.

This battle eventually spilled over into development economics.[35] The insurgent neoliberal theorists within the field of development saw themselves not as representing one pole of two mutually-constituted ontological approaches, but as carrying out a revolution against the structuralist development agenda, especially the ISI-state. Neoliberalism was the coherent vision that emerged from the debates and dissents of the 60s and 70s both in and out of development theory, to replace ISI as the overarching policy vision of the mainstream, and of the policy-makers who decide the fate of millions in LDCs. Its ontology was individualist,[36] its vision spectacularly universal.

The term neoliberalism was coined by Latin American dissenters, and was used to compare the vision behind the NL policies with that of the earlier liberals (free traders) of Latin American history. The term itself seems to have been coined in the 80s in the political arena, once the IMF started putting the policy agenda in place in the wake of the debt crisis.[37] The earlier writers calling themselves dissenters (P. T. Bauer, Lal), neoclassicals (Krueger, Bhagwati), monetarists (Friedman, H. G. Johnson). Their motives were various: anger at the assumption of difference, commitment to the neoclassical analytical framework intellectually, or an agenda for eliminating the interventionist Keynesian state.

Unlike the earlier vision of ISI, which came to dominate the field of development economics, neoliberalism had not yet come to dominate the intellectual field in the early-to-mid 1980s, though it dominated the policy agenda that emerged under structural adjustment in the wake of the Third World debt crisis. Indeed neoliberals, as we will see, would prefer to dissolve development theory as a separate field—a strategy that has succeeded somewhat in the intellectual arena of development economics only in the 1990s. Thus, while there has been much written about, for, against, neoliberalism, there is no *single* text or reader which one can point to as a comprehensive guide from within the field to the arena of neoliberalism in development economics (at the time of researching the dissertation in the 1980s and early 1990s). The closest one gets to a coherent statement of the whole neoliberal agenda in one text is the 1991 *World Development Report,* (World Bank 1991, hereafter WDR) and I will use this as the guide to the neoliberal vision.[38]

As with the ISI paradigm, the neoliberals agree that LDC economies are marked by difference, and would not see any problem with Kuznets' discussion of income disparities, industrial structure, productivity, or with growth theory's emphasis on capital formation and growth as the key solution to collective poverty. What they disagree on is the best mechanism to reach this goal of "eradicating difference."

The WDR opens with the following sentences:

> Development is the most important challenge facing the human race. Despite the vast opportunities created by the technological revolutions of the twentieth century, more than 1 billion people, one-fifth of the world's population, live on less than one dollar a day—a standard of living that Western Europe and the United States attained two hundred years ago.

> The task is daunting, but by no means hopeless. During the past forty years many developing countries have achieved progress at an impressive pace ... So if nothing else were certain, we would know that rapid and sustained development is no hopeless dream, but an achievable reality.[39]

The notion of development as defined by the west, the replicability of the western story, and the focus on growth and technology remain.[40] Poverty is still a marker, and poverty is described in terms of collective poverty (the success of developing nations in the past 40 years is based on average growth in income, and no reference is made to distribution). The zealous tone of the early pioneers can still be heard—the words here mirror those of Hoffman's introduction to Singer (1964) excerpted in note 10 to this chapter.

Thus, neoliberalism, like the earlier ISI theorists it displaced, sees development in exactly the same terms of difference, with a hope for sameness. The tension between sameness and difference remains, and as we will see, creates for neoliberals moments of collapse into structuralism that parallel the collapses of the earlier theorists into individualism.

Here, I examine the neoliberal agenda in detail paralleling the discussion of ISI provided before. First, I examine the intellectual history of neoliberalism. Then I examine how individualist ontology is deployed in neoliberalism, and how and why it collapses at key moments into structuralism. Finally, I examine some of the consequences of deploying an individualist ontology in development economics.

The Roots of Neoliberalism: A History of Individualist Dissent

Chapter two of the WDR is titled "Paths to Development." In this chapter's sub-section on "Changes in Development Thought," ISI is presented[41] (in a grossly distorted form), with a discussion at the end of each sub-topic about the new theories and how they show why the old ones were wrong. In citing sources for the dissenting view, there are two places where one finds sources which go back to the early origins of the field: on Trade Policy (examined in the first sub-section on the roots of NL thought), and on the Role of the State (examined in the second sub-section on the roots of NL thought). Following that, further sub-sections in this section will discuss the Structuralist-Monetarist debate of the 1950s and 1960s, the attacks on the State in the 1970s, and the impact of the debt crisis and the East Asian model in the 1980s. A sixth and final sub-section of this section on the roots of NL thought summarizes the Neoliberal vision.

Trade Policy Debates

As noted earlier, when the protectionist strategies of ISI were first being formulated, a strong dissenting opinion on the relationship between trade and development was voiced by economists like Viner, Haberler, Bhagwati, and Johnson. The arguments of all these authors were based on the neoclassical model of free trade and comparative advantage. They concluded, based on their models, that protectionism would hinder growth, and that a free market, especially free international trade, was the best strategy for development.

These models posed the question of development strategies by drawing on the Walrasian model (or, the Heckscher-Ohlin application of the neoclassical framework to international trade). The basic argument is that as long as nations trade according to the dictates of the free market, the outcome of trade is global efficiency. The gains from trade emerge from a division of labor, with each country producing that which is cost-efficient and then trading. The cost-efficient output emerges because of differences in resources. These gains are divided between the trading countries, with all nations benefiting.

While this position lost the original debates, the theories on which it was based became the basis for the free trade vision of NL in the 1980s. This vision rests on some assumptions about how to undertake economic analysis of LDCs, which I take up here:

a) Markets everywhere operate on the same principles if they are free (differences in how they operate are the result of state intervention). These are the principles of Walrasian microrational individuals, with an auctioneer implicitly guaranteeing that the outcome of individual behavior is coherent and efficient.

b)   In ontological terms, there is no difference between DC subjects and LDC subjects in any sector. Investors follow cost-minimization and profit maximization, consumers practice utility maximization. Thus, the model eliminates difference between DC and LDC subjects.

c)   The LDCs may diverge from DCs because of differences in endowments. This, however, in and of itself should not create LDC *backwardness,* though it may create LDC difference.[42] The market should work to creatively coordinate any of the differences in demand and supply that emerge from differences in resources, resulting in efficiency and optimal growth.

d)   Thus, an additional explanation is needed for the divergence. The single most important divergence between DC and LDC then, is the role that the *state* plays in the LDC. Whereas in the earlier development economics the LDC economy and LDC subject diverged from the DC economy and subject, and the LDC state, like the DC state was the hope for sameness-to-come, in the NL vision, the LDC economy and subject was marked by sameness with the DC subject, and the state was the structure responsible for creating divergence.

The Role of the State

The WDR notes that a key source for the NL vision is Viner and Bauer's early dissent on the state-led ISI strategies for development. As early as 1953, Viner argued (in his lectures at the National University of Brazil [Viner 1963]), that there was little the state could do to help "unleash development," and that most efforts by the state that attempted to do this would hinder development. Viner's 1953 talk also explains some of the differences between the ISI and NL visions in terms of the definition and path to development. The first part of the talk is devoted to examining how one should identify or define development (and hence, what goal one should set for development). He notes:

> A more useful definition of an underdeveloped country is that it is a country which has good potential prospects for using more capital or more labor or more available natural resources, or all of these, to support its present population at a higher level of living, or, if its *per capita* income level is already fairly high, to support a larger population on a not lower level of living. This definition puts the primary emphasis

where I think it properly belongs, on *per capita* levels of living, on the issue of poverty and prosperity, although it leaves room for secondary emphasis on quantity of population. On the basis of this definition, a country may be underdeveloped whether it is densely or scarcely populated, whether it is a capital-rich or capital poor country, whether it is a high income *per capita* or a low income *per capita* country, or whether it is an industrialized or an agricultural country. The basic criterion then becomes whether the country has good potential prospects of raising *per capita* incomes, or of maintaining an existing high level of per capita income for an increased population (Viner 1963, p. 12)

Now, this redefinition has the effect of changing the effect of Kuznets' and Rostow's original emphasis on structural change and take-off in some curious ways:

a) Development has been redefined to move the emphasis *away* from DC-LDC difference, to the question of difference *within* a country between its *potential optimum* (presumably given by the Paretian criteria) and its current state. Thus, suddenly, development is about the distance between the extant economic outcome and the efficient outcome, and not about DC-LDC difference. Everything else—structure of production, capital scarcity, all the other explanations for DC-LDC difference in the earlier definitions— is irrelevant.

This is the only place where I have seen such an explicit statement of how individualism redefines development. As I will show in the next section, the models deployed have in effect defined the maximum possible development of the LDC in terms of this potential market efficient point. While the NL paradigm itself seems unconscious of this implicit redefinition of the meaning of underdevelopment, and as noted above, the WDR starts off its discussion of development by discussing LDC difference from the West, the *specific* goal of development is actually efficiency rather than convergence with the West.

The ideology mixes the two definitions together. In effect, the West is developed because over the years, the West has attained levels of production closest to its Pareto efficient outcome and is reaping the benefits of this. The LDC is underdeveloped because over the years it has not attained levels of production closest to its Pareto efficient outcome, and so is mired in low levels of living. Here, it is not subjective difference, but "outcome difference" that explains the divergence between LDC and DC. To actually show that an economy is underdeveloped, the models deployed discuss how and why the LDC economies have *market outcomes* that are not Pareto efficient, rather than discussing the differences in the production structure, occupational

structure, capital intensity, traditions and norms, of the developed and un-
developed regions.

b) The next question is what accounts for the divergence between reality and efficiency. Definitionally and theoretically, the divergence cannot
be explained by subjective difference or structural differences. Presumably,
the LDCs may be *poor,* but if they follow free markets, *definitionally,* they
could not *underdeveloped* (since they have reached their full *potential* level
of development). Then clearly, the only conceivable reason for the currently
visible lack of full development must be something that intervenes in the
market mechanism—the State.

In the original formulations of Viner in the early 50s, the development
consensus on state-led development had not yet emerged. Viner in effect argued that given the way he defined development, the measure of a country's
development should not be the *actual* rise in per capita incomes that may
emerge with state policy, but the *counterfactual* question of whether this was
the optimal level of output, or the highest possible level of standards of living that the country *could* have achieved if the state had not intervened. In
other words, since development here is defined as a divergence from the *possible* level of production and standards of living, rather than as a divergence
from the *extant* levels of living found in other countries, the relevant measure is the counterfactual.

> Let us suppose, for instance, that a country which has embarked on a
> programme of economic development engages in periodic stock-taking
> of its progress, and finds not only that aggregate wealth, aggregate in-
> come, total population, total production, are all increasing, but that *per
> capita* wealth, income, production, are also increasing. All of these are
> favorable indices, but even in combination do they suffice to show that
> there has been "economic progress," and increase in economic welfare
> rather than retrogression? (Viner, 1963 [1953], p.13, emphases and
> quotes original)

He ends up by arguing that one can have aggregate improvement due to
state intervention, but that this is not to be confused with development since
aggregates can improve while the welfare of substantial numbers of people
is not improved. The state cannot do better than the free market in accumulation, in efficiency, in investment, and in resource allocation. The only role
for the state is in improving the quality of workers (skill development or
human capital development in today's parlance). For the rest, development
will be a slow and painful process in terms of raising standards of living,
since even if the standards of living are low, it is the best the country can do
under its current levels of resources.

Bauer is far more forthright in his condemnation of state-led development. Viner says in measured tones that though poverty is a scandal, all one can do is to wait for the market to work its miracle (he is very clear that he is unhappy that it is going to be slow, but he sees no point in not facing the truth). Bauer speaks in ringing tones, heaping scorn on the "dirigiste dogma" of state-led development.[43]

The key places where Bauer articulates his critique in the early years is in Bauer and Yamey (1951, 1957), and later most famously in his (1972) *Dissent on Development*. The earlier article and book with Yamey focus on critiquing the Kuznets-Rostow-Clark vision of development. Bauer and Yamey, like Viner, reject any connection between industrialization and development, and concentrate on growth alone as the true definition of development. Like Viner, they see little role for the state or for protectionism in generating higher levels of growth. In their section on "Government and Economic Development" (Bauer and Yamey 1957, p 149), they note:

> . . . in assessing policies we tend to use as a yardstick their probable effects on the range of alternative courses of actions open to individuals, and that we prefer a society in which policy is directed towards widening the effective range of alternatives open to members of that society. It follows that we think it should be the function of the state to widen the range of opportunities and facilitate access to them, but that it is for the members of society to choose among the alternative opportunities open to them and to develop them with the aid of their personal endowments and the property they own.

In other words, the state should support the free market. This becomes clearer in their sub-section on "Decentralised Decision-making" (p. 152):

> It is inherent in our conception of economic development that we attach significance to acts of choice and valuation made by individuals, including those which express individual time preferences between present and future consumption . . . Further we favor private economic decision-making, and the diffusion of power which it implies, because they help to safeguard the individual in society, both generally, and also in his capacity as an economic agent . . . However, our preference for an economic system in which decision-making is widely diffused and co-ordinated by the market mechanism is not predicated solely on our criterion of development, nor on the political safeguards which the system provides. We consider that in general this system secures an efficient deployment of available resources, and also promotes the growth of resources. Its efficiency stems largely from two features: mobilization of knowledge and provision of incentive.

The free market is definitionally the basis for decentralized decision making (this is very different from left-wing notions of democratization of the decision-making apparatus). It safeguards freedom, is "diffuse" (thus, they assume that resource allocation is never concentrated—the Walrasian individuals are after all, all price-takers by definition), and efficient because of the role that market incentives play (i.e., because rational maximizing individual behavior is assumed).[44]

What role then, is there for the state? Bauer and Yamey give the following list:

a) *Maintenance of Law and Order* (necessary for a good business environment and to ensure the investment is not jeopardized[45]). The reason for the failure of the private sector to lead development, according to them, is the direct result of the failure of the state to maintain law and order. On p. 164, they say:

> The exercise of business initiative and enterprise and the formation of capital by individuals and firms are likely to be seriously reduced or distorted by the failure of the state to perform its minimum tasks [of maintaining law and order]. The failure of the private sector may then, spuriously, create the impression that the necessary ingredients for economic activity and growth have been supplied by the state itself.

At least they did not mince words—one can see why perhaps a totalitarian state is a precondition for freedom. When a recalcitrant public refuses to accept the existing resource distribution, a totalitarian state can help promote "economic freedom" in private property.

b) *Expenditures Yielding Indiscriminate Benefits:* This is the public goods argument for state intervention.

c) *Distribution of Wealth and Income:* They do not see any role for the state here, since they believe that redistribution is an infringement on the rights of those from whom resources are taken. Further, redistribution from the rich to the poor increases consumption and reduces growth, and so this is, from their perspective, counterproductive. The income, if left with the rich, will generate growth, which in time will make *everyone* better off.

In some cases (remember that this is being written immediately after decolonization, when the question of how some people managed to acquire property rights was still an open question) they do favor redistribution. This would be only in cases where the property rights are so obviously the result of theft and power, and the poor are so destitute, that redistribution makes sense. However, in all cases, if redistribution is to be undertaken, it should be a direct redistribution of property endowments, never a redistribution through taxes, subsidies, and other policies that intervene in the price mechanism.[46]

By 1972, Bauer had abandoned even this muted support of possible resource redistribution. He describes the preoccupation with redistribution in his *Dissent on Development* in his section on "Hostility to the Prosperous" (1972, p. 197):

> Professor Myrdal is generally hostile to the more prosperous and materially successful persons and groups . . . he often clearly implies that the incomes of the materially successful . . . have been somehow secured at the expense of the rest . . . These self-reliant and successful groups, who achieved prosperity from poverty, have contributed greatly to the material advance of the areas in which they have been allowed to operate . . .

The wealthy are wealthy because of their initiative, and what we see in the dirigiste dogma is primarily envy and hostility.[47] By 1984, Bauer has moved to arguing not only that the wealthy are hard working, but that their wealth is itself a just reward. Egalitarianism is not only a misguided form of envy, it is also morally unjust. In Bauer's (1984) *Reality and Rhetoric: Studies in the Economics of Development,* he asks (p. 83): " . . . why is it obviously unjust that those who contribute more to production should have higher incomes than those who contribute less?"

d) *The remaining roles of the government* in Bauer and Yamey (1957) follow the "free market" idea. The government should provide aid to victims of catastrophe (but not too much since resources are scarce, and not too much because it may provide a disincentive for private individuals to provide the aid via charity instead), create an institutional framework in which private investors can then make their free market choices, reform of land tenure (primarily to eliminate communal rights to land which are inimical to growth and to enforce a system of individual tenure), to consolidate landholdings (only when voluntary consolidation via individual exchanges is not feasible), and to overcome possible resistance to economic change.[48]

Thus there was dissent on the role of the state in the development literature from the start. In Viner, it is a muted dissent, primarily arguing that he does not see much of a role for the state. In Bauer and Yamey, and then Bauer, we see this turn into a full-fledged attack on protectionism, and on any role for the state in controlling or shaping the market outcome. There is, however, a role for the state. This is the Lockean role, of the state as upholder of property rights, extended now to include the idea of the state as the *fabricator* of private property rights where such rights do not exist. Thus, right from the start, NL was always torn about its relationship to the state.

The Latin American Monetarist-Structuralist Debate

During the 1950s, a debate arose in Latin America between opponents and supporters of orthodox stabilization programs which is identified as a key source for current debates in the field. Advocates of contractionary stabilization programs in the IMF and conservative governments focused on inflation, and argued for the efficacy of contractionary stabilization of price levels on quantity theory of money grounds. Opponents, most notably at ECLA in Chile, developed a broad-gauged historical and class-theoretic approach to the study of Latin American Economies (the key work from which Latin American Structuralism emerged was widely acknowledged to be Noyola's work in the 1950s which was part of this opposing literature). Some of this work by opponents, in a clear rejection of the terms of debate over stabilization, endogenized fiscal and monetary policy within a broader framework of class conflict.

But this 1950s debate (conducted primarily in Spanish) is not what comes down to us in the English-language literature as the "Monetarist-Structuralist" debate, as represented by such writers as Little (1982) and Arndt (1985). Instead, this debate was mapped into the Cartesian space of the structuralist-individualist duality (as described in chapter two). This mapping occurred in the early 1960s, the result of a curious collusion between supporters of orthodox stabilization on the one hand, and Anglo-Saxon opponents of monetarism and stabilization on the other (Danby 2005). What we have come to know as Structuralism today stems largely from the re-interpretation and codification of the 50s Latin American writings by Anglo-Saxon figures like Seers, and by the way early monetarists like Campos sought to characterize the arguments of their opponents.

The supporters of orthodox stabilization naturally sought to present an attenuated and simplistic version of their opponents' arguments. The key figure to provide the Cartesian interpretation of Latin American Structuralism among the conservative supporters of stabilization is the Brazilian Roberto de Oliviera Campos, who in 1961 named the two poles of the stabilization debate "monetarist" and "structuralist" (the Latin American critics of orthodox stabilization in the 1950s did not use the term "structuralist"). Naming the anti-orthodox position "Structuralist" was part of Campos' rhetorical strategy of a) presenting the opposing position as one of ad hoc assertions of inelasticities of supply, and b) arguing that if such inelasticities existed, they were probably caused by the state. It is hardly accidental that this early individualist critique of the state as obstacle to development arose along with a straw-man version of anti-orthodox arguments. From Campos come all the subsequent neoliberal caricatures of the "Structuralist" position—now caricatures extended to all of ISI—in Arndt, Little, and the World Bank.

But the renderings of anti-orthodox arguments by those who claimed to be its champions in the world of Anglo-Saxon economics probably did even more damage. To make a long story short, Cambridge economists like Seers (1962a, 1962b) used the debate to put forward a Cantabrigian theory of an imperfectly competitive real sector in which price "signals" were ineffective in directing allocation of resources. They spiced this with sneers at Chicago school monetary orthodoxy (their own obsession and enemy at the time), and presented this approach as a formal and rigorous version of what Latin American structuralists were saying.[49]

Latin American Structuralism, then, was reinterpreted by both neoliberal critics and Anglo-Saxon supporters in the 1960s as nothing more than the Cantabrigian obsession with imperfect markets, supply inelasticities, production bottlenecks, and "sticky prices," all described through the "rigorous" application of a Cartesian equilibrium framework. Not surprisingly, as the 60s and 70s saw the attack by microfoundationalists in the West on the Cantabrigian analyses, this version of Structuralism became a key target of neoclassical critics. In the 1980s, as the debates about stabilization and development policy were taking on the strident tone found in neoliberal writers like Bauer, Lal and Little, this interpretation of Structuralism was roundly criticized for positing "ad hoc" assumptions about how markets operate. Little (1982), in particular, argued that the Structuralist "sees the world as inflexible." He argues (in chapter five) that Structuralists "held that the basic cause of inflation lay in structural rigidities of one sort or another," a language that mirrors Campos' criticisms of "arbitrary bottlenecks."[50]

The final description of Structuralism deriving from Campos and the Cantabrigians, and drawing on Little's genealogy of Structuralism is found in Arndt (1985). Arndt argues that Latin American Structuralism, coming from the post-WWII debates in England, was primarily an argument about:

a) Whether prices in markets gave the right signals: Here he includes the works of Pigou, Sraffa, Robinson and Keynes as the key sources for this argument.

b) Whether factors of production responded to price signals: This argument he traces to economists at Oxford who suggested that supply responses are inelastic.

c) Whether factors are immobile and so cannot move to new markets even if they wish to respond to price signals: This argument is traced back by Arndt to Arndt (though he gives no evidence or indication that Noyola or any of the other Latin American Structuralists were familiar with his work).

Latin American authors are curiously missing from this description of the Latin American Structuralist-monetarist debates.[51] Ultimately, Latin American Structuralism becomes key for neoliberal critics since it has been reread as the Western battle between Anglo-Saxon critics of free markets and neoclassical champions of free markets. It is these neoclassical champions of free markets and critics of Cantabrigian economics who are the intellectual progenitors of modern neoliberalism.

Neoliberals like Little (1982) and Arndt (1985), seeing Cantabrigian approaches as the source of Latin American Structuralism, note the obvious *similarities* between the Latin American monetarist-Structuralist debates and *Western* debates about market failure in *DC* economies. But despite these parallels, the conception of development economics as a project of capturing the sources of LDC *difference* was left intact. Thus the critics (and current supporters) retained the notion that Structuralism was pinpointing specific structures which described LDC *difference*.

The original codifier of Structuralism, Campos (1961), never claimed that Structuralists were drawing on Cantabrigian economists. He saw them as arguing that LDCs were different from DCs. Thus, he attacked Structuralism's implicit assumption that poor countries differ from rich ones. He argued that all countries have the same underlying economic model of individual agents who maximize, and whose activities are coordinated by markets which clear. Thus "bottleneckism" made no sense, since if relative prices were allowed to adjust freely, agents would respond to price changes and there would be no supply bottlenecks or inelasticities. Thus, in the earliest critiques of Structuralism, we find the use of universal humanism, rational maximizing individuals, and *sameness* to describe LDC economies. This parallels Bauer's and Viner's arguments above, and became a key plank of NL ideology.

If individualist sameness was the hallmarks of all economies, what then explained LDC difference? Campos argued that the "alleged bottlenecks" could only arise if something *intervened* in the markets. He blamed the bottlenecks on state intervention. Again, the earliest critique of Structuralism mirrors the perspective of "state as cause of difference" found in the writings of Bauer, and the subsequent writings of Neoliberal theorists.

The Latin American monetarist contention that the state created inflation by oversupplying money was also endorsed by later neoliberal theorists like Harry G. Johnson, who used the *microfounded* version of the quantity theory of money provided by Friedman to uphold this conclusion.

The monetarist vision did not win the battle in the 60s, but laid the ground for NL formulations in the 1970s in Latin America. The earlier Quantity Theory Tradition of the monetarists was reformulated as the later micro-founded monetarism, since many Western neoliberal economists saw a resonance between this debate and the debate in the West between Keynesians and Monetarists. The monetarist criticisms were added to the criticisms of planning by Western economists and conservative monetary policies became a crucial plank of NL ideology. The interpretation of the Structuralist perspective as "bottleneckism" was repeated until it became *truth* for all the participants in the development debates, and the critique of the state in Bauer was strengthened with the vision of the state as *creator* of the bottlenecks and shortages and market distortions that LDC structuralists were pointing out.

The Growing Body of Dissenting Literature: The State as the Enemy

Following the 50s and 60s Latin American controversy about the origins of inflation and the nature of LDC economies, one saw a growing body of literature in development economics in the late 60s and through the 70s, which slowly mounted to a crescendo. Viner (along with Haberler) had already argued in favor of free trade in the early debates. Bela Balassa and Associates (1971) argued that LDCs did not face any declining terms of trade, and that export promotion and free markets were the best path to development. Bhagwati and Desai (1970) also argued that import substitution and tariff barriers hurt LDC welfare, using a Walrasian framework. Johnson (1955, 1958, 1965, 1967a, 1971a) joined Bhagwati (1969, 1978, 1983, 1985) and Krueger (1975, 1977, 1979, Kreuger et al 1981, Krueger ed. 1988) in arguing for free trade, again using a Walrasian framework. Thus, not only was the Prebisch-Singer hypothesis attacked empirically, the arguments for *laissez faire* were presented in carefully Walrasianized models.

Johnson (1959, 1962, 1976, 1977a and 1977b) also extended Friedman's microfounded monetary theory to the open economy, and formulated the monetary approach to the Balance of Payments. This provided the theoretical apparatus that allowed the microfounded vision to handle that trickiest of market prices, the exchange rate. McKinnon (1973, McKinnon ed. 1976, also McKinnon and Mathieson 1981) and Shaw (1973) argued that intervention by the state in financial markets promoted inefficient resource allocation and lowered investment. To the early Latin American monetarist critique was thus added a carefully microfounded theory of the macroeconomy and of the financial system. And finally, Schultz (1964) attacked Lewis' labor surplus model, and used Walrasian microrational economics to claim that there was no labor surplus in LDCs, and that agriculture in LDC followed Walrasian market principles.

State participation in production had already been criticized by Bauer and Yamey, by Viner, and by the Latin American Monetarists. Krueger (1974) added to this using a carefully Walrasian framework, and argued that in fact the LDC state was a "boondoggle," extracting rents via ISI policies and hurting the economy. This allowed the neoliberals to not only argue that the state created the problems found in LDC economies, but that the reason the state did this was to extract rents. Thus at the same time that Latin American Structuralism was being carefully "de-classed," and its theory of the state was recast from one of policies pushed under conditions of political class struggle, neoliberalism had found an alternative explanation for the behavior of the state. Neoliberalism suddenly transformed the earlier ISI vision of state as helper of the underdeveloped poor, and the Structuralist vision of state as caught in political class struggle, to the vision of market as pro-poor, neoliberals as champions of the masses, and the *state* (not the exploiter) as the enemy of the working poor.

The key break with previous literature found here is that the state was not just *ineffectual* in promoting development (as the early Bauer and Viner had argued), but that state was actually a *barrier* to development. How did these theories show that the state was a barrier to development? By showing that intervention in markets by the state prevented efficiency. This was shown by identifying the theoretically possible market outcome (which was efficient), and comparing it to the outcome under state-intervention (which was inefficient). Here we see that development economics had moved to a new way of defining development. The extent of underdevelopment was known *not* by distance from the West, but by distance from the free market outcome of the possible growth which *may* have occurred *if* the state had not intervened. The ISI state then, had to be dismantled, and replaced by the Lockean one.

In effect, sameness and difference have been reconfigured in this literature. The earlier vision explained LDC difference from the west in terms of the structural differences which prevented LDCs from emulating DCs, and saw the State as the source for the future sameness-to-come. Here, the "end result" of sameness is already postulated in the models. LDC individuals and DC individuals are the same, governed by the same subjectivity of individualist microrational behavior. The state is the source of difference, the structure that defines LDC deviation that is responsible for existing LDC difference. As with the earlier literature, the structure that accounts for difference is identified primarily so that it can be eliminated. Here too, the goal is to eradicate the structure that fabricates difference. NL reformers took up the agenda of eradicating the LDC state and remaking it in the image of the Lockean state they presumed was found in the DC.

This theoretical insight came at a time when many people in both the West and non-West were dissatisfied with the development project as it had actually been put in place. Already, in many countries the promise of ISI seemed to have lead to corrupt bureaucrats and the promised poverty alleviation, dynamic growth, and fast rises in standards of living seemed to be nowhere in sight. Bauer and Lal give ideological voice to this emerging literature on the inefficiency of the ISI policies, and vocalized a coherent vision of NL as being about dismantling the dirigiste state.

Dirigiste Pessimism and Laissez-Faire Optimism: Debt Crises and the NICs

If the theories were primarily grounded in the ideology of laissez faire and free market individualism, they still may not have swept the field so completely. The earlier theories, as noted, attacked the state and argued that free-market efficiency based on the counter-factual was the relevant measure of underdevelopment, rather than any actual rise in closeness to the West or living standards. While theoretically coherent, and slowly gaining resonance among people in the LDC who had lived with the corruption and inefficiency of the ISI state, this in itself would not have triggered the wholesale adoption of the NL agenda.

This is because the NL vision, while theoretically coherent, was not an optimistic one. Viner and Bauer were promising a slow process of development. While marginally better than ISI, there was no promise here of growth, of rising standards of living, of rapid prosperity. The NL approach called on the LDC to stick to what it is good at—agriculture and primary product exports—and stop engaging in "DC envy" or trying to reproduce the Western industrial economy.

But the 70s and then 80s saw two events that magically transformed the implicit pessimism of the NL agenda into a very optimistic vision of growth unleashed, and of quick changes in the standards of living in LDCs. These two events were the debt crisis, which rang the death knell for the promise of development through ISI, and the success of the East Asian economies (NICs) who followed a strategy of development that was not based on ISI (and which was very happily reinterpreted through the NL ideology to be "laissez faire").

The debt crisis in effect turned many countries following ISI policies into net debtors who were unable to cover their payments deficits. The crisis this triggered led economists and policy makers to hunt for a structure that had generated this crisis. Neoclassical economics had just such a structure ready and waiting: the dirigiste state. The argument seemed compelling to the policy makers.[52]

At the same time, the success of the NICs seemed to indicate that here was another path to development, which promised rapid convergence with the West. Just as under ISI the West had been the marker of development, and an effort was made to reproduce the historical path to development in the West in the non-West, the NICs were seen as the new success story. And, just as the West had a story about "stages of development" which had to be followed, the path that the NICs took was carefully examined—if the rest of the LDCs could just follow the historical path that the NICs took (instead of looking to the historical path that the West took), then they too would grow and develop.[53]

The WDR draws heavily on the interpretation of the NICs success given in the World Bank Policy Research Report on the *East Asian Miracle* (World Bank 1993). The vision requires a complete elision of the role of State policy in the actual East Asian experience. The miracle is seen as the result of free markets, an open economy, and private property. Export promotion industrialization became the key to development, with the "promotion" part of it being curiously converted into "free market." The reasons for the success are apparently "orthodoxy in macroeconomic management" and "open markets." These two assumptions are basically a reading of the monetarist free market ideology (macroeconomic stability) and Walrasian free market ideology (open markets and no price distortions) onto the NICs, and become the two pegs of the NL policy agenda.

There was one small anomaly left to explain. The neoclassical vision of the free traders and of Walrasian comparative advantage had said that the path to growth was trade based on comparative advantage. The works of Bauer and Yamey, and of Viner, did not advocate industrialization, and saw no gain for the LDCs from attempting to follow Hirschmanian linkage effects by moving to high productivity industrial production. But the NICs were clearly able to raise living standards not just because they had followed free market advantage in primary products and agriculture, but because they had been able to export the products of the kind of industries specified by ISI. While the strategy was of export-promotion rather than import-substitution, the structural change in production and the targeting of Hirschmanian industries was clearly part of the success story.

The NL vision explains this by simply arguing that the NICs in fact followed their comparative advantage. They were labor-rich, and so they exported labor intensive products. And, like good neoclassical investors, they invested in their area of comparative advantage by investing in labor. So, if the economy had to invest in the area of its comparative advantage, it would have to invest in its labor force. Thus, skill development and human capital formation entered the neoliberal agenda. But since the generation of labor market skills required education, and education was a public good, the private sector could not undertake it. Thus, what had looked like an anomalously strong role of the state in the NICs' experience was not anomalous at all—it was simply a market-friendly role played by the state, investing in the public good of education so as to enhance their comparative advantage.

Suddenly the second source of "difference" between LDC and DC/NIC was found: human beings. There was a key role for the state to play under NL after all—to subsidize and finance human capital investment (but to do it in a manner that kept actual wages low). Thus, the story of the NICs was brought into conformity with comparative advantage despite their entry into manufactures and industrial production. Suddenly, NL pessimism becomes unbridled optimism, even as ISI is killed off by the pessimism generated by the debt crisis and the rise of inefficient bureaucracies.

The Final Vision of NL: Stabilization, Liberalization, Privatization

The WDR, after dismissing the Structuralist and ISI approaches, outlines its vision of development. The rest of the WDR discusses the following (chapter headings followed by a brief synopsis):

Investing in People: This chapter argues for education, and improvements in health and nutrition. It pays special attention to women's education (primarily because it results in reduced population growth).[54] This creates a strong role for the state in eliminating the second bottleneck to development (the first being the dirigiste state itself)—the poor quality of the people. Vocational training is added to basic literacy, so that the LDCs can trade according to their comparative advantage in their abundant resource (labor). Apart from human capital development, there is no other role for the state to play—the state delivers these newly developed workers to the entrepreneurs, who undertake the actual business of producing and investing and exporting.

The Climate for Enterprise: The "climate" basically involves two things. First, it requires *macroeconomic stability,* which is interpreted primarily as low inflation and low fluctuations in exchange rate, along with a public guarantee of liquidity in financial markets via central banking.

Employment and income stability have disappeared from the standard Keynesian macroeconomic definition of stability, and are replaced with the monetarist definition of price stability. Not mentioned, but key to such price stability, is the necessary elimination of large non-discretionary spending on social welfare, since budget balancing and low levels of public debt are necessary for macroeconomic stability as defined here, making any serious budgeting for social safety nets difficult.[55] Also not mentioned is that price stability requires the elimination of possible wage-price spirals, and hence the elimination of any form of collective struggle for maintenance of living standards or for wage increases. Thus the two traditional avenues for income redistribution—social transfers and collective bargaining over wages—have disappeared from the agenda for social change in LDCs as inimical to the interests of investors.

The second plank of the "climate for enterprise" is *liberalization.* Liberalization advocates target three arenas: a) Trade Liberalization, which should increase exports, and make domestic industry competitive by opening it up to the stick of foreign competition (the application of free market Walrasian theory to trade by Bhagwati, Krueger and Johnson); b) Financial liberalization, which should eliminate any effort to control investment financing, and should leave lending to the private banking sector, which should ensure efficient resource allocation (the application of free market Walrasian theory to the banking sector by McKinnon and Shaw); and c) Industrial deregulation, which would eliminate all controls on domestic production (the application of the free market Walrasian vision to the domestic economy, most forcefully articulated by de Soto, Krueger, Bauer and Lal).[56]

In effect, the policy is one of dismantling the interventionist state, and replacing it with a state that protects the interests of private property and free enterprise. This is presented not as a policy of *doing* things in favor of any group, but as one of *undoing* past policy.

The end result is a vision of free markets, with the state ensuring a secure climate for enterprise and free markets. The policy itself has two prongs: *Stabilization,* which puts in place the orthodox monetarist vision of anti-inflationary state policy, and *Structural Adjustment,* which dismantles the previous policies via privatization and liberalization. The third prong, left unstated but still clear, is that after undertaking stabilization and structural adjustment, the state will operate as a Lockean civil state, guaranteeing private property, upholding contracts, and eliminating all efforts to disturb free enterprise and push for redistribution by recalcitrant workers or other Third World 'interest groups.'

Individualist Ontology in NL Ideology

Having examined NL's origin and final visions, let us now look at its ontology. NL ideology draws on two key types of economic theory for its theoretical and policy vision: monetarist theories of inflation and macroeconomic stability, and Walrasian theories of market efficiency in trade, finance, agriculture, and industry. Underlying these theories is a vision of unleashed individualism and the freeing of the individual from the state. I will not examine the ontology of NL theories in the same detailed way that I examined the structuralist theories in the previous major section, since I will examine the monetarist theories of macroeconomic stability in the next chapter, and I have already examined the Walrasian models in the previous chapter.

The actual theories of the NL critics in trade, in finance, in labor markets, in industry, are nothing more than a straightforward application of Walrasian general equilibrium to the sector being examined. The theories postulate rational individuals with preferences and maximizing firms, who meet in free markets governed by an auctioneer. The result of this interaction is efficiency. Anything that prevents the auctioneer from clearing the market is a structure that causes inefficiency: the state intervention in the market in effect prevents the auctioneer from clearing the market. The overt structure of the state is to be replaced by the minimal structure of the market. On reading NL theory, one notes that we see the same analysis in all the articles. All that differs is the area the theory is applied to (exports and imports in one story, consumption and investment in another, asset portfolio choice in yet another), and the specific intervention being decried in the model (minimum wages in one, quotas in one, tariffs in one, interest rate ceilings in one). Since I have already explored the Walrasian theory in detail in chapter two, I will not repeat the discussion here.

Instead, let me examine the overall vision, the general ideology of individualism that lies at the heart of this model. The vision of NL reform is that of a new broom sweeping away the cobwebs of the dirigiste ISI state, and unleashing the thwarted Walrasian individual-entrepreneur. The story told is of rational, maximizing, enterprising individuals, capable and fully formed, innately able to generate the best results with nothing but the most minimal of structures: the implicit and unacknowledged structure of the auctioneer, along with the explicit and acknowledged structure of the Lockean state. Thus, unlike the earlier development vision of ISI, the LDC subject here is already fully formed, individualist, maximizing, and deviates not a jot from his or her DC counterpart. Where Kuznets argued that the civil state and culture were structures that fabricated the individualist of the

DC, NL reformers argue that the individualist of the DC is actually transhistorical, acultural, innate, and already fully extant in the LDC. The NL vision then is implicitly arguing that individualism *is* the human condition, and that humans everywhere are pre-structurally, pre-socially, and innately calculating microrational entrepreneurial subjects. Hence it is individualist.

But if subjectivity is innately pre-structural, then what explains deviance? LDC deviance, as noted before, cannot be explained by universal individualism (unless one wishes to posit eugenic or racialized theories of the innately differing nature of LDC subjects). It requires some call on structuralism, a structure that causes deviation. The structure posited is the *dirigiste* state. This accounts for LDC deviance—underdevelopment, presumably, would not *exist* in LDCs were it not for the ISI state.[57] Thus, interestingly, the theory in effect claims that the LDC-DC difference is a mere fabrication of recent history. What they never explain (and have never felt compelled to explain) is the existence of poverty and of underdevelopment long before the emergence of the *dirigiste* state.

This logical conclusion is found most clearly on the literature on the informal economy. While the earlier literature examined informal labor markets in terms of dualism, or petty commodity production, in Hernando de Soto's (1989) *The Other Path,* the informal economy was seen as a way of avoiding the *dirigiste* state. The informal sector is the hope of the LDC, since it is the site of capitalist entrepreneurship, innovation, and free markets. It is the proof of persistence of the atomistic innately microrational individual. Its existence is also the proof that underdevelopment is a creation of the dirigiste state. Most mainstream literature on the informal sector accepts this characterization.

But while NL postulates pre-existing microrational subjects, it still has difficulty in its theoretical apparatus in positing development and change. If microrational subjects have already adapted to the extant *dirigiste* state, then will not the elimination of this state destabilize the minimal structure of market information and contracts? How will the price-taking individuals move from the old inefficient equilibrium to the new one? The auctioneer does that job.

But even if the auctioneer moves individuals from the old equilibrium to the new one, the question left unanswered is this: if individuals are innately prestructural atoms who merely respond to the exogenous environment, and if their exogenous environment is the dirigiste state, then what gets rid of this structure? This structure is "exogenous," outside individuals, and hence there is no reason for any individual to seek to remove it. If individuals sought to change the structures by which they operated, then the auctioneer story becomes unstable, and rationality has to be restated as subjectivity, politicization, activism. Thus, lacking any story of how atomistic individuals become socially aware, active political subjects who can do more than simply respond to exogenous environments, NL reformers hit up against a theoretical lack (one which is never articulated). Someone has to do the job of dismantling the dirigiste state, and that someone has to be a structure outside the individualist microrational Walrasian framework. The job is handed to the dirigiste state which is to be dismantled.

Thus, even as the neoliberals have the elimination of the state as their goal, they are heavily dependent on the state for doing the dismantling. The structure of difference, as with the earlier development theorists, requires a structure capable of transforming difference into sameness. There is only one clear structure identified by the NL theories: the state (the other structure, the auctioneer, is not very helpful in this regard). NL theory depends on the state to enact the reforms and to carry them through, enforcing them with harsh measures if need be.

The second problem that NLs face is that the actual experience of reforms in many countries does not seem to be one of dynamically unleashing entrepreneurial production under free trade. While the WDR and the general literature on NL reform draws heavily on the East Asian economies, there was a second group of countries that embraced NL reform in the 70s and 80s: Latin American economies. Chile embraced these reforms even before the debt crisis (Foxley 1983). With the debt crisis, many other countries embraced such reforms in the 80s. The decade following these reforms has been one of much turmoil, with country after country experiencing not stability and growth, but financial instability, crises, recessions. Further, the reforms did not eliminate even the problems they were supposedly designed to address—balance of payments deficits and the ability to grow via exports which would eliminate the debt crisis presumably triggered by the dirigiste state.

Clearly, simply adopting the NL reforms did not automatically lead to the Walrasian efficiency, entrepreneurial investment, growth, and stability promised by the reformers. Something else was going on. What emerged was the "sequencing" literature. The sequencing literature of the 1980s (Choksi and Papageorgiou 1986, Edwards 1984, McKinnon 1991) postulates that while the *end* result of the NL reform is as promised, the actual success of the strategy depends on the sequence in which the reforms are enacted—macroeconomic stability first, then domestic financial liberalization and industrial deregulation, then trade liberalization, and finally liberalization of capital markets.

Why should the sequence of reforms matter? The argument is that the markets do not all adjust to the new regime at the same rate, creating a possibility of crises. In other words, the actual structure by which the markets can all coordinate needs to be put in place before the individualist entrepreneur can be safely unleashed—the auctioneer is not always going to call out the right equilibrium prices in all markets right away. As noted in the previous chapter, the move from equilibrium to equilibrium poses a problem for the individualists, and they rely on the auctioneer actually calling out the prices to individuals at the right speed, and the right order, for the new equilibrium to emerge. The move from the old equilibrium to the new one creates a problem for the individualists. Thus, the sequencing literature creates a second structural collapse—the collapse of the Walrasian market into a *flawed* structure in the auctioneer. This then requires a second structure—the State—to ensure that the move to the new equilibrium is actually undertaken in the right manner, since the auctioneer does not seem to get it right. The State, by supplying the correct sequence of reforms, can replace the flawed auctioneer and ensure that the path from the old equilibrium to the new one is correct.

Consequences of Deploying Individualism in Development Economics

Here, I examine some consequences of deploying Walrasian Individualism in Development Economics. What emerges is that for all its postulation of being different, of being a new vision, individualist development economics shares many perspectives and consequences with the earlier structuralist vision it replaces:

a) *Like the earlier theory, NL individualism understands development in terms of sameness and difference.* Where the earlier theories focused on the difference, the NL theory focuses on the sameness of DC and LDC individuals. But like the earlier theory, the cause for underdevelopment is found in a structural difference, a difference which is automatically "bad," and must be eliminated. The difference is the dirigiste state.

b) *As the earlier ISI vision, NL theory too collapses into its opposite.* The theory draws on structure to explain difference, and draws on structure to create sameness. The structure that creates difference is the State, and the structure which will create sameness by eliminating difference is the State.

c) *The maintenance of this polarity retains the tendency for pendulum swings between the two ontologies.* Just as the difficulties of describing difference and postulating sameness-to-come lead ISI theorists to collapse into individualism at their key weak point (investment and the behavior of the LDC entrepreneur), so individualism faces difficulties in postulating the mechanism by which difference will be transformed into sameness-to-come. It immediately falls into it opposite—structuralism (structuralism is drawn on to explain how the old policies will be dismantled, structuralism is drawn on to explain why the new policies fail, and structuralism is drawn on to suggest the solution for the failure of the new policies).

d) *As with the earlier ISI theories, NL theories also elide class and retain the notion of the well being of the nation state and national weal as the goal of development.* Specifically, they assume that everybody will partake of the growth and entrepreneurial opportunities unleashed by the reforms. The individualist vision elides class in its very theory, since individuals are postulated as pre-social entities, and markets are postulated as realms where freely choosing individuals exchange to mutual benefit. While NL theory does have to recognize class in some arenas (such as the need to discipline a recalcitrant working class, and to enforce reforms despite the harm they do to workers), it simply asserts that the resistors just have to be forced to adapt, since they may not realize it, but they too will benefit in the long run despite their short-term discomfort.[58]

e) *As with ISI, the NL theories elide history.* The existence of underdevelopment is attributed to the dirigiste state, while their path to development is seen primarily in terms of divergence: in this case, divergence from the NICs. Of course, poverty, the informal sector, and divergence from DCs all predate the protectionist ISI state, but one almost feels on reading the NL theorists that one had thriving decolonized nations with no problems reduced to poverty because of the ISI state.

CONCLUSION

The ISI-NL debates are a product of the specific ways in which development economics has developed as a field. The debaters have more in common than they realize, since they share a common vision of development, a common role for ontology, and a common tendency for collapse into their opposite. The key points made in this chapter are:

a) The goal of the LDC is to be like the DC (or like the NICs). The theory that explains the DC (or the NICs) is the Walrasian individualist vision, which has the absolute minimum of structure (correct working of market signals) for coherence. The goal, then, has always been marked by reference to the primarily individualist vision of the DC (or NIC) economy.

b) The definition of the LDC is difference. The way to explain difference is by reference to structures that prevent individualism from flourishing—be they structures within the LDC economy or structures imposed by the dirigiste State. The explanation of the existing state of affairs in LDCs, then, is marked by reference to structures.

c) The development problematic always had recourse to both individualism and structuralism, since it always needed to keep both the explanation of underdevelopment (structuralism) and goal (individualism) before it.

d) Structuralism, as deployed here by both the ISI theorists and the NLs, has always seen structures as obstacles or constraints. All the structures identified are reflections of LDC difference and LDC lack. Thus all the structures identified are identified primarily so that they can be abolished.

e) This vision of structure as restraint and of individualism-driven society with the bare minimum of structures needed for coherence as goal, which implied policy to eliminate these restraining structures, is shared by *both* the pro-trade neoclassicals and protectionist structuralists. All they disagree on is the path from structure-bound society to individualist society.

f) The ISI theories saw the structures as social or cultural: tradition, subsistence. These were structures that shaped inadequate agents, and would be removed by the agency of the state. The NL theories of the 80s that replaced ISI saw the LDC agent as no different from the DC agent. Then what explained LDC difference? They identified the ISI state as the source of structural difference. As with earlier theories, the goal remains the elimination of structures, since structures identified were inherently "bad" since they explained deviance. So, NL set out, like the earlier theories, to dismantle the structures that produced difference—in this case, the ISI state.

g) The debates about trade and development made sense to its participants *despite* the different ontologies deployed, since there was actually agreement on the vision of difference and future sameness, and agreement that structure, where identified, was a bad thing. It was identified in order to be dismantled.

h) The actual move from structure bound society to individualist society is left fuzzy for *both* individualists and structuralists. As noted in chapter two, the use of an equilibrium framework makes it almost impossible to describe the dynamic process of change from structuralist social order to individualist one. Each theory then draws on its opposite to close the gap and invoke a story of change.

i) Thus, the polarity between structure and agent is a precarious one, and depending on whether one is using a theory that takes the end-result or using a theory that focuses on the structures found in current LDC economies, one will deploy individualist or structuralist theories. The pro-traders were using a theory that presented the end-result, the growth emergent when one kept the goal in mind. The protectionists were using a theory that presented the structures that prevented the goal from being realized.

Thus, this chapter has shown how for all their differences, ISI and NL theories have certain commonalties. The commonalties emerge from the tension between sameness and difference in development economics, which leads to a proclivity for swings from one pole of the structure-agent dichotomy to the other within the field. In the next two chapters, I continue to examine, in greater detail, the terrain of the debate between structuralism and individualism in development economics. Exchange rate theory and the CDD will be taken up respectively to show how this debate plays itself out in policy discussions.

Chapter Four

The Balance of Payments
and the Exchange Rate

The contractionary devaluation debate (CDD) concerns the impact of exchange rate devaluations on LDC economies. Exchange rate devaluations are recommended by the IMF for countries that are unable to meet their foreign exchange payments obligations, a situation often termed as a Balance of Payments (BOP) crisis. New Structuralists have charged that these devaluations cause stagflation. In order to examine the ontological bases for the arguments of the two sides of the CDD (examined in detail in chapter 5), this chapter examines their theories of the exchange rate and international markets. The chapter builds on the general exposition of structuralist and individualist ontologies in development economics presented in chapters 2 and 3, and focuses on one key market in the economy: the market for foreign exchange.

The *exchange rate* is the rate at which domestic currency is exchanged for foreign currency. It is set in the market for foreign exchange either by market forces (floating exchange rates), or by the relevant foreign exchange authorities (fixed exchange rates). The literature on contractionary devaluation is concerned with fixed exchange rates. A devaluation is an increase in the official price of foreign currency undertaken by the foreign exchange authority. In the context of neoliberal policies, it is undertaken to eliminate a deficit in the balance of payments.

How a particular theory understands the impact of devaluation depends on how it interprets the imbalance in payments that provoked the devaluation. Devaluation will only be undertaken if it is expected to have "real" effects. If changing the exchange rate is to have any real effects, one has to specify those real effects, and how they will emerge. Therefore, the literature on devaluation has to pay attention to price and output determination, and resolve such questions as the role of money supply or wage structures in this process. Thus much of the CDD is concerned not just with the market for foreign exchange, but with the exchange rate's relationship to the real economy.

The *Balance of Payments* is simply an accounting statement of the various sources and uses of foreign exchange by a country, and represents all the economic interactions between domestic and foreign agents. As an accounting statement it must balance. A theory of the "real effects" of a devaluation must describe which components of the BOP are affected by the devaluation, and how. This requires some understanding of agent behavior and agent response to devaluations. Further, it must describe how some components in the BOP adjust to the others to bring about a balance in the accounts.

As noted above, the *exchange rate* is conceived of by both structuralists and individualists as a price: the price paid for foreign exchange by the domestic economy. As such, it reflects the price of access to foreign exchange for undertaking international transactions. But since prices are determined by different rules in both theories,[1] it is not surprising that beyond agreement on this definition, there is not much agreement about either the mechanisms by which the exchange rate is determined, or the impact of a change in exchange rates on the macroeconomy.

In this chapter, I first introduce the Balance of Payments and the concept of a payments disequilibrium in the section "The Balance of Payments," since devaluation is a policy designed to cure the shortfall in foreign exchange. The rest of this chapter will then discuss how individualists and structuralists comprehend economic agency in international markets, and examine their theories of the BOP and the exchange rate. The section "Individualist Analyses of the BOP and the Exchange Rate" examines the individualist theories of the BOP and exchange rates, and "Structuralist Approaches to the BOP" examines the structuralist approaches to them.

In each of the sections on individualist and structuralist theories, I ask four questions in assessing the theories presented:

i)   What is the ontology underlying this theory?
ii) How is an "imbalance" in the BOP understood?
iii) What is the "adjustment mechanism" to a BOP imbalance? That is, how does the logic of causality in the theory describe responses to BOP deficit? and
iv) What role (if any) is there specified for devaluation?

Table 4.2 at the end of these two sections provides a synopsis of the various theories examined in this chapter. The last section, "Conclusion: Differences and Similarities between Individualists and Structuralists," synthesizes the key points made in this chapter, and highlights the commonalities and differences between the individualist and structuralist perspectives on the BOP and the exchange rate.

THE BALANCE OF PAYMENTS

The Balance of Payments is an account which summarizes all of the transactions between the domestic economy and the rest of the world. The simplest version of the BOP consists of the current account, the capital account, and "Official Settlements" or Change in Reserves (Table 4.1 below provides a sample BOP and describes the various components of the account).

The BOP, as an account of all sources and uses of foreign exchange, must balance. But while the account must always balance, it still leaves the question open of how a particular economy *attains* a balance in its accounts.[2] In international finance, this is often presented as a question of which of the elements of the BOP are *"autonomous"* or reflect the decisions of individuals to engage in foreign transactions, and which are *"accommodating,"* and *adjust* to bring about balance. This in turn requires a theory of the subjectivity of the economic agents and the operations of the various elements of the BOP to make a decision about where to draw the "line" between autonomous and accommodating expenditures in the BOP. This distinction has evolved in part as a way to define a BOP crisis: a situation of unsustainable accommodating flows.

The conversion of the accounting identity into a framework of equilibrium balance is common to both individualists and structuralists. As I will show, they disagree on what the various autonomous and accommodating flows are, and on what the behavioral equations describing agent decisions in the autonomous flows are. But both agree that a theory of BOP crises can only emerge when one converts the accounting identity into an equilibrium framework. Further, both agree on the distinction between autonomous and accommodating flows, though they may disagree on which flows are autonomous and which are accommodating. Their definition of BOP crisis rests on this distinction since crisis is defined as the inability to sustain the accommodating flows and thus ensure closure, self-regulation and systemic self-reproduction at equilibrium. This common mode of analysis reflects the shared Cartesianism of the two ontologies, since it assumes that one can carefully separate out the various components of the BOP, and divide it up into "parts" which are autonomous and accommodating. I will return to the shared Cartesianism of the two approaches in the last section of this chapter.

To explore the forms that the distinction between "autonomous" and "accommodating" flows can take, we can use a simplified statement of the BOP with an equation format rather than the account shown in Table 4.1.

Table 4.1 The Balance of Payments

The table below provides a sample Balance of Payments (BOP). The BOP is an account which tracks the flows of income, expenditures, and capital across national borders. It represents the aggregate economic transactions undertaken by the members of a nation and the rest of the world. The entries on the Left hand side represent economic activities that generate foreign exchange, and the entries on the Right hand side represent economic activities that use foreign exchange.

Sources of Foreign Exchange	Uses of Foreign Exchange	"Balances"
Current Account		Trade
1. Exports	Imports	Balance
2. Income received on factor services	Income paid for factor services (including interest on past debt)	Current
3. Private Remittances from Abroad	Remittances to foreign residents	Account
4. Unilateral Receipts (Official)	Unilateral Disbursements (Official)	Balance
Capital Account		
5. Direct Foreign investment from abroad	DFI undertaken abroad	
6. Long Term foreign Borrowing	Long Term Foreign Lending	Global
7. Short Term Foreign Borrowing	Short Term Foreign Lending	Balance
Official Settlements		(where
8. Reductions in Reserves	Additions to Reserves	this line
Sales of Gold	Purchases of Gold	should be
Sales of Foreign Exchange	Purchases of Foreign Exchange	is disputed
Sales of Other Assets by Central Bank	Purchases of Other Assets by Central Bank	in policy debates)

NOTES

a) All items on the Left Hand Side are POSITIVE or inflows, while all items on the Right Hand Side are outflows and so have to be DEDUCTED from the BOP when the account balances.

b) The balance between the items in 1, Exports less Imports, is called the trade balance.

c) The balance between the inflows and outflows on the current account (items 1-4) is called the current account balance.

d) The items on the Left Hand Side in the capital account are capital imports and represent an inflow of foreign exchange. The items on the Right Hand Side are capital exports and reflect a use of foreign exchange. One could, if one wished, present net flows of capital: Net inflows (or imports of capital) would be added, Net outflows (or export of capital) would be subtracted.

e) The balance on the current account and capital account combined (items 1-7) is also referred to as the Global Balance. There is some disagreement about how to define this, however, since the idea behind the Global Balance is to separate out the "autonomous" from the "accommodating" flows. There is much disagreement among economists about whether Short Term Capital Flows should be included in this figure.

f) The final entry represents reductions in or additions to official reserves. A reduction in reserves represents an increase of the foreign exchange available in the economy, and hence is added, while additions to reserves are a use of foreign exchange and are subtracted. As with the capital accounts, we can use net figures: a net reduction in reserves is a source of foreign exchange and is added, a net increase in reserves is a use of foreign exchange and is subtracted. Most analysts assume that changes in the government's reserve position represents an accommodating flow.

g) The total account has to balance. Thus, if one added all the items in the account (subtracting those on the right hand side), the sum should equal zero.

As an accounting statement of money flows, the BOP has to balance (Total Foreign Exchange Inflows = Total Foreign Exchange Uses). Placing all items on the left hand side, a simple statement of this accounting identity is:

$$X - M - LTC - STC - R \equiv 0^3$$

where X is exports of goods and services, M is the value of imports, LTC and STC are exports of long term and short term capital respectively,[4] and R is the net increase in official reserves of gold and foreign exchange.[5]

Thus, when one argues that a country is in deficit or facing a "short-fall," one has to define which of these items is a "forced" or *balancing* entry—for example, that the government is taking on loans, or runs down reserves, in order to sustain imports. Where one draws the line will depend on which of the activities represented in the balance of payments account one believes to be reflective of people's "desires" or "behavioral character-istics," and which one believes to be "accommodating" or "balancing" ac-tivities (activities that in effect *finance* the BOP deficit by accommodating to the autonomous activities).

For example, if one believes that exports, imports, and long term cap-ital flows induce short term borrowing and a running down of government reserves, then, one can rewrite the above accounting identity with au-tonomous flows on the left and accommodating flows on the right:[6]

$$X - M - LTC = STC + R$$

If however, one believes that short term capital is also autonomous, with the government having to adjust reserves to suit, one could write instead:

$$X - M - LTC - STC = R$$

A variety of formulations have sought to subdivide STC and/or LTC into au-tonomous and accommodating parts.[7]

But one need not stop there. An OPEC nation might manipulate oil ex-ports to obtain a desired level of reserves, producing the following au-tonomous/accommodating distinction:

$$- M - LTC - STC - R = - X$$

Another country might compress imports to reach a similar goal:

$$X - LTC - STC - R = M$$

The point is this: any item in the BOP may in some places and times be "autonomous," in other places and times be "accommodating." A BOP "crisis" generally implies that changes in the autonomous components have overwhelmed the state's capacity to manipulate the accommodating parts of the balance, *usually* manifested in a vanishing R.

Therefore, any discussion of whether a country is in a balance of payments deficit automatically entails:

1. specific behavioral assumptions about what drives the decisions to export, import, borrow and invest in LDCs, which constitute ontological assumptions about economic subjectivity,
2. the identification of one or more "accommodating" components of the BOP in which a "deficit" is manifested,
3. a diagnosis of the factors leading to the payments crisis based on these assumptions, *and*
4. an implicit outline of a "solution" to the deficit, since the answers to 1 and 3 above will include some notion of why the deficit emerged and how agents will respond to different policy measures.

Thus, though both sides in the CDD might agree that a situation of fast-dwindling reserves represents a "crisis" in the obvious sense that capacity to import or service debt is threatened, there need not be any agreement on the causes, extent, or policy responses to a payments deficit. How one answers these questions depends on one's ontological position on the nature of LDC economies. The next two sections examine how individualists and structuralists assess the BOP and provide recommendations for handling a BOP crisis.

INDIVIDUALIST ANALYSES OF THE BOP AND THE EXCHANGE RATE

As noted above, the BOP consists of two components: a "real sector" flow of goods and services, usually consisting of the trade balance (but also including direct foreign investment and payments on factor services), and a financial market flow of securities in the capital account. Individualists using the Walrasian vision usually separate out the theories of the determinants of real and financial sector decisions, and so have two separate components for their assessment of the BOP. The first component is the trade flows, usually discussed using a neoclassical Walrasian theory of trade, and the second component added to that is a theory of the financial sector, drawing on a variety of approaches to the financial flows of the BOP. I first examine the neoliberal theory of the current account and trade balance, and then examine various neoliberal theories of the full BOP including financial flows. Finally, I conclude the discussion of individualist approaches to the BOP and present the main conclusions of this section.

Trade Theory

The general theory of trade used by the neoliberals draws on Ricardian comparative advantage and the Heckscher-Ohlin reformulation of comparative advantage. Ricardo's formulation of comparative advantage used a labor theory of value and the gold specie flow mechanism to explain both why trade is good, and the mechanism by which it would take place in a manner that ensured BOP equilibrium. In the Heckscher-Ohlin reformulation, Ricardo's labor theory of value is replaced by the carefully individualist notion of desire and technology driving supply and demand to set a series of *relative* values for imports and exports.

In the neoclassical theory of international trade, nations undertake exchange in a *barter* framework and under conditions of full employment. Thus the question of the capital account and financial flows does not arise. The argument is that free trade is beneficial to both nations (in the simple two-country models employed), with each nation producing the commodity in which it has a comparative advantage due to factor abundance. Trade not only raises the total value of output globally because of production specialization, it also increases consumption efficiency because nations, through exchange, can consume goods produced elsewhere. The model is exactly the same as the Walrasian model described in chapter two. The auctioneer calls out the correct relative prices at which all markets—including the markets for imported and exported goods—clear. In equilibrium, since each individual and each country meets its budget constraint, trade is balanced, with each country exporting exactly enough to meet the relative cost of its imports. This model of free trade underlies the neoliberal support for free markets. The ontology used here is entirely individualist.

But a theory of trade among nations must also include some notion of the exchange rate, since it is the exchange rate that agents use to determine the relative prices of imports and exports. The exchange rate is absent from the picture. The individualist framework cannot seriously be saying that there is no such thing as an exchange rate. So we must construct the implicit exchange rate in this theory.

The free market system is described in a Heckscher-Ohlin world as a barter economy where relative values determine real outcomes. Actual price levels are simply set in terms of a numèraire. Money then is a veil, and the quantity of money sets the *price level*, since there is no real theory of a *demand for money* in the sense that money enters the utility schedules of people as something that is desired in the way *real* goods are. Money is "held" to facilitate exchange, and any utility it has is simply as that, a numèraire, through its ability to acquire other goods.

The exchange rate is a price. It is the price of acquiring foreign currency. As such, it is set in the market for foreign exchange. *It is not a policy tool.* Why would you desire to buy or sell foreign exchange? Because of your desire to acquire foreign goods or services. The foreign exchange market equilibrates to bring the supply and demand for foreign exchange in line, and in doing so translates one numèraire into another, based on the extent to which the two economies trade. The relative price of imports and exports is set by the underlying real variables.

Ontology: The framework for this type of supply-demand analysis is a simple extension of the neoclassical model described in chapter two. Trade arises through the interaction of priorly defined individuals maximizing desire, in an environment of given technology, resources, and property distribution. The implicit exchange rate is set by the action of supply and demand to reflect the real terms of trade, which are expressions of the underlying preferences, technology, and resources.

Adjustment mechanism: Since the theory defines equilibrium as the condition where supply equals demand, supply equals demand in all markets, including the one for foreign exchange. There is no explicit "adjustment" mechanism: the theory provides a description of equilibrium. In a comparative static sense, a very small change in some variable leads to instantaneous price adjustments that produce a new equilibrium. But it does not provide a description of a situation in which there is a large disequilibrium (imbalance in payments), nor a mechanism of how to attain equilibrium when out of it.

Concept of imbalance and role for devaluation: There is no role for any policy to deal with imbalance in this theory *because there can be no imbalance.* An imbalance implies that the value of outflows of currency exceeds the value of inflows. This means an *excess demand for foreign exchange* in a debtor country. So imbalances arise only when one is "out of equilibrium," and some sort of *intervention* is preventing the movement to equilibrium and balanced trade.

Note that so far, we do not have money, since the Walrasian world does not have any role for money except as a numèraire. Any one of the goods produced can be used as a numèraire, and so there is no theory of money. In addition, the model cannot have two numèraires and thus though the Walrasian model accommodates direct foreign investment and real capital flows with some modifications, it stumbles when attempting to incorporate financial flows or trying to accommodate the concept of two monetary units (two numèraires) and the relationship between them. Thus, the pure Walrasian model which forms the basis of neoclassical trade theory has no explicit conception of the exchange rate. To accommodate this idea, neoliberals need something more than the simple model of trade and the current account. They need some theory of the relationship between trade flows and financial flows, and a theory of the exchange rate. The next subsection examines the various sources for the neoliberal theory of the BOP and the exchange rate.

Theories of Money and International Payments Adjustment

Here, I examine four key theories of international financial flows, BOP imbalance, and the exchange rate in an individualist framework. The theories examined here form the basis for the general neoliberal perspective on macroeconomic balance and international payments equilibrium: the specie-flow mechanism, the neoclassical elasticity approach, the monetary approach, and the rational expectations approach.

The Gold Standard

The concern in the literature on the gold standard was not so much with a balance of payments problem, but the adjustment mechanism in the international economy. In this approach, the gold specie-flow mechanism maintained the exchange rate within stable limits and ensures payments balance as follows. Gold was the numèraire, and money was pegged to the gold that backed it. If the price of gold was $1 per lb. in the United States, and Rs. 10 in India, the exchange rate would be near Rs. 10 per dollar.

If there was an "imbalance in payments," and the excess demand for dollars caused the exchange rate to increase to Rs. 15, there would be room for arbitrage. If the cost of shipping gold to and from India was Rs. 1 per lb., one could buy one lb. of gold in India for Rs. 10 and ship it to the United States at the cost of Rs. 1. One could then exchange it in the United States for a dollar, thus acquiring foreign exchange for Rs. 11, and resell the dollar in India for Rs. 15, thus netting Rs. 4. Or demanders of foreign exchange could acquire dollars for Rs. 11 directly, circumventing the exchange market in India. This would push the exchange rate back to the limits set by the price of gold.

Thus, in the specie-flow mechanism, the demand for dollars will be met by the inflow of gold to the United States, and the outflow of gold from India. The central bank holdings of gold in India start declining, those in the United States start increasing. As India's monetary base shrinks, the U.S.'s increases. It is at this point that the theory of price determination and money becomes crucial for describing how the imbalance would disappear.

These changes in the monetary base are assumed to affect *price levels* in the two countries through the Quantity Theory of Money (rather than the monetary changes affecting *output levels*). In other words, as the money supply in India falls, the price level in India starts falling. Similarly, as the United States' money supply increases, price levels increase. These changes in price level (lower in India, higher in the U.S.) constrict the excess demand for U.S. imports and restore external balance. The exchange rate was thus set within stable limits, and the imports and exports of a country were determined by the relative values of production in each country.[8]

Ontology: This mechanism derives its momentum from the flows of gold set loose by the individual desire for profit. More importantly, it translates these flows into *price* changes through the Quantity Theory of Money, which assumes that all markets clear because of Say's law. Say's law assumes that supply and demand forces will operate to clear all markets, thus ensuring full employment and sufficient demand for sales. But what generates these supply and demand forces? It is a vision of priorly specified agents each acting in his or her own self-interest. This is therefore an individualist conception of agent behavior.

But for the mechanism to work, the central bank had to play its role, standing ready to exchange currency into gold on demand. Further, policies for credit creation were to follow the "rules of the game," tightening credit and raising interest rates in deficit countries and vice versa in creditor countries, thus speeding the adjustment process.[9] So there was an institutional role for the monetary authorities, a rule or structure that would allow the individual decisions to mesh harmoniously.

Adjustment mechanism: Adjustment took place by gold flowing naturally from deficit to surplus countries backed by complete currency convertibility, causing changes in the price level until the external balance was restored. This adjustment comes from the previously defined maximization drive of the individualist ontology, which is given unfettered play by the government's readiness to convert currency to gold on demand.

Concept of imbalance and role for devaluation: International imbalance, or inability to pay for foreign goods because of trade deficits, is not an issue in this framework. This is because the maximizing behavior of individuals will automatically set the adjustment mechanism working, preventing any persistent imbalance.

Also, in this description of the gold standard there is no role for devaluation as a policy if money supply does not affect real values. This is because the whole apparatus rests on relating money to gold at a fixed rate. A devaluation implies changing the monetary unit (changing its relationship to gold), but as long as the government buys and sells gold on demand, the price level in each country adjusts to the total gold supply in the economy. As long as the theory of relative price determination and output levels does not depend on the money supply, all devaluation implies is a change in numèraire.

The Elasticity Approach

The elasticity approach to the balance of payments is based on the supply-demand analysis described above in the neoclassical approach to trade theory. What makes this theory interesting is that it does not actually discuss the reasons why money is held in a Walrasian system. Instead, it simply postulates that nations have exchange markets for their currencies, and these markets are presumably reflections of the various "autonomous" sources and uses of foreign exchange in the BOP. Since according to the individualist vision all sources and uses of foreign exchange reflect individualist desire, and all markets clear in equilibrium, presumably the market for foreign exchange will clear as well. Thus, while there is no actual theory of why money is held or demanded, the theory simply starts by asserting that there is a market for foreign exchange. Presumably all one has here is a transactions demand for money, and foreign exchange is demanded or supplied primarily to facilitate transactions in foreign markets.[10] If all markets clear then, of course, the foreign exchange market will clear too. Its price will reflect the *relative* demands for foreign goods by domestic residents, and for domestic goods by foreign residents, giving the appropriate conversion of one numèraire into another for the relevant markets. If this market does not clear, then clearly some other market (market for imports and/or exports) is not clearing by Walras' law.

Thus, the elasticities approach examines the equilibrium in a single market, the market for foreign exchange, without actually explaining why money is held at all. Taking this market as a given, the approach asks, what is the equilibrium exchange rate? Note that since the exchange rate ultimately facilitates numèraire conversion, and the Walrasian equilibrium is an equilibrium of *relative* prices, the theory is implicitly defining the equilibrium exchange rate as the price that equilibrates the foreign exchange market to ensure that *relative prices* for real goods and services across borders are market-clearing. Thus, the equilibrium exchange rate referred to here is the *real* exchange rate. The *real exchange rate* is the rate at which the actual *relative* value of the two numèraires ensures market-clearing. It is defined as the nominal exchange rate relative to the price levels found in the two countries (since the price level will, by giving *real* purchasing power of a Rupee and the *real* purchasing power of a dollar, give us the correct *real* value of the numèraire conversion contained in the nominal exchange rate).

The definition of the equilibrium with reference to the real exchange rate which ensures equilibrium market clearing then gives us the definition of a payments imbalance. If one is out of equilibrium so that numèraire conversion does not take place at the correct level to ensure that agents can respond to the correct underlying relative prices, then the foreign exchange market will not clear and there will be an excess demand (or excess supply) of foreign exchange, matched by an underlying real excess demand (or supply) for goods and services in the current account. If the excess demand for foreign exchange persists (which can only happen when the foreign exchange market fails to clear and hence when one is out of equilibrium) one faces a BOP imbalance. When one is in equilibrium and the exchange rate adjusts to ensure the correct numèraire conversion, the autonomous sources of foreign exchange exactly match the autonomous uses of foreign exchange at the going price level (which reflects the *underlying* real relative prices facing agents correctly) and there is no excess or shortfall in payments, and hence no BOP crisis.

The impact of a devaluation (a change in the *nominal* price of foreign exchange) is analyzed in terms of the response of demand and supply of foreign exchange to the price change. But in supply-demand analyses, the *real* exchange rate is set in the market for foreign exchange as a *price*. So how does "devaluation" enter the picture? Implicitly, the elasticity approach must be assuming that if the foreign exchange market fails to clear then it must be because something *prevented* the move to equilibrium and pushed the economy into a situation where equilibrium does not attain. This can only happen when something—the state—holds the *nominal* exchange rate fixed at the "wrong" level vis-à-vis the market-clearing *real* exchange rate (given the price levels of the two countries). In other words, when the state fixes the nominal exchange rate at which currency conversion will take place, the auctioneer, faced with two incommensurate numèraires cannot call out the correct underlying *relative* prices that should underlie the demand and supply for transactions across borders at equilibrium. Devaluation, then, implies a change in the *nominal* exchange rate so that the numèraire conversion reflects the *correct* conversion of the purchasing power of the two currencies given price levels, so that the economy can move to the correct real exchange rate and hence to equilibrium.[11]

Another way of looking at the exchange rate in the elasticity approach is to ask: if something (a sudden shock, inflation, a change in the underlying real variables) caused the demand (or supply) for foreign exchange to shift, then does a change in the value of the exchange rate move one back to equilibrium (whether the change comes from the state setting the "correct" real exchange rate, or from the free market creating a change in the nominal exchange rate so that the correct numèraire conversion ensues when exchange rates are flexible)? No matter which way one examines the impact of a change in the exchange rate, the end result is in effect to ask—will the responses of agents to changes in the price of foreign exchange in the foreign exchange market ensure that the move to equilibrium will take place and the BOP deficit eliminated?

The elasticity literature is interesting in the light of our discussion (chapter 2) about the need for some story of how the economy moves from one equilibrium to another in the Walrasian approach. The auctioneer calls out prices, and follows a rule of increasing the price when there is an excess demand, and of decreasing the price when there is an excess supply. But can we be sure that the agents' responses to the auctioneer's calls will ensure a move to a new equilibrium? While not providing such a mechanism or alternative to the auctioneer in the real world, this literature recognizes the problem sufficiently to provide a stability condition for the equilibrium (in this particular market).[12]

The issue of devaluation or exchange depreciation in this approach can better be understood as a short-run movement to equilibrium. Assume that for some reason (like an outward shift in import demand) there arises an excess demand in the market for foreign exchange. The market should presumably shift to the new equilibrium exchange rate (or the state, via a devaluation in the nominal exchange rate should allow the economy to move to the correct equilibrium real exchange rate). Is the equilibrium *stable?* Does the adjustment process actually move one to the new exchange rate (through a process of depreciating the currency), or worsen the problem? This amounts to asking about the relative slopes of the supply and demand for foreign currency. Figure 4.1 shows the different possibilities.

The statement of the stability condition finds mathematical expression in the Marshall-Lerner condition, that the sum of export and import elasticities (the underlying *real* demands for goods and services) be greater than unity.[13] Subsequent refinements of this condition more carefully specify the impact of the dynamic adjustment mechanism in terms of domestic and foreign currency, examine whether the depreciation starts from a position of balance or imbalance, and so on. Haberler (1949) provides an excellent synopsis of this approach.

The following graphs show the different shapes and positions that the S and D curves for foreign exchange can take. Under the elasticity approach, whether or not devaluation improves the BOP will depend on the relative slopes of these curves. In graphs A, B and C, a shift in demand for currency from D to D' causes an excess demand for $ at the old exchange rate e. In A and B, a rise in the price of $ (a devaluation of the rupee) in response to the excess demand, decreases the BOP imbalance and moves the economy towards the new equilibrium at e'. In C however, the slopes of the two curves are such that the Marshall-Lerner conditions are not satisfied. The rise in the price of $ in response to the excess demand at e *worsens* the BOP imbalance, moving the economy further from equilibrium.

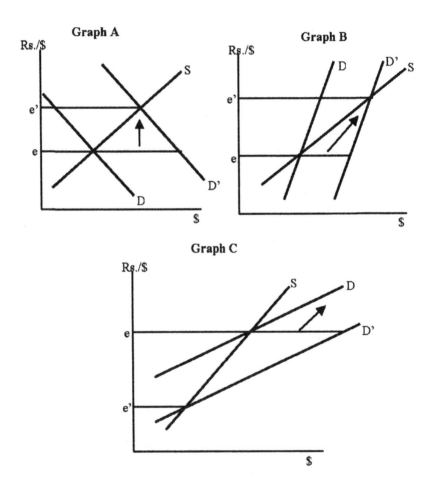

Figure 4.1 The Elasticity Approach to the Balance of Payments

Ontology: Note that this entire approach is individualist. The discussion is based on the shapes of demand and supply curves for foreign exchange, that are in turn derived from the maximizing decisions of priorly specified agents (though why the priorly specified agents hold money or use money is never actually explained in the barter world of Walrasian general equilibrium).

Adjustment mechanism: The dynamic analysis derives from images of adjustment from one equilibrium to another, through *static* or non-historical time. The adjustment process itself will not change the original technology, property distribution, or tastes from which the demand and supply curves are derived. The particulars of the underlying indifference patterns that generate these curves will determine their slopes in much the same way that the leisure-income tradeoff can generate a negatively sloped labor supply curve. The case of the inability of devaluation to correct an imbalance in payments is simply the dynamic impact of a Giffen good.

Concept of imbalance and role for devaluation: The concept of an imbalance here is one of an economy out of equilibrium in the market for foreign exchange. The issue is not whether devaluation can be used as a policy tool, but whether the equilibrium is *stable*. If it is unstable, there is no role for a "devaluation" policy, since this will move one still further from the equilibrium. If it is stable, market adjustment should get the economy to the new equilibrium, unless the state had intervened by fixing the exchange rate to begin with (in which case devaluation is nothing more than an effort by the state to mimic the market it sought to replace).

The description provided of the Gold Specie mechanism and the elasticities approach to the exchange rate so far shows that there is no room for a balance of payments imbalance and devaluation in a free market economy. Something will always adjust in the free market (either price levels or exchange rates) to create balance in the BOP. This is a crucial element in the particulars of the devaluation debate to be discussed later. The remaining sections will deal with individualist theories of fixed exchange rates that do discuss devaluation explicitly.

The Monetary Approach to the Balance of Payments

The monetary approach to the balance of payments is based on the insights of Friedman (1959, 1963, 1969, Friedman ed. 1956) and the works of H. G. Johnson (1959, 1977a and 1977b, also Frenkel and Johnson 1977)). It represents a clever attack on Keynesian and New Structuralist approaches to the BOP (discussed in the section on "Structuralist Approaches to the BOP" below). The monetary approach to the BOP draws on Milton Friedman's reformulation of the Quantity Theory of Money, and provides an explicit theory of monetary flows in an open economy. Thus it includes not only the trade flows discussed under the Walrasian vision, but also financial flows.

The theory of money added to the Walrasian vision is a theory of asset portfolio choice. Money now is held for two reasons—to meet transactions, and as a store of value. But, individuals will not actually use money as a store of value because there are other financial stores of value—bonds, securities, and debt instruments—that pay interest. Thus, the actual demand for money holdings in the portfolio of individuals is for meeting transactions, and not for storing value. Left to themselves, financial markets operate like any other market, and clear to ensure the optimal allocation of savings and resources to investors.

Since money itself is held primarily for transactions purposes, and other assets are used as stores of value, what happens when the state prints too much money? As money reaches individuals' portfolios they find themselves holding too much money, and so start to "discard" the excess by spending it. This generates an excess demand for goods and other financial assets. But, since supply is set at full employment, the excess demand will push up prices. And, as prices rise, the transactions demand for money increases. This process continues till the economy reaches a new equilibrium with real values unchanged, but higher price levels. Thus financial flows or movements into securities and goods are linked to inflationary pressures and the effort by the state to raise the money supply, as individuals make an effort to spend the excess money printed by the state. While in the long run the excess supply of money has no real effects, in the short run it causes instability, and affects financial markets.

More troubling for monetarists is the state's undertaking deficit spending and issuing government bonds to finance deficits. The reason is that the state, by issuing government-backed bonds, has in effect introduced a new asset for individuals to hold as a store of value—an asset which pays an interest and which is risk-free. The state by using such risk-free bonds to fund budget deficits has the ability to draw resources away from the private sector. This means that the interest rate paid by the state does not reflect the appropriate market assessment of the risk-return profile of an investment undertaken by the state. Instead it reflects the state's guarantee of repayment due to its ability to tax the public *regardless* of the appropriate risks or returns associated with state expenditures. This diverts resources towards the state and away from private investors, and reduces growth as the resources are used to fund wasteful and inefficient expenditures by the public sector.

The monetary approach to the BOP adapts Friedman's theory to the open economy. The primary idea behind the monetary approach is that the balance of payments deficit is simply the excess of foreign exchange payments over foreign exchange receipts by the residents of a country, reflecting an excess of nominal expenditures over income. The residents have to finance this deficit by running down their cash balances, transferring them to the foreign exchange authority. This starts an automatic adjustment mechanism, as the cash balances drop below equilibrium levels, creating a rise in interest rates and a reduction in credit creation. As expenditures start falling, the excess of payments over receipts should correct itself, eliminating the imbalance. Johnson (1958) provides a framework for this type of analysis.

In chapter seven of his book, Dornbusch (1980) provides an excellent description of this model, where he starts with an economy at full employment, with a fixed exchange rate. Nominal expenditure is related by the stable velocity of circulation to the level of domestic money supply. Nominal income is the price level multiplied by real income (which is set at full employment). The trade balance is the excess of expenditure over income, and shows up as a cash flow from deficit to surplus country. This sets off a long term adjustment process in the price levels of the two countries, and there is no long run equilibrium trade deficit.

Note that in this approach, when the nominal exchange rate is fixed, something *else* has to give so that the net result of the changes is a change in the *real* exchange rate so that one is again at the underlying real Walrasian BOP equilibrium. In effect, whether the adjustment comes from credit reductions via changes in the interest rate (so that the *real* value of purchasing goods from abroad by taking on debt changes) or by changes in the price level (so that again, the *real* value of purchasing goods and hence the real relative value of the numèraire changes), the nominal exchange rate can be fixed only when some *other* mechanism will then ensure that the numèraire conversion can take place at the correct level to ensure that the underlying real decisions are based on the correct market clearing relative prices. In the monetary approach, it is a flow of assets across borders which will itself change the actual purchasing power of money in the two countries so that they reflect the correct market-clearing real relative purchasing power of money in the two countries at the going nominal exchange rate. This shows up as a stabilization in the value of *nominal* expenditures (if the value of nominal expenditures stabilizes when real income is fixed, the stabilization can only occur via a change in the purchasing power of the nominal unit).

Ontology: By conceptualizing the balance of payments categories as monetary macroeconomic phenomena, the monetary approach eliminates the possibility of any long-term imbalance in the BOP regardless of the fixed nominal exchange rate. The payments imbalance sets up its own adjustment mechanism, whether it is by the interest rate adjustment reducing credit, or by money flows reducing nominal expenditure. These adjustments are driven by individuals responding to market forces based on their rational decisions to maximize the utility derived from the real value of their asset-portfolios. Though this individualist aspect of monetarist theory is not explicit in the monetary analysis, it becomes clearer in the rational expectations framework of the next section.

Adjustment mechanism: Note that we are back in the world of the gold standard. The trade deficit is a "flow excess supply of money" (Dornbusch 1980, 125), and emerges as individuals move out of money and into goods. As an excess supply, it is a disequilibrium problem. Left to itself the market will adjust to eliminate the disequilibrium by removing excess spending either by monetary flows which translate into changed price levels (Dornbusch 1980) or credit reduction in the domestic market (Johnson 1959).

Concept of imbalance and role for devaluation: Again, an imbalance cannot be understood in this individualist framework except as an aberration from equilibrium. Why would we have an imbalance? Johnson identifies two reasons i) Individuals' decisions about the stock of money they wish to hold could change, creating a temporary flow excess demand for money, which shows up as a surplus. But once the new equilibrium stock is reached, the surplus disappears. ii) Individuals have a flow excess demand for goods, based on the current money supply and exchange rate. Left to itself, the flow imbalance will correct itself. Thus an imbalance can arise in the course of a movement to a new equilibrium, or as a temporary aberration that corrects itself as the economy returns to equilibrium.

What is the impact of a devaluation in a free market economy? Devaluation increases the relative value of foreign money. Foreign spending in domestic currency rises[14] creating a *temporary* improvement in our balance of payments. In the long run, money flows wipe out this short run effect through changing nominal spending (Dornbusch 1980) or interest rate rises causing a reduction in credit (Johnson 1959). This is analogous to the gold flows changing prices to render devaluations useless as a long term policy under the gold standard. Devaluation or credit policy could be useful if the *short run* process of attaining the new equilibrium is to be speeded up, but for lasting real effects, the underlying decisions of agents need to be examined.

As with the elasticity approach then, the only reason to recommend a devaluation is when the state, by intervening in the adjustment mechanism, *prevents* the move to equilibrium. This would occur when the state has set the nominal exchange rate, and then via some *additional* controls prevented the market from clearing the imbalance through a flow of assets and changes in the interest rate and the purchasing power of the currency. For example, if in addition to setting the exchange rate, the state intervenes in financial markets to *also* set the interest rate and prevents a credit squeeze from clearing the imbalance, then the adjustments cannot work, and a change in the nominal exchange rate to reflect the correct market-clearing real exchange rate becomes essential.

Or, when the state consistently prints money to finance deficits, then there is a continued and sustained flow excess supply of money, which creates a long term imbalance (because the state in effect continually pumps new excess supplies of money into the system before the market can finish adjusting to equilibrium). Or, when the state by printing money and issuing state-backed international debt keeps creating short term imbalances, which over time accrue as continued and unsustainable levels of national debt.[15] Devaluation as a policy of getting the "real exchange rate" right is only necessary when something *prevents* the move to equilibrium where automatic market mechanisms correct the imbalance.

The Rational Expectations Formulation

The rational expectations formulation can be seen as the final closure of some gaps that were left in the monetary approach to the balance of payments. The monetary approach to the balance of payments respecified a trade deficit as showing a flow excess supply of money (see above). But in the monetary approach, the discussion of the flow excess supply of money was undertaken purely in terms of decisions to purchase goods and services on the current account. Neoliberal theory still has to specify how and why *assets* are demanded on the capital account. In particular, exchange rates provide the conversion from one form of money holding *or* asset to another. If there is a difference in the return to money or to financial assets across national borders, then individuals will rearrange their asset portfolio to take advantage of interest rate differentials across borders, which will itself create changes in the exchange rate until the interest rate differential and differences in returns to the two numéraires is wiped out.

One of the contributions of Keynes' *General Theory* was to specify transactions, precautionary, *and speculative* motives for demanding money. In addition to being a medium of exchange, in an uncertain world money is held as a hedge (precautionary demand), or in the course of movements in and out of assets, based on expectations about the future bond prices (speculative demand). If a financial investor expects future bond prices to rise, she will buy bonds now to sell later, and so move out of money. But if she expects the future price to fall, she will sell bonds now and hold money so as not to make a capital loss. Thus the demand for money for speculative purposes is highly unstable, based on perceptions and expectations. It was in this context that Keynes developed his idea of liquidity preference.

While neoliberal theory has a story of the flow excess demand for goods and services on the trade balance, based on a flow excess supply of money across borders, money so far is held purely for transactions purposes. The monetary approach has no story of the speculative demand for money or of the possibility of sudden movements in and out of money in response to changing expectations about the value of asset-prices. Further, if the state does print money, or engage in issuing bonds (one key source of the flow excess supply of money), this should result not only in a change in the purchasing power of money, but also an expected change in interest rates. What if the flow excess supply of money also generates changes in the asset-portfolios of individuals in response to such expectations? If such movements in and out of assets and money emerge, then the flow excess supply of money can become unstable and there is no guarantee of the economy automatically reaching equilibrium. What is needed is a theory of the demand for assets and the movement in and out of assets and money based on expectations.

In the rational expectations reformulation, individuals' expectations are based on perfect knowledge. This perfect knowledge includes knowledge of the actual equilibrium level of interest rates across borders, of the coming changes in the underlying real exchange rate and price levels in all countries during a move to equilibrium, and of the path that the economy will take in reaching the new equilibrium. Individuals then decide to purchase assets based on such perfect knowledge. With rational expectations, individuals *can predict all the changes that a policy action which generates a flow excess supply of money would bring* (they know where the new long run equilibrium will be). They make their decisions based on this perfect foresight. Asset markets adjust instantaneously to cause interest rates to fall or rise (under fixed exchange rates) to move individuals to exactly the right money (and asset) demand position, so there will be no excess demand or supply for money, and thus no trade imbalance (since a trade imbalance is merely a reflection of the excess supply or demand for money).[16] Note that the adjustment mechanism is instantaneous, since individuals can always tell exactly where the market is moving, and how fast. Thus there is not even a short term description of a trade imbalance in these models (even in descriptions of overshooting, see note 16 of this chapter).

Ontology: In this framework, every aspect of the economy, right down to the possible move to the new equilibrium is captured in the knowledge, preferences, and maximizing calculus of the individual. This is the most absolute of individualisms because it precludes any structuralism. Any structural phenomenon that might exist is automatically known to all and hence made individualist.

There can be no moment "out of equilibrium" unless adjustment speeds of prices are not instantaneous. But since individuals would know what the adjustment speeds are, and rational expectationists assume that *money and financial asset markets* always have infinite adjustment speeds, these particular markets will never be out of equilibrium. In the asset market the adjustment will automatically clear the excess demand for money at all times. This is a refined version of the Walrasian demand-supply analysis described in chapter 2, with "expectations" defined to derive the demand for money from an individualist position.

Adjustment mechanism: The mode of adjustment to a "disequilibrium" comes from individuals instantly assessing what the equilibrium would be, and asset prices changing to reflect that knowledge. Occasionally one can get "over-adjustment" (if the speed of adjustment in one market is slower that in another, say) as shown by Dornbusch (1980) in chapter 11, section 2. But essentially, the adjustment in the asset market (under fixed exchange rates) wipes out money excess supply and thus balance of payments deficits.

Concept of an imbalance and role for devaluation: As noted above, with all the individualist assumptions in place, the BOP imbalance can only be understood as an extremely short term phenomenon that occurs when the economy is out of equilibrium because of an *unanticipated exogenous shock.* Otherwise, rational expectations ensure that the economy is never out of equilibrium. Persistent BOP imbalance can then only be understood as the result of *persistent, unpredictable, and erratic* exchange rate and money supply policies by the government, coupled with direct intervention in the market mechanism (through quotas, subsidies, fixing interest rates too low, or other such relative price affecting behavior), rendering the automatic mechanism of the market useless.

What role is there for a devaluation? If the devaluation is anticipated, individuals will fully anticipate the relative fall in the value of domestic currency. The asset market will adjust to instantaneously change the interest rate to reflect this, and the devaluation will have no real effect even in the short run. If a devaluation is unanticipated, it will have some short term effect, but once the markets adjust, the effect will be eliminated. Thus the ability of devaluation to have any impact depends on the extent it is unanticipated (i.e., the extent to which people can be "fooled" by the government for a short moment).

It turns out that a carefully articulated rational expectations model runs into problems that are not perceived by the practitioners of this school of thought. In particular, the image of complete foreknowledge on the part of investors raises thorny issues. The theorists cannot conceive of a persistent trade imbalance under perfect foreknowledge. But note that if there *is* such an imbalance, *then a broad macroeconomic policy like devaluation cannot restore balance*. This is because under perfect knowledge, whatever the underlying *real* cause of the imbalance, it is known to the investors, and they make their decisions accordingly. If the government decided to devalue, and the investors knew about the decision, the investors would know where the new equilibrium would be, and compensate accordingly. There would be no change in any real values (including the balance of payments). Thus not only can the theory not explain a persistent trade surplus under free markets, an anticipated devaluation cannot fix such a problem.

In such a theory, as with the previous individualist stories, the only way in which a persistent payments imbalance can arise is if the state actively intervenes in *more* than one market to prevent market clearing (setting the exchange rate alone will not do the trick, since markets will then adjust all values for real interest rates and prices to reflect the correct numèraire conversion—the correct conversion for equilibrium being *known* to the rational agents armed with perfect foreknowledge). Even here, the state's interventions are known to the agents. Thus, though an unanticipated devaluation to get the real exchange rate in line with correct numèraire conversion may work for a short time, the only long run solution is for the state to clearly and credibly eliminate the market interventions that prevented the move to equilibrium.[17] When the state is not credible in its reforms, agents believe that the reforms are temporary and do not adjust to the new equilibrium (since they base their decisions on the equilibrium that will emerge when the state soon reverts to its old policies). Instead, they simply adjust their decisions to reflect the move to the new equilibrium they think will emerge once the state reverts to its old policies.

Conclusion: Individualists and BOP Crises

The result that emerges from the discussion of the various individualist approaches to the BOP and exchange rate above is that individualist theories cannot conceive of a persistent payments deficit except as an aberration, a moment out of equilibrium. In each individualist story, there is a description of some automatic mechanism that would restore balance if markets do not clear. No matter what the mechanism (gold flows, credit reductions, instantaneous adjustment under rational expectations), the force behind this adjustment is the action of priorly specified individuals maximizing utility or profits. The underlying equilibrium the economy will reach is the one specified by the Walrasian model of trade and foreign investment. Financial flows emerge only as a reflection of these flows of real foreign investment.

But LDCs in the 1980s were clearly marked by persistent and long term payments deficits. To explain this long run deviance from equilibrium neoliberal theorists need a theory of some *structure* that prevents the move to equilibrium. In the LDC, this structure was identified as the ISI state. Thus the only way to explain persistent payments problems, in these frameworks, is that the *government* is intervening in the market (by pegging the interest rate, creating too high a money supply, misdirecting resources) and thus *preventing* the move to equilibrium.

Balance of Payments problems thus indicate some intervention in the market by the government, *and since any intervention in the market is bad, because left to itself the market will always generate full employment and efficiency,* it also indicates the existence of policies aimed at social change which are undesirable from the individualist standpoint. Macroeconomic policy in this context can be understood as "correcting past mistakes," or eliminating misguided intervention, rather than as policy to correct problems that the market could create. This individualist reasoning has a profound impact on the set of policies prescribed by debtor nations in LDCs, since the IMF utilizes individualist analyses to set their policy agendas as part of IMF conditionality in providing debt-servicing and help to nations facing a payments crisis.

The above discussion provides the underpinning for the general neoliberal policies. In effect, individualists do not see any role for intervention by the state, and argue that left to itself, the market will ensure that the BOP is in equilibrium. There should be no long term payments imbalance. Why then did LDC economies face payments imbalance? The answer is, not surprisingly, the state (chapter 3 discusses why the neoliberals define LDC difference in terms of the state). Note that a policy of setting the nominal exchange rate *alone* does not result in a payments imbalance, as long as something else adjusts to ensure that the real exchange rate can provide the correct numèraire conversion. Thus the reason for a persistent payments imbalance is when the state in addition to setting the nominal exchange rate, intervenes in markets and thus prevents the correct real exchange rate from emerging to clear the market. There are three possible reasons for a persistent payments imbalance:

> a) The state, by its policies of tariffs, quotas, licensing, and price and wage controls has intervened in the trade account, squeezing exports which generate foreign exchange by making them unprofitable and expensive, and promoting imports which use foreign exchange. This is a direct intervention in the trade account which can prevent the optimal level of trade from emerging, and create too high a demand for imports.

> b) Though the policies of tariffs, quotas, licensing, and so on will create a reduction in foreign exchange by reducing exports, this in and of itself would not have created a problem in the BOP (though it may have resulted in low growth and inefficient production) since left alone, the BOP would balance since the market would ensure that import demand was constrained by the available resources, unless the state additionally followed policies to maintain the fixed exchange rate by *accommodating* the excess demand for foreign exchange. By printing too much money, by borrowing in international markets, and by guaranteeing foreign borrowing, the state created and accommodated the flow excess supply of money, and the corresponding excess demand for overly-cheap foreign goods.

> c) Further, by controlling financial markets and setting the interest rate, the state prevented the natural market mechanism of the credit squeeze from operating to ensure that the equilibrium was reached.[18]

Thus, state intervention directly created the long term imbalance in the BOP. In each of these reasons for a persistent BOP imbalance, the state is postulated as a structure which then explains LDC deviance by its rules and activities.

From this emerges the policy agenda for neoliberal reform from the IMF:

> a) The immediate policy has to be to get the nominal exchange rate higher, so that the autonomous flows can respond to the correct prices for market clearing given by the appropriate real exchange rate. Devaluation thus has to be the first policy, making access to foreign exchange prohibitively expensive in the market for foreign exchange, and putting an end to the excess demand for foreign exchange. The state should devalue the nominal exchange rate so that the real exchange rate reflects the "correct" market-clearing Walrasian equilibrium price for foreign exchange given the relative purchasing power of the currency vis-a-vis the rest of the world (in effect, it is a call for a "corrective devaluation" which will set the nominal exchange rate higher so that the correct market-clearing real exchange rate emerges).

> b) The new real exchange rate has to be maintained, and the flow excess supply of money which caused the BOP imbalance has to be stopped.

Thus, the state should balance its budget and cut back on increasing the money supply. Above all, inflation, which causes the currency to become "misaligned" with the rest of the world (since with inflation, given a nominal exchange rate, the real exchange rate no longer reflects the correct conversion of purchasing power across numèraires), and causes an increase in imports and decrease in exports has to be curtailed.

The above policies of "corrective devaluation" and anti-inflationary fiscal and monetary policy form the heart of IMF stabilization policies which should eliminate the BOP imbalance in the short run. In the long run, neoliberals advocate liberalization of all markets and privatization of all state enterprises. The logic behind the liberalization and privatization is to ensure long run efficiency and to ensure that the BOP imbalances do not reappear in the future.[19] Taylor (1993) provides an excellent description of the logic behind the reforms. The full set of reforms (stabilization, liberalization, privatization) is simply an application of the logic behind neoliberalism explained in chapter 3. All of these reforms are seen as "corrective policies" which undo past mistakes, rather than as "proactive" policies. In effect, this is about removing the structure (interventionist ISI state) that caused LDC deviance.

In terms of a policy for the exchange rate in the long run, the exchange rate is no more than a conversion of one numèraire into another, and the market will ensure through arbitrage that the conversion does take place. But since the exchange rate is something that affects relative prices in many markets, it is important that its value be stable. Thus ideally, the exchange rate should be fixed, and the state's ability to undertake policy that can "distort" the numèraire conversion, by making the value of domestic money too high or too low for the correct relative prices to emerge, must be curtailed. In effect, the state should get out of the business of making structures that are rightly the prerogative of the auctioneer.[20]

As noted in the previous two chapters, individualists have an extraordinarily hard time explaining change, or movement from disequilibrium to equilibrium. Thus, both in terms of explaining LDC deviance, and in terms of explaining the move from deviance to sameness, they rely on the state. The LDC state is a moment of structuralist collapse for individualists—they explain deviance from equilibrium via the state, and it is the same state which will undertake to instill sameness by "dismantling" itself and re-configuring its role as the Lockean state. In addition, there are some key moments when describing the actual move to the new equilibrium that the neoliberals collapse into their opposite. I will discuss these moments of collapse the next chapter, on the CDD.

STRUCTURALIST APPROACHES TO THE BOP

This section examines the structuralist approaches to the BOP. First, I examine the two key macro-structuralist theories of the BOP, then I discuss structuralist conceptions of BOP crises.

Structuralist Theories of the Open Macroeconomy

The structuralist approaches do not create a separate set of theories for trade relations and for discussions of the exchange rate and macroeconomic balance. Thus, unlike individualist approaches, we do not find two types of theories, some devoted to the trade relations between nations and others devoted to financial relations. Instead, structuralist theories combine all these flows into a single model of macroeconomic outcomes in open economies. Here, I examine the two main structuralist theories of the BOP: the Absorption approach, and the New Structuralist approach.

The Absorption Approach

The absorption approach to the balance of payments developed as an extension of the neoclassical-Keynesian descriptions of demand behavior and pricing. I do not have space here to describe all the ways in which Keynes himself provided structural and institutional analyses of different aspects of the economy. But as described in chapter 2, two very specific aspects of Keynes' work, i) his theory of aggregate demand behavior and ii) his description of market output (rather than price) adjustment were incorporated in the neoclassical-Keynesian synthesis. This description of the economy draws on structuring rules (the marginal propensity to consume or import, the wage structure in the labor market) to describe the operation of markets.

In the simplest form of the absorption approach, price levels in each country (except the relative price of imports) are fixed, supply of all goods is perfectly elastic (because of unemployment), and the total level of output is set by total absorption or the level of demand. Each country has a marginal propensity to import (analogous to the marginal propensity to consume). The balance of trade is described by the value of $(X - M)$ that emerges in the equilibrium condition

$$Y = C + I + G + (X - M)$$

where C, I, and G are the components of domestic absorption, and $X - M$ is net foreign absorption (X, our exports, is the foreign country's imports, and hence will depend on the rest of the world's marginal propensity to import based on *their* income levels). Clearly, whether or not there is an imbalance will depend on what the equilibrium levels of X and M are. Note that here the exchange rate is not set by market forces, but is instead an exogenous variable set by state policy (otherwise the above equation of equilibrium with a trade imbalance would not hold, since the trade imbalance would then set off changes in the exchange rate). Decisions to buy and sell goods on the current account are autonomous, and reflect agent decisions based on the structural rules linking imports and exports to domestic and foreign income respectively.

What would the impact of a devaluation be? If world prices and income were unchanged, our exports could increase, because they are now cheaper. This would set off a multiplier effect (the trade multiplier), increasing consumption and imports. The net effect on the trade balance will depend on how much income improves as consumption increases (based on the marginal propensity to consume and the Keynesian multiplier), and how large the induced increases in imports are (based on the marginal propensity to import). Thus employment will improve, but the trade balance may or may not improve.

If the relative increase in import prices does not translate into a general price increase, but induces an initial switch to domestic consumption, we again see multiplier effects. If imports contract as domestic C is increased, Y starts increasing. This in turn increases M. Again, employment improves, but whether or not the trade balance does will depend on the induced increase in import demand.

If the increase in relative import prices does get translated into an increase in general prices, reducing real income, C starts to decline, setting off a multiplier contraction in Y and M. Here the trade balance definitely improves, but only by increasing unemployment and inflation.

Finally, if the devaluation does affect world prices and income, a contraction in imports could create unemployment abroad. As foreign income shrinks, domestic exports shrink. This would in turn reduce domestic spending and employment. The devaluation sets off a generalized employment crisis, and the net impact on the trade balance would depend on foreign and domestic import propensities.

Clearly, the final impact of a devaluation would depend on the specification of i) import and consumption propensities in each country, ii) the theory of how prices are set, and iii) the specification of real wage determination in the labor market. Chapters 3 and 4 of Dornbusch (1980) provide models for all the mechanisms described above.

Ontology: The neoclassical-Keynesian synthesis is a much watered-down version of Keynes' *General Theory.* But even in this version, aspects of Keynes' formulation provide a structural basis for understanding the economy. Demand is derived from underlying rules governing the relationship between economic aggregates. Prices are set by institutional forces. Finally, price-elasticities define the rules by which the various components of demand respond to changes in relative prices created by the devaluation, especially changes in the relative prices of traded and non-traded goods.[21]

Adjustment: The balance of payments can have a persistent deficit or surplus. Markets do not automatically clear through price adjustments, nor is there any automatic mechanism to remove payments imbalance. The impact of a particular policy is described by an adjustment mechanism captured in the multiplier. The multiplier translates the impact of a policy by looking at the various channels by which the change feeds into the system through the different structural rules, in effect translating the structural rules and relationships into a final multiplier.

Concept of imbalance and role for devaluation: Unlike the individualist approaches, in the structuralist framework we see imbalance in payments as a possible long term problem that does not automatically solve itself. We are not always at a market clearing equilibrium, nor does the structure automatically provide us with a way to reach a trade balance. Devaluation emerges as a possible policy tool, either to ensure full employment or to restore external balance. But whether and how it does this will depend on the particular structuring variables (e.g. how large is the marginal propensity to import, are there any repercussion effects, how do prices change, and so on).

The New Structuralist Approach

The New Structuralist approach is an extension of the absorption approach, with a more explicit attempt to i) retain and highlight some elements of neo-classical-Keynesian structuralism, particularly the specification of demand ii) add more explicitly a theory of markup pricing along Kaleckian lines, as the economy reaches equilibrium by output adjustment iii) make some attempts to incorporate income distribution in the Keynesian theories of demand, and iv) use a Sraffian or Leontief style input-output description of production relations. Since this school of thought is less homogeneous, with different authors using different elements of these four rules, I will give a general description of the framework here, and point out the importance of the structural assumptions for these models. I will discuss the New Structuralist approach in more detail in the next chapter when discussing the CDD.

As in the absorption approach, the balance of payments is the excess of domestic spending over domestic income. The spending categories are the same as in the Keynesian absorption approach. Output levels are dictated by demand levels as in the Keynesian framework. Prices do not adjust to ensure market clearing, but instead are set by a markup on costs (Kaleckian pricing behavior). Thus one can have equilibrium imbalance in payments.

The Kaleckian pricing (prices are set as a markup on production costs) introduces interesting channels through which the impact of a devaluation can be felt. If the cost of imported inputs rises, domestic prices will rise to maintain the markup. The cost of the devaluation gets "passed on" to workers through a reduction in real income. If workers have a higher marginal propensity to consume than capitalists, this real income redistribution will cause expenditures to fall, and set off further output contractions.

Another extension of the Keynesian demand driven model in this framework is the use of input-output matrices to describe production. These matrices come from the works of Leontief and Sraffa, and describe the various inputs needed to produce a unit of output by each sector. The use of such matrices turns out to be an important extension of the absorption approach. The key to understanding them is to look at their implicit theory of input demand. Decisions to purchase inputs are a derived demand from these matrices. *The input decision is not made on the margin.* This is crucial, because one of the rational expectations critiques of the New Structuralist position is that the ability of firms to move in and out of an industry, based on changing the marginal decision to invest in any given industry will bring forth supply adjustments. This would be one way the market eliminates payments problems in the individualist theories.

It is possible to interpret such matrices as "short run," since they argue against substitution between inputs, exports, and imports in an easy fashion. This is analogous to reinterpreting Keynesian demand as "short run," since individuals do not substitute between consumption and savings in the marginal propensity to consume approach. But there is another interpretation of such matrices. These matrices describe underlying structural rules, governing the relationship between inputs and outputs in a particular economy. Firm decisions are not "absent," they are governed by the limits imposed by the rules. Firms act to meet demand and maintain a profit margin (through the markup), given the way different sectors of the economy depend on each other. In fact, for many New Structuralists, this structure of production reflects the underlying structures that explain LDC deviance (see chapter 3 for a discussion of how production structures and "bottlenecks" are a reflection of LDC difference for structuralists).

Keynes argued that in an uncertain world, where money shapes behavior and outcomes, decisions to hold assets or to invest in productive capital need not automatically ensure full employment. Similarly, in a world where production is guided by ability to invest in fixed capital and by access to inputs, decisions to move in and out of a particular input cannot be made easily "on the margin." In an LDC economy, lacking infrastructure, technology, resources, and appropriate conditions for entrepreneurs to undertake decisions in response to markets, the production structures themselves are constrained by the structure of relationships within the LDC economy.

The networks of production require that for a particular shift in input structure, *all firms down the production chain adjust according to the rules governing production relationships.* If there is no certainty about the ability to sustain such changes, then it would be "rational" (in the sense of the limits enforced by structure, rather than in the sense of "maximization") to stay with existing input coefficients. This is particularly true if the types of input changes needed "on the margin" are changes in fixed capital, plants, and equipment, which take time to put in place and require resources beyond the reach of capital-scarce LDC economies. Thus the input-output coefficients can be seen as broad rules governing firm demand decisions for inputs, in much the same way that the marginal propensities to consume can be seen as broad rules governing household demand behavior. Whether or not an economy has a trade deficit in equilibrium will thus depend not only on the marginal propensity to import by consumers, but also on the extent to which domestic production requires imported inputs. New Structuralists argue that developing economies attempting to create growth and industrialization require a high level of imported inputs.

How the pricing behavior, income distribution, or production coefficients are set up in these models thus opens many more channels for an equilibrium imbalance of payments, and for devaluation to have an effect on the real economy. The key to the formulation of an equilibrium imbalance for both the absorption approach and the New Structuralists, however, is the break with market-clearing behavior in prices. As long as i) the labor market does not clear automatically, and ii) investment does not automatically adjust to ensure that a payments balance is maintained in equilibrium, it is possible to i) specify equilibrium deficits, and ii) for a devaluation to have long run real effects (since export and import demand respond to income rather than price, while supply matches effective demand and maintains the profit margin through markups).

Ontology: This mode of reasoning extends the structural specification of the neoclassical-Keynesian vision to the supply side. Input-output coefficients specify structural relationships within the production economy. Markup pricing reflects the overall relationship maintained between costs and profits. Thus though there are many more elements to this description of the economy, it retains the structuralist ontology of the absorption approach.

Adjustment mechanism: As with the absorption approach, there is no automatic adjustment to a new equilibrium that corrects deficits in international payments. If a devaluation is undertaken, the final impact on demand and supply depends on marginal propensities to import and export, on input requirements, and on the redistributions set up by the devaluation. Whether or not the devaluation will correct the imbalance depends on the response of each sector. Further, even if the trade balance was improved, it is possible that this would take place through inflationary and recessionary means which are undesirable.

Concept of imbalance and role for devaluation: The imbalance is not an out-of-equilibrium aberration. In this theory, it is possible to have persistent equilibrium payments deficits. The appropriate policy to create both internal and external balance would depend on the specific structures governing the economy. Note that this literature has focused on the harmful effects of devaluation. This is because it has concentrated on the particular structures identified as key to developing economies. Theoretically, it is possible to construct a model of an economy with structural parameters that ensure that devaluation has only beneficial effects.

Conclusion: Structuralists and BOP Crises

Structuralist theorists, by and large, focus on real flows of exports and imports across borders, or on flows of real capital (imported inputs and investment). However, there is no reason for the BOP to clear in equilibrium. Financial flows are therefore *accommodating*, since in effect they must implicitly adjust to the unbalanced autonomous flows in the BOP at the equilibrium, and the autonomous flows are derived purely from real flows in the goods markets. In and of itself, a BOP disequilibrium is not a problem as long as the deficit country is financially accommodated by the rest of the world. Indeed, as shown in chapter 3, two-gap models were used by the structuralist proponents of ISI as an argument in favor of foreign aid (in effect, an argument in favor of global financial accommodation of LDC deficits to finance investment and imported inputs). A crisis only occurs when accommodation is no longer forthcoming, or if factors outside the control of the state create a sudden change in the payments requirements of a country. If long term accommodation is a problem, then adjustment to a new equilibrium will require state policy in both countries, and preferably, more of the costs of adjustment will be borne by stronger economies.

Further, BOP deficits in and of themselves are not bad. A deficit used to finance future growth by the state is eminently desirable in resource constrained LDCs trying to change their production structures. Devaluations may or may not hurt the economy, depending on the actual parametric values of the structures in the economy. The parametric specifications of LDC difference describe resource constrained and technologically backward economies with high imported input demand and low savings and low investments. These specifications imply that devaluations will hurt LDCs, and especially hurt the investment and growth potential of these economies.

However, despite their Keynesian legacy, and despite Keynes' key contributions in the area of a theory of money, structuralists, particularly, New Structuralists, lack a well-formulated theory of the balance of payments. Their discussions of the impact of devaluations, and the possibility of a payments imbalance, concentrate on the goods markets, and examine real flows of income across borders. Some models may include flows of capital across borders, but these flows are usually postulated, not explained as the endogenous outcome of the various structural rules governing investment decisions across borders. Further, these flows, when postulated, describe real flows of capital.

Financial flows here are purely accommodating. Structuralists lack a theory of why or how finance accommodates these flows or why foreigners accept foreign currency debt to meet these real flows. This is indeed peculiar, given Keynes' key contributions in the area of liquidity preference, demand for money, and uncertainty in financial markets. Unless these models can fully specify why or how the financial flows accommodate the trade imbalance, they remain "real sector" focused, and lack any theory of the exchange rate or financial decisions in currency markets. Implicit here is the assumption that the exchange rate is set by the state exogenously (it is an exogenous policy parameter, and does not function like the exogenous behavioral parameters like say, the mpc or the theory of prices governed by mark-up pricing). Further, if finance accommodates to the current account deficit, then presumably, unless the entire financial system behind the IS-LM approach is left out, the state is the primary maintainer of the exchange rate, and accommodates the imbalance in the autonomous flows by running down reserves, or issuing state-guaranteed debt to foreigners as a way to generate the requisite foreign exchange.

The approach needs an extremely active policy for the model to describe any longer term equilibrium position in the economy. The state sets the exchange rate and stands ready to constantly accommodate all flows via reserve changes. Policy is virtually endogenized here, since the model actually cannot work unless the accommodations to the real sector are undertaken by the state. Unless policy is implicitly endogenized and the state stands ever-ready to accommodate all flows, these models are at a rather less-than-general level and describe a "less than fully closed and self-reproducing" economy.

This is because most structuralist models of the open economy do not have a good theory of money. New Structuralists draw on the completely real-market theories of Kalecki, Robinson, and other Cantabrigian theorists of imperfect markets. In these theories, finance even in the closed economy is purely accommodating, and the results are derived entirely from the goods market and the behavior of capitalists, consumers, workers, all described (with the exception of the given nominal wages) in terms of real variables. The Cantabrigian tradition of imperfect markets and the neo-Ricardian tradition which concentrates on theories of distribution of real output do not have any well-formulated theory of financial decisions even in the domestic economy (I exclude Keynes from this category of theorists). Lacking a theory of autonomous financial decisions and money even in the domestic economy (money is purely accommodating to the real sector decisions of capitalists even in the domestic economy), it is hardly surprising that these theories similarly lack any discussion of financial decisions across national borders (there have been some efforts by New Structuralists to create a theory of finance—I take these efforts up in the next chapter).

While IS-LM Keynesians can explain money in a closed economy, most founder when attempting to discuss the role of money across national borders, or in explaining why people hold money in more than one form. If financial flows are made autonomous (i.e., are determined by structural rules governing agent behavior), the models start to fall apart. A fully-specified self-regulating and closed model would have to add rules governing liquidity preference and asset-speculation for both domestic and financial assets, and rules governing the relationships between domestic and foreign interest rates, as well as rules governing the choices to invest either at home or abroad. When these many rules are added, there are not enough equilibrating mechanisms (IS-LM has two equilibrating variables—interest rate in the money market, and income in the goods market) to ensure that the rules governing the goods markets equilibrium and the rules governing money market equilibrium will always cohere. In particular, there is no mechanism to ensure that the autonomous flows in the goods market thrown up by the goods market equilibrium will exactly match the autonomous flows of finance across borders thrown up by the money market equilibrium.[22] Thus, structuralist approaches to the BOP are left vulnerable, because they are not quite fully structuralist and lack adequate equilibrating mechanisms to ensure full articulation, closure, and systemic self-reproduction in a theory which includes autonomous financial flows.

The inability of structuralists to explain the financial flows across borders is a result of their commitment to Cartesianism (explored more carefully in the concluding section of this chapter). If one accepts that the only way to theorize the international transactions of an economy is by converting the accounting identity of the BOP into an equilibrium theory, then logically, one needs to have some internal mechanism that ensures that the autonomous flows cohere. Otherwise, some element in the BOP has to accommodate the imbalance in the autonomous flows. If there is no part of the BOP that is accommodating *and* no mechanism to ensure coherence among the autonomous flows, the structuralists cannot have any explanation for how the economy attains equilibrium. Thus for both New Structuralists and the IS-LM Keynesians, it is absolutely essential that one element of the BOP be left untheorized so that it will be purely accommodating and implicitly adjust to the equilibrium imbalance in the autonomous flows. Finance then, *must be accommodating*. If it is not accommodating, the models of equilibrium break down.

For structuralists, the various structures that create the goods market flows define LDC difference and explain why LDCs ran up large trade deficits under ISI. The deficits, however, were necessary to finance development and move to LDC-DC sameness. When pushed on why they have no real theory of asset-flows, or on why the state will undertake the requisite accommodating policies in LDCs, structuralists are unable to respond with a theory of *how* financial accommodation will take place. Instead, they argue that if there is no endogenous mechanism guaranteeing accommodation of LDC deficits, then, by an international policy of foreign aid, such accommodation *should* be provided. Without accommodation, there can be no mechanism to finance the goods markets deficits necessary for investments in industrialization and growth. When accommodation fails to emerge, the enforced cut-backs in imports and investment, operating through the various goods market and production structures, will destabilize LDCs in the short run. Further the loss of resources to finance investment will set back the development agenda and reduce growth in the long run. The debt crisis for structuralists is a crisis which emerged *because* the requisite accommodations to LDC deficits were not made, and thus reflects a failure of global policy.[23]

CONCLUSION: DIFFERENCES AND SIMILARITIES BETWEEN INDIVIDUALISTS AND STRUCTURALISTS

In this chapter, I examined individualist and structuralist approaches to the exchange rate and the BOP. This section will pull together the key conclusions of this chapter. The first part of this section examines differences between the two approaches; the second presents some commonalities between the two approaches.

Table 4.2 Different Approaches to the Exchange Rate

Different approaches to the exchange rate use different ontologies, and come to different interpretations of an imbalance in payments, and a role for devaluation. This table provides a synopsis of this chapter's conclusions.

	Concept of imbalance	Adjustment mechanism	Role for devaluation
INDIVIDUALIST ONTOLOGIES			
Gold Standard	Only out of equilibrium	Automatic money flows	none
Neoclassical Trade Theory	Only out of equilibrium	Automatic price adjustment	none (since prices adjust)
Elasticity approach	Only out of equilibrium	Dynamic stability requires D and S curves with right slopes	No consistent conception of role, analyzes possible direction of BOP response
Monetary approach	Only out of equilibrium	Money flows or credit adjustment	No long run role for devaluation, only corrective devaluation
Rational expectations	Only out of equilibrium for very short periods	Instantaneous price adjustment by agents with full knowledgerole	no long run role, only corrective devaluations
STRUCTURALIST ONTOLOGIES			
Absorption approach	Equilibrium imbalance	No automatic mechanism attention on multiplier type adjustment when devaluation takes place	Ability of devaluation to get BOP balance or increase employment depends on particular structure (e.g., mpc)
New Structuralists	Equilibrium imbalance	No automatic mechanism, attention to all channels through which devaluation will affect economy	Ability of devaluation to get BOP balance or improve employment depend on particular structure of the economy

Key Differences between Individualist and Structuralist Approaches

Table 4.2 provided a synopsis of the key points to emerge from our discussion so far. Below, I first synthesize the main aspects of each approach, and then present the main differences between the two camps.

Individualist Approaches

a) Individualist approaches understand *all* the flows found in the BOP to be autonomous in the sense of reflecting the individual decisions of maximizing rational agents. In equilibrium, since markets ensure that relative prices bring the autonomous decisions of agents into coherence, there *cannot* be any imbalance in the BOP, and hence there is no need for any accommodating flows.

b) The exchange rate is a price for individualists. It is the price of foreign exchange. But since money is acquired primarily to finance transactions, foreign exchange is primarily demanded or supplied in order to undertake the real transactions in international markets. As such, the exchange rate is a price that works merely to clear the foreign exchange market by ensuring the correct numèraire conversion from currency to the other. Thus, the relevant price is the real exchange rate which reflects the correct currency conversion based on the relative purchasing power of the two currencies in global markets.

c) In all the individualist theories, the key to equilibrium in the BOP is some mechanism that ensures correct numèraire conversion. This may be a change in the exchange rate itself under a system of flexible exchange rates. But even if the exchange rate is fixed in nominal terms, as long as there is some other mechanism that is set loose to produce the correct real exchange rate, there can be no imbalance in the BOP in equilibrium as the correct real exchange rate and correct numèraire conversion will emerge.[24]

d) Since individualists see nominal devaluations as purely a change in the numèraire, the end result in all theories of fixed exchange rates is that devaluations can have no impact on the equilibrium real values of goods and services in markets.[25]

e) All individualist theories have to draw on some form of structure—state intervention—to explain why there may an imbalance in the BOP. This is because they cannot explain any long term imbalance, since in equilibrium the BOP always balances.[26] Thus, for individualists, it was the profligate and interventionist ISI state that *caused* the BOP imbalances in LDCs.

f) In all cases, a devaluation is a "corrective" devaluation, which brings the exchange rate to the correct equilibrium real exchange rate.

Structuralist Approaches

a) Structuralist approaches focus on the goods markets determinants of the BOP.

b) The equilibrium in the goods markets is set by the structural rules governing agent decisions to import and export.

c) The rules are varied, and encompass consumption rules (both rules linking consumption to income, and rules linking consumption responses to price changes), production rules (which determine the need for imported inputs), and distributional rules (via mark-up pricing and fixed nominal wages), depending on the theory deployed.

d) There is no inherent reason for the goods market equilibrium to generate a payments balance.

e) Implicitly, financial markets fully accommodate the BOP imbalance, or else the state has the requisite resources to fully accommodate the imbalance. The exchange rate is a policy tool, and is not endogenously set by the markets to clear the BOP.

f) There is no inherent reason for a payments imbalance to signal a BOP crisis, as long as the accommodating flows continue. Crisis only occurs when the accommodation from financial flows is no longer available.

g) Devaluations may or may not improve the deficit, and could cause contractions. There is no inherent reason to believe that a devaluation can eliminate a payments deficit. In the long run, only a change in the structures governing the demand for imports and/or the supply of exports can generate equilibrium without a payments deficit.

h) In the short-to-medium term, financial accommodation is necessary in order to change the structures governing LDC economies and to create growth. In the long run, as long as the structures change correctly, there should not be any need for continued financial accommodation since LDC difference will be converted into sameness, and the economies will be able to generate both resources for investment (via growth) and foreign exchange (via exports).

i) In the interim, the BOP crisis in LDCs reflects the failure of international agencies to ensure accommodation of the deficits. The crisis is not the result of market intervention, but instead reflects the failure of DC policies to accommodate the needed resource transfers to finance development.

Key Difference between Individualists and Structuralists

The key differences between structuralists and individualists are in their views of the mechanisms by which an economy reaches equilibrium (one using individualist ontology and the auctioneer, the other using structural rules). Individualists have a fully articulated model of all the autonomous components of the BOP. The articulation comes from their conception of equilibrium. But in all cases, full articulation via equilibrium is carefully constructed to ensure that the priorly specified agents are not changed by the equilibration process, and the equilibrium prices are reflections of the pre-given desire, technology, and resources which define the individualist agents. Every mechanism by which adjustment takes place derives from the profit-maximizing and utility-maximizing behavior of pre-specified agents.

But in constructing such a carefully Walrasian model, where eventually equilibrium in the BOP will take place with the correct numèraire conversion, so that the correct equilibrium relative prices across national boundaries emerge, individualists cannot explain the existence of BOP imbalances. Nor can they explain why the state needs to undertake a devaluation since the automatic mechanisms unleashed by microrational agents should generate the correct equilibrium even with fixed nominal exchange rates in many of the models. Faced with such a problem, individualists collapse into some structure to explain LDC difference. They pinpoint the ISI-state as the source of the BOP deficit and the cause of LDC difference. They also have to depend on the state to then undertake the "corrective policies" which will undo the past policies and put the correct market prices and appropriate market mechanisms for generating equilibrium in place.

Structuralists draw on structural rules and parameters governing agent behavior to describe LDC difference. Equilibrium for them is simply a condition where all the rules are met. Thus, they have no trouble explaining LDC difference—LDCs have deficits in their BOP precisely because the deficits are the logical outcome of the structures governing LDC behavior. There is no inherent reason for equilibrium to clear the foreign exchange market or to ensure balance in the BOP.

However, if the BOP does not balance in equilibrium, then implicitly, some element in the BOP must be accommodating the deficit. Structuralists implicitly assume that financial flows will accommodate the real flows in the goods market, and hence assume that the capital account implicitly accommodates the BOP deficit. Thus, they must be assuming some extra-structural agent who ensures that financial accommodation takes place. Structuralists assume that the state will accommodate the BOP deficit by undertaking the appropriate policies of borrowing and of running down reserves. This means that the structure described is not self-reproducing and closed.[27] Thus the structuralists, unlike individualists, do not have a fully articulated, closed and self-reproducing international economy.

This leaves them vulnerable, since they are unable to explain *why* the equilibrium described by their models will emerge, and how it will be self-reproducing. Structuralists facing the dilemma of an unsustainable equilibrium in the long run, fall into individualism. In the medium term, they argue that international accommodation of LDC deficits is sound policy. In the *long term*, the structures governing LDC economies will change to make the accommodation unnecessary. But how will the structural parameters governing LDC economies change? As discussed in chapter 3, at this point structuralists fall into individualism. The LDC economy will change when, with a little help from the state (via accommodation of the current account deficits to finance imported inputs and industrialization), the *individualist* profit-maximizing entrepreneur is unleashed to generate growth and investment. The long run will be the moment of LDC-DC sameness, when the structures governing LDC difference are eliminated and the unsustainable accommodations to the incompletely specified structure of the international economy are no longer necessary.

Similarities between Individualists and Structuralists: Cartesianism

As noted above, individualists and structuralists often fall into their opposite and draw on each others' ontology when trying to sustain their arguments. But though they draw on each other, note that the underlying differences in the ontologies they use to define the LDC economic subject generate vastly different perspectives on economic policy. They have very different theories of how agents respond in markets. They have differing notions of what causes a BOP crisis, and what constitutes equilibrium in the BOP. They thus have differing assessments of the correct policy to follow when a crisis emerges. They also have very different notions of the role played by the state in promoting development, and propose different policy solutions to promote LDC sameness.

But they also share some key assumptions. In particular, both agree that the best way to proceed when faced with the accounting identity given by the BOP is to distinguish accommodating and autonomous flows, and to use the distinction to provide a theory of BOP equilibrium. They also agree that the best way in which to define equilibrium is by reducing the various flows of the BOP to underlying economic subjectivity (either an individualist subjectivity or a structuralist subjectivity), and then postulating some mechanism by which the various decisions mesh to produce a closed and self-regulating whole.

Thus, both agree that a BOP crisis occurs when the accommodating flows (which adjust to the BOP deficit created by the autonomous flows) cannot be sustained at the current level. This situation occurs when market-created equilibrium (for individualists), or when state ability to maintain systemic reproduction and regulation (for structuralists) breaks down. They have different theories of what the various autonomous and accommodating flows are, and how the BOP reaches equilibrium. Individualists see *all* flows in the BOP (except those coming from the state) as autonomous. All flows (except those coming from the state in the "Official Settlements" account) are autonomous because they reflect the autonomous decisions of priorly-specified rational agents. The various autonomous components of the BOP are *simultaneously* determined and brought into balance via the market mechanisms which ensure that agent decisions mesh. For structuralists, the goods market is autonomous since it reflects the decisions made by agents governed by behavioral rules and generates the possible imbalance in the BOP. Finance accommodates then, either because financial sectors are assumed to *always* accommodate the real sector (as with most New Structuralist theories), or because the state is implicitly guaranteeing accommodation.[28] In both stories, crisis only occurs when something happens to make the equilibrium unsustainable—state intervention preventing the automatic adjustment of the autonomous agent decisions in one story, and a failure of the international organizations and DC states to provide financial accommodation in the other.[29]

The shared commitment to equilibrium and ontological reductionism (the autonomous flows are reduced to the underlying ontological essences governing agent behavior) reflects the shared Cartesianism of the two approaches. As described in chapter 2, Cartesian analyses specify the economic totality as a space or plane, where the aspects that make up the space/plane completely determine it. Each aspect of the totality can be specified independently of the totality, and capturing the various aspects of the totality results in fully grasping and specifying the totality. Cartesianism deploys two key conceptual techniques (discussed in detail in chapter 2):

i)   exogenous/endogenous distinctions which describe both the totality under consideration and the parts from which such a totality is constructed; and

ii) equilibrium, which is the process of "reassembling" the parts to
ensure full articulation, self-reproduction and closure.

The Exogenous/Endogenous Distinction

The Exogenous-Endogenous distinction, as described in chapter 2, identifies
the various parts that make up the economic totality. In economics, the specification of the parts of the Cartesian plane involves specifying the variables
and parameters in the analysis. Specification of these variables fully captures
all the totality, and explaining the various parts fully explains the economy.
In specifying the variables that make up the economic totality, economists
distinguish two types of variables: exogenous variables, and endogenous
variables. Endogenous variables are those parts of the economy which adjust to create coherence, closure, and self-reproduction in equilibrium. Their
values are the ones the economist seeks to explain. In the theory of the BOP,
the various flows of the BOP and the equilibrium level of the payments balance are endogenous, since the differing theories seek to explain whether
there can be a payments deficit in equilibrium.

Exogenous variables are the different parameters and variables which
are given, and which determine the value of the endogenous variables.
Economic analysis deploys two types of exogenous variables. The first set of
exogenous variables includes those which are "extra-systemic," and which
are changed by some external agency which is properly conceived of as external to the economy. Changes in these variables can change the values for
the endogenous variables thrown up by the economy at equilibrium, but
their presence or absence does not destabilize the analysis. The second set of
exogenous variables includes those which reflect the underlying ontological
essences of the theory. These variables play a key causal role in the analysis,
and cannot be changed or allowed to become unstable. Any effort to describe changes in such variables or any attempt to endogenize these variables
will cause the analysis to explode as the behavioral essences of the models
become destabilized.

In the structuralist and individualist approaches to the BOP, just as the
Cartesian theorist reduces the totality into its constituent parts, all the analysts proceed by decomposing the BOP into its constituent parts—the decisions to import and export goods in the current account, the decisions to
borrow and lend or to hold assets abroad in the capital account, and the decisions by the state to run down reserves in the "official accommodation"
part of the account. The accounting identity in effect describes the various
components or parts of the social totality being studied—the international
economy. The analyst then proceeds by examining the behavior underlying

each of these parts, and fits them together to provide a theory of the BOP. Here, I show how the common use by individualists and structuralists of the autonomous-accommodating flows distinction reflects their common Cartesianism, and their common effort to identify those flows in the BOP associated with their second set of exogenous variables (coming from their ontological priors) from all other flows. Any effort to endogenize the specifications of how these flows emerge destabilizes the analysis.

In individualist analyses, we find the following parts brought to the analysis of the various portions of the accounting identity of the BOP: microrational agent behavior which governs decisions on the current and capital accounts, and state behavior which shows up in the official accommodation section of the BOP. Let us start by examining a BOP which may be in deficit (I will examine the move to equilibrium in the next sub-section). The BOP can then be divided into two portions—the autonomous flows which result in a deficit, and the accommodating flows which accommodate the deficit. The careful separation between autonomous and accommodating flows when the BOP is out of equilibrium requires one the distinguish between those flows whose values come from *within* the system and reflect the ontological priors of the system, and those flows whose values come form outside the system and *accommodate* to the values thrown up by the ontological priors.

Individualists clearly see the *real* parts underlying the BOP as microrational agents responding to price signals. Their behavior, their preferences, the initial endowment of resources, and production functions, are all carefully specified exogenous parameters in the system that fully defines the parts. These cannot be destabilized and define the ontological components of the system. The flows that come from these decisions *at the going prices* are always autonomous, since they reflect the exogenously given *ontological priors* of the system. When the system is out of equilibrium, the only way the system can *maintain* the disequilibrium is if something *accommodates* the autonomous decisions of the priorly specified agents. This accommodation comes from the state running down reserves to meet the demands of the agents. Accommodation comes from those flows in the BOP that reflect the behavior of the only participant in the BOP transactions who is *not* governed by the priorly given ontological essences of the theory.

Structuralists bring the following parts to their analysis of the BOP: Structural rules governing agent decisions on the goods market, and financial markets and/or the state. Again, let us start with a BOP deficit (I will take up the issue of whether this can be seen as a closed and self-regulating equilibrium in the next sub-section). When there is a deficit, the BOP is divided into two portions—autonomous flows which result in the deficit, and accommodating flows which accommodate the deficit generated by the autonomous flows. For structuralists, the parts underlying the BOP deficit clearly come from the *structural rules* governing agent behavior: marginal propensities, production structures, and mark-up pricing. These ontological rules are the exogenous variables whose values generate create the BOP deficit. The flows in the BOP that come from the exogenously given ontological priors defining the rule-governed behavior of agents in the goods markets are identified as the *autonomous* flows. *Accommodation,* then, must come from the state or from financial markets which are *not* defined by the exogenously given structural rules. Again, accommodation comes from those flows in the BOP which are *not* governed by the rules describing the underlying ontological essences of the theory.

Thus for both structuralists and individualists, the autonomous/accommodating flows distinction is primarily a distinction that chops up the Cartesian whole of the BOP into two neat parts. Autonomous flows reflect those activities in the BOP which come from the priorly specified behavioral essences of the theories. Since these decisions come from the ontological priors, their specification cannot be touched. They will change as the economy moves to equilibrium or if the equilibrium changes (since the value of the flows themselves is endogenous), but they have to change according to the causal rules set down by the ontological priors. This is what makes them "autonomous"—the rules governing these flows cannot be touched.

Accommodating flows reflect the adaptation to the BOP imbalance from those parts in the BOP which do *not* reflect the underlying ontological rules of the theory. They are exogenous in the sense of reflecting the activities of parts *not* specified by the theory, and so their behavior *can* change or adapt. Thus their behavior can be described as accommodationist, since it does not *have* to derive from the ontological priors of the theory, and so be assumed to adapt without destabilizing the analysis. Since both theories agree that the state is exogenous in the sense of being extra-systemic and not bound by any ontological priors, it is not surprising that *both* see the state as the source of accommodation. The distinction between autonomous and accommodating flows then, requires that the accommodation come from the one source whose behavioral attributes are *outside* the logic of the system.

Equilibrium

Having specified the various parts in the analysis, and identified those variables which are exogenous and reflect the ontological priors of the system, the theorists now have to describe the totality by using equilibrium. In equilibrium, the specification of the different parts of the totality are brought together, and the social whole is fully determined. The process of bringing together the various parts of the Cartesian totality requires that the different rules and essences described by the exogenous variables which form the Cartesian whole must fully determine the whole. As noted in chapter 2, "equilibration" is the process of bringing together all the parts of the social totality, and ensuring that their various specifications "mesh" with one another, *without changing any of the independently specified logic of each part.* For equilibration to be met, the process of fitting together these parts must be seamless and timeless. "Seamless" in the sense that *no* interaction or relationship between economic parts can be left loose or unresolved in the equilibrium. "Timeless" because given the absence of history and change in *both* ontologies, the point when all rules are met must also be the point where there can be no more change.

In the theory of the BOP then, all the flows resulting from the specification of the behavior of economic actors must "mesh." The rules governing economic decisions must completely describe the BOP in equilibrium, and the various maximizing decisions of the agents (for individualists) or rule-governed decision of the actors (for structuralists) must cohere. Technically, then, since the *autonomous* flows are properly speaking the flows emerging from the full specification of the agents, equilibrium requires that the autonomous flows cohere. The accommodating flows describe the activity of an *extra-systemic* agent, and their behavioral specifications are not theorized by the models. If Cartesian equilibrium requires that the parts are fully specified, and that they mesh, then equilibrium properly speaking is when the totality is fully captured by the autonomous flows, and does not *depend* on the accommodating flows (which are, after all, left untheorized). While the flows undertaken by the untheorized state may *affect* the outcomes in the economy, it should be possible to specify the outcomes in the economy *without* such flows.[30]

Individualists ensure that equilibration takes place when the state does *not* offer accommodation to the autonomous decision of agents. In such a situation, the exogenously specified logic of microrational agent behavior, or the exogenously given auctioneer, sets loose a series of changes in the numéraire conversion and hence in the relative prices which govern autonomous agent behavior. The autonomous flows then adjust in accordance to the ontological rules governing agent behavior, until full coherence in all autonomous decisions is reached. Equilibration here is carefully specified to ensure fully meshing, seamless, timeless results. There is no need for "accommodation" in equilibrium, because by definition, the system is self-regulating and self-reproducing based on the autonomous flows.

As noted in chapter 2, the equilibration process presents some difficult issues for individualists, and spells their moment of collapse into structuralism. When the system is seamlessly and timelessly in equilibrium and all autonomous flows cohere, how does one explain payments imbalances, or the need for change? One cannot draw on the exogenous variables underlying the accommodating flows—the underlying essence of microrational agent behavior. Instead, one has to draw on some extra-systemic structure to explain payments deficits—the behavior of the untheorized actor undertaking accommodating flows, namely, the state.

Structuralists have a much harder time with equilibrium in the open economy (though as noted in chapter 2, the closed-economy models of the structuralists do not face such problems with equilibrium). For structuralists, equilibrium simply implies a state in which all the structural rules governing agent decisions are met. Thus, they can have equilibrium without the autonomous flows in the current account automatically clearing the BOP. But this definition implicitly requires that the accommodating flows work to sustain the equilibrium deficit in the current account.[31] Structuralists, then, give up full articulation and closure for tractability in their models,[32] and specify equilibrium based on a partial set of behavioral rules. Equilibrium here still means that all the behavioral rules are met. But it no longer means that the equilibrium result is fully specified and capable of self-regulation and closure (self-regulation and closure depend on the untheorized accommodating financial flows being sustainable). Thus, in addition to the difficulties in specifying a move *from* equilibrium and discussing how the structural rules change to eliminate LDC difference, structuralists have to explain why their structural rules hold at all given the lack of closure and self-regulation. At this point, they collapse into individualism, agreeing that the rules are not sustainable in the long run, but insisting that they hold in the short-to-medium term.

Structuralists not only need the LDC state to actively *accommodate* the extant structural rules, but to *also* work via policy at *changing* the extant rules (it is the state's efforts to change the structural rules governing LDC economies which forms the heart of the structuralist development project). How does the state manage to both ensure coherence of the extant structural rules and change in the rules simultaneously? Structuralists argue that the act of accommodating the current rules which generate a BOP imbalance will *itself* generate the resources that create the growth and industrialization which will then change the rules. In this way, the two requirements of the LDC state are brought into conformity—both closure via accommodation in the short-to-medium term and an end to LDC difference and a change in the structures in the long run will come from the same policy. Just as the individualists draw on the state *both* to explain LDC difference and the mechanism by which LDC sameness will come (the state will be the agent which enacts the neoliberal reforms and dismantle itself), so too do the structuralists draw on the state to explain *both* how the system which described LDC difference can self-regulate and *also* how there will be a change these structures to generate sameness-to-come.

The moment at which the structuralists create a role for the state to ensure both medium-term maintenance of the structures via accommodation, and long term change in the structures via industrialization and growth, is the moment of their collapse into individualism. As shown in chapter 3, the structuralist models of development implicitly rely on the *individualist* entrepreneur who will (with a little help from the state) dismantle extant structures of LDC difference and generate long-term transformation in the developing economy. The only reason that a policy of accommodation can create both medium term systemic closure and long-term structural change is the implicit reliance on the individualist LDC entrepreneur. If the entrepreneur who will use the resources generated via state borrowing to convert structural difference into LDC-DC sameness is not forthcoming, the policy of structural change and development cannot bear fruit.

Thus we see that structuralists and individualists have very different ontologies, and hence different definitions of a BOP crisis, and different solutions for such a crisis. However, they share a commitment to Cartesianism which creates a tendency for each to collapse into its opposite at key moments in discussing the BOP in LDC economies. The next chapter will examine the CDD in greater detail, to show exactly how the debate about international finance and exchange rates in developing countries pulls together the concepts of structure, individual, and LDC difference raised in this chapter and the previous one.

Chapter Five
The Contractionary Devaluation Debate Revisited

This chapter uses the insights of the previous chapters to examine the contractionary devaluation debate (CDD). First, I provide a brief history of the debate. Then I analyze the Neoliberal and New Structuralist perspectives in the CDD in detail. In the section after that, I draw on the previous analysis and shows that the CDD is best understood as a debate about ontology. Though the two perspectives differ in their ontology, they have some commonalities, coming from their shared Cartesianism and shared understanding of the project of development as eliminating LDC difference. Then, in the fourth section of this chapter, I examine the differences and commonalities between the two perspectives, and show why the ontological differences between the two perspectives leaves the CDD empirically unresolvable. The final section of the chapter briefly draws out the consequences of the terrain of the CDD, and provides some conclusions.

THE CONTRACTIONARY DEVALUATION DEBATE: A BRIEF HISTORY

Nations undertake devaluation in order to eliminate a balance of payments deficit. Two questions arise: i) Does devaluation reduce the deficit? ii) If it does so, what are the macroeconomic consequences for the economy? The former question has its origin in the elasticity approach. The latter concern has entered the literature in discussions of the "transfer problem," under the absorption approach.

The first questions about the ability of a devaluation to improve the balance of payments came in the debate over Marshall-Lerner conditions. In "Devaluation and the Trade Balance: A Note," A. O. Hirschman (1949) reexamined the Marshall-Lerner conditions for countries that did not start devaluing from a BOP equilibrium. He concluded that even though a country could reduce its trade deficit through devaluation, in terms of domestic currency the gap between the revenues generated by exports and the cost of imports might increase. The obvious conclusion was that devaluations might be able to correct payments deficits, but the ability to correct a balance of payments deficit via devaluations may come at the expense of growth and full employment.

This note, though influential, did not trigger a debate on how a fall in the domestic currency balance of payments could adversely affect employment and growth. Though most literature reviews date the origins of the contractionary devaluation debate to Hirschman, the subsequent debates on devaluation do not seriously question the *ability of devaluation to reduce the trade deficit*. The focus of the debate has been to question the costs of maintaining external balance through devaluation. That is, when real adjustments to relative prices take place, they are assumed to do so in the appropriate directions, *even by those authors who do not think that agent behavior in markets is guided by marginal principles* (i.e. structuralists).[1] This is despite that fact that within structuralist models themselves, there is no inherent reason for the net impact of a devaluation to be payments-improving. Instead, the current debates focus on the growth effects of devaluations.

In 1963, C. F. Díaz-Alejandro first put forward the view that devaluations are contractionary. In Cooper (1971a) this idea was expanded. Until the 1978 publication of an influential article by Krugman and Taylor, however, the dominant view was that the net effect of devaluation on economic output was positive. Since then, a whole school of thought critiquing devaluation has emerged. Barbone and Rivera-Batiz (1987), Branson (1986), Buffie (1986a), Hansen (1983), and van Wijnbergen (1986) further examined the demand-reducing possibilities of devaluation. Bruno (1979), Buffie (1986b), Taylor (1983) and van Wijnbergen (1986) have extended this to examine supply-reducing effects of devaluations. All of the authors who critique devaluation for producing economic contractions, following Krugman and Taylor's lead, have used New Structuralist models to generate their results.

In opposition to this view, Khan (1990b), Guitian (1981), Lizondo and Montiel (1989), Khan and Montiel (1987), Edwards (1989a and 1989b), and many others argued that critiques of devaluation are based on a *short run* conception of the economy, and do not use an appropriate framework to assess the impact of devaluations. If markets operate to clear, and interventionist policies are removed, the economy will be fully employed with no imbalance in payments in the long run. But at the very least, devaluations will reduce payments deficits by reducing the excess demand for foreign exchange. Thus, while devaluations *could* perhaps be contractionary in the short run movement to equilibrium in some cases,[2] in the long run devaluations are necessary and will create both external balance and growth (especially if accompanied by a full package of structural adjustment policies).

Many empirical studies have been undertaken in an effort to resolve the issue.[3] But despite voluminous data sets and twenty years worth of empirical investigations, the conclusions have been ambiguous. Further, the opponents and proponents of devaluation have been unable to reach a consensus on the appropriate modes of analyzing the data and interpreting the empirical results. Thus, efforts to assess the possible contractionary effects of devaluation via empirical adjudication have failed, and the debate remains unresolved.[4]

NEOLIBERAL AND NEW STRUCTURALIST THEORIES IN THE CONTRACTIONARY DEVALUATION DEBATE

Supporters of the IMF position advocating devaluation use an individualist framework i) to present their position, and ii) to reformulate the structuralist position from an individualist perspective. The critique of devaluation comes from a structuralist extension of the absorption approach. This section illustrates this difference and shows that the debaters often collapse into their opposite, and the contours of the debate are shaped by the general project of development described in chapter 3. First I examine the neoliberal perspective, and then I examine the New Structuralist perspective.

The Neoliberal Position

In the contractionary devaluation debate, the neoliberal or individualist position uses a monetary approach to the exchange rate. In particular, the models it uses come from the "monetary approach to the balance of payments" combined with a Walrasian microeconomic understanding of individual demand and supply behavior in "real" markets. When it explicitly recognizes the role of uncertainty in agent decisions, it uses a rational expectations approach.[5] Thus, the sources for the orthodox models are individualist, since (as discussed in chapter 4) the Walrasian, monetarist and rational expectations frameworks are explicitly individualist.

In the last two chapters, I have already provided the basic framework for neoliberal policies. Here, I show how individualism is deployed within the CDD. I first look at two models, one a presentation of the neoliberal logic by Edwards and Montiel (1989), and the other a presentation of the neoliberal critique of the New Structuralist perspective by Lizondo and Montiel (1989). I then examine the moments of neoliberal collapse into structuralism more carefully, using the "sequencing literature."

Individualism in the Neoliberal Perspectives in the CDD

In "Devaluation Crises and the Macroeconomic Consequences of Postponed Adjustment," Edwards and Montiel (1989) develop a model to "explore the relationship between the dynamics of macroeconomic adjustment and the timing of the implementation of an adjustment program featuring a nominal devaluation" (p. 875). What is important to note is that this is a rational expectations based model, where individual agents are maximizers.

As they themselves say, "the model is derived from well articulated microfoundations and distinguishes between equilibrium and disequilibrium movements in real exchange rates" (p. 876). As noted above, in the rational expectations framework, to get any real impact by devaluation, one has to identify *disequilibrium* movements (since in equilibrium, there is no long run impact from a devaluation).

The devaluation is described as a *corrective* devaluation, that is, one that takes the exchange rate to its appropriate equilibrium value (where supply would equate demand) after an exogenous shock. Again, the description of an initial deficit has to come from some exogenous disturbance, because in equilibrium, there can be no imbalance.

The exchange rate market then operates on supply and demand principles, and the deviation from equilibrium exchange rates causes a balance of payments deficit. Depending on the type of exogenous shock disturbing "macroeconomic" equilibrium, the particulars of the consequences of postponing a return to equilibrium are different. But the longer a move to the appropriate exchange rate is delayed, the worse the consequences for the economy.

Interestingly, the model has to postulate a corrective devaluation, since the traditional routes for adjustment (money flows or asset redistributions affecting prices or interest rates) are absent in the model—some structure (the state) prevents the usual modes of automatic adjustment to equilibrium from emerging. Since the authors wish to point out the dire economic consequences of failing to adjust, it is not surprising that they do not provide the usual individualist channels for adjustment in the model. This necessitates the "corrective devaluation."[6]

But the particular "corrective devaluation" is one that takes the economy to the right exchange rate, where the right rate is derived from the supply and demand curves that reflect individual behavior. Thus we have here a short run individualist model that makes room for a devaluation by postulating i) an out of equilibrium moment, and ii) a policy to return the economy to equilibrium. Note that these involve moments of collapse of the models into structuralism. As noted in chapter 4, there is no mechanism in a fully articulated Walrasian rational expectations model to actually generate either a payments disequilibrium, or to require any policy by the state to move the economy back to equilibrium. The moment out of equilibrium is postulated via a sudden "shock," some extra-individual force that pushes the economy out of equilibrium. The "shocks" postulated in such models should be understood as structural moments, a quick draw on some force external to the agents, to describe the emergence of a moment out of equilibrium.

Further, the move out of equilibrium now requires an additional structure—the state—to intervene via devaluation and restore balance. This is necessary because the model lacks the mechanisms that the auctioneer usually draws upon—maximizing individuals responding to arbitrage opportunities and engaging in money or asset flows which will then change prices and restore equilibrium. Having eliminated the mechanisms for the hidden structure of the auctioneer to work the move to equilibrium, Edwards and Montiel then have the structure of the state step in. In fact, the failure of the state to step in or to continue with the "wrong" exchange rate policy is itself a structural moment— a wrong policy by the state which has dire consequences for the macroeconomy. Thus both the explanation for the continued problems in LDC economies and their solution, lies with the structure of the state.

More interesting are the grounds on which the new structuralist position is attacked. In "Contractionary Devaluation in Developing countries: An Analytical Overview," Lizondo and Montiel (1989) offer a critique of, and an alternative model to, the New Structuralist position. They note that though most of the profession does not think that a devaluation could actually worsen the trade balance (despite Hirschman's article), and most agree that it will cause some inflation, the issue of output contraction is still unsettled.

At the outset, they note that since they are trying to build a model that incorporates the general assumptions of the new structuralist position, their analysis is subject to the general limitations of that literature. What are the limitations they identify in the New Structuralist position (p. 184)?

a) Lizondo and Montiel note that where the exchange rate is the only exogenous nominal variable, *a nominal devaluation has no real effects.* Thus, the New Structuralist argument that devaluations can create contractions in the economy makes no sense at all to them. Now, from an individualist perspective, this is quite correct. As noted above, for individualists using a fully specified and completely articulated model of the exchange rate, devaluations in fact do not have real effects if i) the model uses rational expectations (Lizondo and Montiel critique the New Structuralists for not using rational expectations) or ii) the model argues that changes in monetary variables translate into price, rather than output effects. (This is another way of saying that there are no wealth effects from the nominal change in value, or that money does not affect any real values since individual decisions depend on relative rather than nominal values). The gold standard and the monetary approach both make just this assumption, as does the rational expectations approach.

Thus, from the neoliberal perspective, it is almost impossible to explain how a nominal change in the numèraire could result in real changes in the economy. To do this, one would have to posit some structure that prevents the result from emerging. The neoliberals do not accept the behavioral structures identified by the New Structuralists, and thus find their position "limited."

However, as seen in the article by Edwards and Montiel (1989), the neoliberals themselves call on structure to explain a move away from equilibrium, and also have to posit some structural inability on the part of the economy to move back to equilibrium. Without positing these structures, there is no logical justification for the state undertaking a devaluation that could have real effects—how else would there be any real "consequences" of postponing devaluation? By Lizondo and Montiel's own argument here, a devaluation postponed should have no consequences at all! Thus we see that while neoliberals critique the New Structuralists for the limitations and lack of rigor in their theories, the neoliberal perspective is itself required to call on structure in order to explain why a devaluation is necessary at all, and why the market does not just automatically adjust without the help of state policy.

b) Lizondo and Montiel understand the contractionary devaluation debate as a debate about the *path taken to the new equilibrium*. This is not surprising, since in the individualist approaches, trade imbalances and a role for devaluation can emerge only out of equilibrium.[7] Indeed, the structuralist results are often seen as arising from "odd rigidities in arbitrary markets" (Nunnenkamp and Schweickert 1990). From an individualist perspective, these rigidities which generate the structuralist results can only be explained as:

i) short term phenomena arising because some markets take longer to adjust, or

ii) structural impediments in the adjustment process which are *created* by the state.

But devaluation and the neoliberal policies are above all the *removal* of state-created structural impediments—thus one cannot argue that the contractions associated with *these* policies come because of structures created by the state. The only way to recast the structuralist position in a "general" model, then, is to look at this as a short term problem along a path to equilibrium due to differential adjustment speeds in some markets.

But if prices do not all have the same adjustment speeds, then the adjustment speeds are an extra-agent structure. The adjustment speeds, in effect, are the explicit rules that govern the mechanism by which the (usually implicit) auctioneer ensures coordination. Interestingly, New Structuralist structures then are precisely recast as some flaw in the key structure used by individualists—the auctioneer is slightly flawed (or more precisely, the auctioneer is a little slow in some markets and hence is flawed in the short run, but in the long run the auctioneer eventually gets it right[8]). Note that the auctioneer still gets the job done eventually, just not instantaneously, or with complete coordination in all markets immediately. Thus even while recasting the "arbitrary rigidities" of structuralists into the individualist paradigm, the individualists striving to make sense of the New Structuralist perspective *cannot* recast this model in any way that destabilizes the underlying rational agents or see this as a reflection of agent *behavior*. They can only recast it in the one structural space within their models that does not destabilize agent specification—the auctioneer.

c) Finally, Lizondo and Montiel are particularly critical of the New Structuralist use of supply-side rigidities and use of an input-output framework. It is this framework that identifies supply side relationships that could mean contraction of output due to rising costs of imported inputs. The use of this framework is criticized by neoliberals as "bottleneckism," and as a failure by the structuralists to recognize agent maximizing behavior which should generate substitution effects in production which would overcome the cost effects on imported inputs. Thus profit-maximizing microeconomic firm behavior is employed to attack the structuralist position on production, and the structural rigidities are interpreted as a short run lag in supply response.

But again, if there is an "adjustment speed lag" in responses, then presumably there is no reason why this should not translate into such large scale instabilities and failures to move to equilibrium that the suppliers' behavior is no longer governed by microrational calculation but by structural rules in production (this was Keynes' point about uncertainty and the move to convention in making production decisions). But while adjustment to market prices at faster or slower speeds can be accommodated in the Walrasian vision, mark-up pricing and production structure which does not reflect underlying agent profit-maximization cannot be incorporated into the neo-classical models. Thus, it is not surprising that this particular assumption is picked out for special criticism by the neoliberals and reinterpreted through the lens not of behavior, but of lagged response.

Neoliberal Collapse into Structuralism

As shown above, and in the previous three chapters, individualist analyses collapse into structuralism at some key points. First, the purely individualist model (except for the minimal structure provided by the auctioneer), cannot actually explain why LDC difference exists, and has to call upon some form of structure in order to explain LDC deviation from equilibrium. For neoliberals, this structure is the state. Within the exchange rate debates, for individualists, we see that the only reason for LDC problems with debt and balance of payments is clearly the ISI state. Further, we find that explaining the move to equilibrium and sameness also poses problems for neoliberals. This is especially true in the arena of exchange rate policy. To see why this happens particularly in this arena, we need to examine the exchange rate a little more carefully.

As noted in the previous chapter, the exchange rate is the price that converts one currency into another. But it is not a "simple" price, since it acts as a price for a *nominal* value—money—and the individualist vision of perfect foreknowledge and full rationality cannot handle individuals who may be less than perfect and respond to *nominal* rather than *real-relative* price signals from the auctioneer. If individuals demand foreign exchange for some purpose other than to conduct transactions, or if they demand foreign exchange in response to the *nominal* signals sent out by the exchange rate,[9] then the perfect coordination and carefully specified maximization behavior of agents breaks down (full coordination with money as a "veil" breaks down when agents responses are governed by "money illusion," and they make decisions based on nominal rather than real prices). Thus, the exchange rate *must* actually be reflecting the *real demands* for goods and services and capital across borders, and cannot be purely about money demand (except for conducting actual transactions across borders—foreign exchange is never demanded as a store of value).

But this makes matters worse. If the exchange rate is a price that reflects the *underlying* "real" demand for various elements of the balance of payments found in the current account and real capital flows, then it is one price that equilibrates too many markets. The exchange rate will be used to calculate the real-relative price of domestic and foreign tradables and equilibrate the demand and supply for exports and imports in the trade balance so that price-differentials in tradable goods across national borders are eliminated. And, the *same* exchange rate will *also* be used to calculate the real-relative interest rates which give the demand and supply of financial assets in the capital account and will adjust to eliminate the interest-rate differential in asset markets across borders, to generate equilibrium in the asset market. It will have to equilibrate numèraire conversion so that the correct relative prices and cross-border price equalization emerge in *more* than one market. The auctioneer finds that he has to call out a single price to equilibrate two markets—the asset market and the goods market.

The solution has been twofold. First, neoclassical theory distinguishes between the long run and short run. In the long run, exchange rates act as numèraire converters and via arbitrage ensure purchasing power parity (real-relative prices are equalized since the purchasing power of the two numèraires are exactly equal at the going conversion rate) in the goods markets. In the short run, exchange rates clear the financial market and via arbitrage equate interest rates to clear the money market. The short run effect only arises because state intervention makes interest rates diverge due to excess money creation or deficit financing and so acts as an "exogenous shock" to throw the system out of equilibrium. In effect, the same price has to stabilize two markets, and the long-run short-run distinction helps to artificially bridge the gap.

But if one argues that the market handles numèraire conversion perfectly in the long run, so that the underlying real values are what drives all decisions, the numèraires themselves do not affect final outcomes and hence numèraire conversion should not affect the actual long run outcomes. Since numèraire conversion does not affect real values, it stands to reason that in equilibrium, the actual value of the exchange rate in purely nominal terms cannot affect final outcomes. This was the solution offered by the Gold Standard, the monetary approach, and the rational expectations approach. But if this is true, then why should a country devalue at all? The change in the nominal value of the numèraires should not affect any outcomes.

To handle this, the neoliberals again call on structuralism. For some reason (again, the reason is the interventionist LDC state), the mechanisms by which the numèraire conversion can be undertaken in the long run by the markets is missing—the mechanisms that allow this to happen like monetary flows or credit reductions are either directly prevented by capital controls in the asset markets, or else do not emerge because the market is not "adequately developed." Hence, the state needs to undertake a devaluation to fix this structural problem. While in the real sector one can see the logic behind the IMF position, the insistence that money is a veil makes it very hard for neoliberals to sustain their calls for monetary reform in nominal values like the exchange rate without this type of call on structural "bottlenecks" which prevent the automatic mechanisms of money and asset flows across borders from ensuring that the correct numèraire conversion takes place (what is the assumption that financial flows do not take place "properly" even in LDCs with open capital markets like in Latin America, if not a "structural bottleneck"?)

Finally in recent years individualists have increasingly called on the structure of "adjustment speeds." This response has become necessary as starting with the Chilean crisis in 1982, one country after another has reeled under the impact of highly unstable markets and crises as the policies of neoliberal reform have been put into place. What explains this failure of the individualist policies to generate sameness in the LDCs? Why does the auctioneer fail to handle both the short-run capital market problem of interest rate equalization and the long-run goods market equilibrium? In terms of modeling, individualists cannot actually handle two numèraires for the long run—if something in the system does not force the numèraires to fall in line, then the model starts to break down as the auctioneer is forced to call out prices in two numèraire systems and the mechanism for forcing them to become in effect a single system of numerical values is not in place.

The answer to this problem of failed numèraire conversion is found by yet another recourse to structure, which then explains why LDCs have not managed to produce sameness in their economies. The response is found in the "sequencing" debate (McKinnon 1991, 1993; Edwards 1984, 1986; Edwards and Edwards 1987; Choksi and Papageorgiou 1986) taking place since the 1982 Chilean crisis among neoliberals. Some LDC markets (usually the labor markets, goods market and domestic financial markets), because of the past structures created by the LDC state, have slower adjustment speeds (the international capital market has a faster adjustment speed). Thus, the lagging response of the slow markets sends the "wrong" relative-price signal to the markets which respond more quickly, resulting in a destabilizing adjustment in the wrong direction in the fast-responding markets. Under such conditions, if all markets are opened up simultaneously, then some markets respond to the wrong signals sent out by the markets that have not yet adjusted to equilibrium fully. As pointed out above, this notion is simply an extension of the implicit structure of the auctioneer, the only difference being that the auctioneer is not functioning very well because of the past structures created by the interventionist state.[10]

When an LDC faces such a situation, then undertaking all the neoliberal reforms simultaneously can result in instability and crises. Thus, to handle this problem, an LDC needs to "sequence" its reforms correctly—to first change some markets, and once they have adjusted to the "correct level" (though why that would be the "correct level" given the remaining interventionist policies of the state is left unclear), liberalize the next market. Who is to ensure the correct sequence of reforms, and stand ready to intervene in the market if one market responds too quickly and threatens instability? The state. Thus, liberalization requires a highly vigilant and proactive state—the faulty structure of the auctioneer is augmented and corrected by the appropriate structure of prices from the state. Again, individualists collapse into structure and a reliance on the structure of the state to ensure that the market works correctly during the reforms.[11]

Finally, note that though neoliberalism collapses often into structuralism, it should still properly be seen as individualist. The reason for this is that each of its collapses into structure is carefully undertaken to leave the pre-specified, fully formed, rational individual intact. While neoliberals can conceive of the structuralist perspective (as a story about the short run move to equilibrium), or themselves invoke structure via the state or the faulty auctioneer or the adjustment speeds in markets, at no point can they conceive of these structures in *behavioral* terms. Thus, while adjustment speeds are acceptable structures, they are acceptable precisely because they leave the individualist description of economic agency intact. Neoliberals can accept flawed auctioneers, but not human agents with a differing subjectivity. This distinction is important for understanding the inability of the two camps to resolve their differences.

The New Structuralist Position

The New Structuralist critique of devaluation uses the absorption approach to the balance of payments, and extends the Keynesian demand categories with a Leontief or Sraffian input-output production structure, and a Kaleckian theory of mark-up pricing. Thus the sources of this framework are explicitly structuralist (as discussed in the previous three chapters). Here, I first examine the structural mechanisms by which this literature argues a devaluation can cause a contraction, and then take up the moments of structuralist collapse into individualism.

Structuralist Ontology in the New Structuralist Perspective

Hamilton (1988) provides a review of the contractionary devaluation literature. In it he identifies eight "primary mechanisms" through which a devaluation can cause a contraction. The first five are from the demand side, and the remaining three from the supply side. I will follow his schema and then discuss the ontology implicit in these results.[12]

i) Trade deficit effect: By increasing the domestic cost of imports, the devaluation reduces real income. The reduction in real income causes a fall in real expenditure that sets off a multiplier effect. This is an extension of the discussion on whether and how devaluations stimulate expenditure on domestic products (exports) in the elasticities approach.

ii) Wealth effect: The devaluation increases the price of imports, and can set off an inflation. The inflation may increase the desire to hold nominal money balances (so as to maintain the real money balances). This causes expenditures to drop, and so reduces income (Connolly and Taylor 1984). (Note that in this theory, the desire to hold more nominal balances—a "flow excess demand for money"—is met by reducing expenditure, rather than showing up as a "trade surplus" as in the monetary approach.)

iii) Redistributive effects: If export revenues increase, and wages do not rise enough to "catch up" with inflation, the devaluation redistributes income away from workers to profit recipients. Some of this extra income of the rich goes to the government under a progressive tax structure. If the marginal propensity to save for the government is higher than for profit recipients and wage earners, then there is a reduction in total expenditure, setting off a contraction in output (Krugman and Taylor 1978).

iv) Effect of foreign debt repayment: Devaluation raises the domestic currency cost of servicing the debt. The improvement in the trade balance due to increased domestic value of imports is partially offset by this increase. If the debt-service burden is extraordinarily high, the net effect could be to worsen the trade balance (even without the Marshall-Lerner conditions being violated) and set off a contraction (Hamilton 1988).

v) Effect of repatriated profits: Devaluation redistributes income away from wage earners to profit earners. If the share of foreign ownership in the export sector is large, the redistribution could increase outflows due to profit repatriation, and reduce expenditure. This would set off a contraction (Barbone and Rivera-Batiz 1987).

vi) Intermediate imports: If there are no domestic substitutes for imported inputs, the devaluation will reduce the amount of inputs available (by making imports more expensive) and thus reduce supply (Hamilton 1988).

vii) Interest costs of working capital: If devaluation increases the demand for money balances, it can raise the interest rate. Rising capital costs can cause an output contraction. Further, as inflation reduces the real money supply, demand will shrink, reinforcing the output contraction (Taylor 1981, 1983).

viii) Investment response: The higher cost of imported investment goods might reduce investment demand, and thus cause a fall in expenditures. This would set off a contraction in income and output (Buffie 1986b).

In addition to the eight mechanisms identified by Hamilton, there is a ninth one on the demand side, identified by Krugman and Taylor (1978).

ix) Ad Valorem Import Tax Effect: If the state derives most of its revenues by taxing tradables (a common source of tax revenue in poor LDCs with a small taxable income base), and import taxes are ad valorum, then the rising real price of imports will cause a proportional rise in rise in the real tax burden. The reduction in disposable income will reduce expenditures, which will cause a contraction in income and output.

In each of the nine mechanisms described above, the following assumptions stand out:

a) The labor market did not necessarily clear. Thus the structure of the labor market determined wages, but did not push the economy to automatic full employment. The level of employment was set by the level of demand. This is a structural rule, where wages are determined by convention and by the ability of labor to maintain real wages, rather than by supply-demand considerations.

b) The various demand side effects all worked by translating some initial change created by the devaluation (like a redistribution) into a real change through expenditure contraction. What determines expenditure levels? Income, with Keynesian demand functions (adapted in this model to specify differing marginal propensities for workers and capitalists), rather than complete adjustment to relative prices. Thus the description of consumer behavior is based on Keynesian structural functions.

c) When monetary changes take place (as in the wealth or real balance effect), they do not set off automatic price adjustments to correct imbalance. Instead, they work themselves out by output contractions, since the economy is not automatically at full employment. This is an extension of the Keynesian demand functions that describe aggregate demand behavior as a function of expenditures (and now also as a function of wealth) rather than as a function of prices.

d) Cost effects operate through markup pricing raising the price because costs went up. In a microeconomic framework, the increased costs of inputs would create substitutions away from expensive inputs. But in a world governed by the production structure of the input-output matrices, such switching is not easily and costlessly possible. Further, the producers described here do not follow microrational pre-specified behaviors of profit maximization, but follow a structural rule governing capitalist behavior via mark-up pricing.

Thus each of the above results and mechanisms was arrived at by invoking some structure, to both allow for long run imbalances in payments, and to describe why the cure could be worse than the symptom.

New Structuralist Collapse into Individualism

The New Structuralist perspective, as noted above, draws on structural rules to specify economic agency. But there are important places where this perspective too collapses into individualism. The reasons for this collapse can be traced both to Cartesianism and to the hegemonic position occupied by the individualist perspective within the field of economics today. In effect, the structuralists, like the individualists, have to handle the issue of exchange rates equilibrating two markets—money markets and goods markets. While the New Structuralists, drawing on their Kaleckian-Cantabrigian roots, have a well developed theory of structural rules governing the goods market (note that all the effects of a devaluation work through either expenditures on real goods and services or via supply effects), they do not have a well developed theory of the financial sector or of the behavior of agents in the capital account.

This leaves them extremely vulnerable to the charge of "short-termism," since in effect, their financial system and the capital account implicitly accommodates fully all the imbalances in the current account. Either the financial markets must be fully accommodating, or the state's policy has become completely endogenized, with the state standing ready to take on debt and run down reserves—a position that is unsustainable in the longer term (how is the state to respond when it finally runs out of reserves?). If this is true, then indubitably the neoliberals are right that the short run and myopic policies of the state which accommodated the current account deficits led to the BOP crisis.

In effect, the real sector focus of the New Structuralists leaves them in a bind—they have a system with too few variables and inadequately specified structural rules to ensure full articulation and equilibrium. The only way to respond to such a critique is to create some additional structural rules about the money market, or to endogenize some variable (i.e., eliminate one of the extant rules which creates the inability to close the model properly).

Endogenizing the money market and creating rules that govern money market behavior has been done by the neoclassical-Keynesian synthesis for the closed economy (via liquidity preference and the marginal efficiency of investment schedule). But if the New Structuralists accepted this, they would have to give up their production structures (since investment would now be given not by the profit share or production structure, but by the money market). Further, if asset portfolio choice could determine goods markets outcomes, they would no longer have a stable marginal propensity to consume and/or import in the international markets.[13]

In addition to the problems of trying to open up the full Keynesian system with both monetary and goods flows mediated by a single variable, the New Structuralists face the following problem. We need to remember that the New Structuralists are not the progeny of Keynes, but of Cantabrigian imperfect markets along the lines of Robinson, Sraffa and Kalecki. Their predilection is for corn models and distribution-determined outputs via mark-up pricing and given production structures. This approach is extremely real-sector oriented, and lacks a well-specified financial sector. While the demand side comes from Keynesian marginal propensities, two key variables—profit rates and investment decisions—come not from the IS-LM story, but from the real-sector determined supply side of mark-up pricing, reinvested profits, and supply-determined input coefficients. If the financial sector of Keynesian theory is introduced with the interest rate set in money markets and investment responding to the interest rate, then the real-profits and mark-up pricing determined investment rule disappears. New Structuralists prefer to avoid that route.

If New Structuralists cannot accept the Keynesian formulation of money markets and are required to stick to a real-sector determination of output and investment given their commitment to Neo-Ricardian models from Cambridge, then they have to endogenize something for their models to close. The Goods Market demand side is already endogenized. Supply or financial markets cannot be touched without destabilizing the mark-up and the production structures. This leaves only two possible options: the labor market, or the state. Respecifying the labor market would either open the Pandora's Box of class struggle and historically determined mark-ups— something that Structuralism has avoided historically (see Appendix B in the dissertation [Charusheela 1997]), and that New Structuralist approaches have inherited in their model-formation even though they are aware of this. *Or* one would have to endogenize the wage-rate along individualist lines— again something that structuralists cannot do without destabilizing their mark-up pricing theory and their discussion of production structures. It would also generate the individualist result of full employment, and structuralists are (with good reason) unwilling to take that route.

The alternative is to respecify the state and endogenize policy. De facto, the structuralists, by assuming that the current account flows are fully accommodated by the state, have done that. But they are loath to admit this, for two reasons. First, as noted in Chapter 3 [see also Appendix B of the original dissertation, Charusheela 1997], this was precisely the point made by Noyola, and such a route opens up the issue of class struggle (as in historical struggles and mass movements, and not as in "equilibrium-generating structural parameters generating wage-share and profit share") and the question of *whom* the state accommodates and under what circumstances. Structuralism's history has been that of replacing Noyola's historical class struggle-determined endogenous policy accommodation[14] with Cantabrigian imperfect markets, and true to their roots, New Structuralists have avoided endogenizing policy. In effect, endogenizing either the labor market[15] or state policy moves one away from the Cartesian terrain of prespecified fully articulated structures to the open-ended moment of class struggle and historically determined outcomes—something that New Structuralists with their commitment to Cartesian equilibrium are unwilling to do.

The additional reason for not endogenizing state policy is that New Structuralists are above all development economists operating within the development paradigm. This requires a specification of difference, and a specification of the agency that will move one from difference to sameness. The sameness-to-come is to be brought about by the state freeing up the individualist entrepreneur waiting to be unleashed. If state policy is endogenized, then one can no longer call upon the LDC state to generate sameness-to-come!

Faced with such impossible demands, the New Structuralists fall into their opposite. They agree that their description of the open LDC economy is short run, and that of course in the long run the individualists are right that the New Structuralist models need a theory of finance to close the gap. Taylor (1983) makes an effort to bridge this gap by introducing a financial sector in LDCs—but cannot bring himself to include a financial sector which may destabilize the rest of his carefully specified behavioral assumptions on the production side from the Neo-Ricardian models. Thus, while the formal financial sector in these models basically consists of public sector lending to accommodate development agendas and promote industrialization along standard ISI lines, the informal sector and black economy or "curb market" for finance is purely individualist![16] The curb market in finance is driven by individualist behavioral rules in the New Structuralist models, and is thus more efficient than the formal banking sector and provides full and allocationally efficient financial intermediation. The curb market sets the interest rate by equating savings (which come purely out of profits) to investment in working capital. Thus the interest rate is the *one* price that works to equate supply and demand in the market in these models. Cho (1986) notes that the New Structuralist and Neoliberal theories of financial intermediation and financial markets are virtually indistinguishable—there is no hint of financial market imperfection in the New Structuralist models. Their perspective on the role of financial intermediation, and assumptions about agent behavior in the informal financial sector are exactly the same as that of the Neoliberals.

Though the New Structuralists fall into individualism to generate a financial sector, they carefully specify that financial markets only determine working capital costs, and are not related to profits (coming purely from the mark-up) or investment in productive capacity (coming purely from reinvested profits).[17] The results in their models are therefore not the same as the individualist results, since structural rules still govern production structures, labor markets, and pricing mark-ups. The individualist curb market is carefully deployed in a manner that leaves the ontological assumptions governing all other areas of agent behavior undisturbed. But once New Structuralists accept individualism in financial markets, they have a hard time explaining why their production side does not follow microrational behavior as well.

Further, though a financial side has been introduced in the models, it cannot be deployed to close the gap in their analyses of the capital account in the BOP. Financial market accommodation is purely for working capital and not for longer term imported inputs (since long term investment is profits-financed). Informal financial markets are not integrated with the international markets, and their perfectly competitive interest rate only works to clear the domestic financial market, and not to determine the demand and supply of assets in the capital account. This is because the real exchange rate in New Structuralist models is still determined by state policy and not by curb-market or black-market determined flexible real exchange rates. This is essential, since if the individualist financial markets *also* gave accommodation to current account deficits on the capital account, they would do so via efficient changes in the real exchange rate. If the curb markets determined real exchange rates perfectly and efficiently, then nominal devaluation by the state would not generate contractions since the real exchange rate would adjust via the capital account, and the real costs of imported items would remain unchanged. The mark-up then stays the same, there are no redistributions, and nominal devaluations cannot affect real output. Thus the individualist financial markets New Structuralists stipulate is confined to the domestic economy. Their financial markets do not actually close the gap left in their analysis of the BOP, and implicitly, current account deficits are *still* accommodated by the state.

Finally, New Structuralists have to explain how the state manages to accommodate the current account deficit without the model collapsing into "short-termism." They end up arguing that the deficit *should* be accommodated in the short-to-medium term since LDCs are savings-constrained. As long as the international debt taken on by the state subsidizes development and growth, there should not be any long-run problem, as the growth itself will generate the revenues needed to pay back the current-account deficit. But who will undertake the investment that generates the growth from this state-accommodated international borrowing? The investor is the LDC entrepreneur, who now has access to foreign resources and inputs, and who will presumably find a way to break free from the production structures, the limits of mark-up pricing, the demand constraints, and the infrastructure inadequacies to maximize growth. Again, the New Structuralists, as their older ISI counterparts, fall into individualism when explaining why in the long run their strategy for development will generate sameness. Thus, New Structuralists remain open to attacks of bottleneckism and short-termism from individualists, and fall into individualism in order to close their models and explain the LDC sameness-to-come.

THE ONTOLOGICAL CONTOURS OF THE DEBATE

As described in chapter 4, any theory of the balance of payments and devaluation requires a conception of payments imbalance, agent response to policy changes, and preferred policy solutions. Here I demonstrate that both structuralists and individualists have assessments of all three, coming from their own ontological perspectives.

Individualists in the CDD

The models used by advocates of devaluation rely primarily on a marginalist flex-price description of the economy. They use a Walrasian equilibrium framework, which assumes *pre-given*, fully specified individuals, who have preferences (for consumption, for labor, for savings, and in the monetarist versions, for money balances). Along with the pre-formed agents, there are resources (both total available resources, and the distribution of those resources) and technology (production functions). These agents are then let loose in free markets with full information and complete coordination provided by an (implicit) auctioneer. Their interaction will generate equilibrium, which should, via the responses of agents to the flexible prices system, bring into balance (definitionally), *all demand and supply decisions in all markets—including the market for foreign exchange.*[18]

By Walras' Law, two points can be made: First, if any one market is out of balance, that imbalance is exactly matched by imbalances in the opposite direction in other markets. (Thus, if the foreign exchange market is out of balance, that implies systemic imbalances in other markets, including financial markets for money, and perhaps, the labor market). Second, if there is systemic (or general) equilibrium then *all* markets, including not only the foreign exchange market, but *also the money markets and labor market*, should clear. This is assumed to happen if relative prices are allowed to adjust via a flexible price system to the general equilibrium values.

A payments crisis will be characterized by an excess demand for foreign exchange at the going exchange rate. The excess demand for foreign exchange should drive up the price of foreign currency (reduce the exchange rate), making imports more expensive and exports cheaper. This should reduce imports, increase exports, and thus eliminate the foreign exchange gap.

The theory described so far does not discuss the role of money and financial markets in the macroeconomy. In the monetarist approach to the BOP (Johnson 1977a and 1977b, Frenkel and Johnson 1977), this excess demand in the foreign exchange market is a direct reflection of the flow excess supply of domestic currency (or an excess of domestic expenditures). With flexible prices and interest rates, and free and open international markets, this excess demand should translate into rising domestic prices, and an outflow of domestic finances, that will correct the price imbalances and restore equilibrium. In the long run, since all savings are assumed to flow into investment, and since money is neutral (there is no money illusion in individuals' decisions to hold money balances, and all decisions are made based on relative price levels), appropriate price responses should eliminate the deficit.

Regardless of whether a theorist uses the real side approach (examining the mismatch between the underlying real variables in this market), or a monetary approach (examining the mismatch between the overall expenditures on demand including imports of goods and exports of capital, and the overall supply of goods including the exports of goods and imports of capital), the underlying model uses individual decision-makers operating in a Walrasian world. Since in equilibrium, in such a flex-price system, there is, by definition, no excess demand, payments deficits are definitionally situations that emerge in an economy that is out-of-equilibrium.

The IMF's mandate is to prescribe policy for *long term*, persistent payments problems. By virtue of their definitional ontological position, individualists cannot define equilibrium (or long run) payments crises within their model. Thus, the only solution is to argue that something must be systematically disrupting the free market flex price system: government interference. The appropriate policies for payments crises are then self-evident: restore the right prices, and ensure that government intervention is eliminated.[19]

In policy terms, this is exactly the IMF logic for devaluation. Definitionally, if there has to be undesired or accommodating adjustment in order to meet international settlements, that implies that the economy needs to adjust back to equilibrium.[20] First and immediately, in the market under consideration, one adjusts by letting the price of foreign exchange rise. This should eliminate the excess demand for foreign currency. Thus devaluations become the policy most frequently deployed as soon as a country faces payments problems. From the monetary approach, this imbalance in the foreign exchange market is a reflection of the excess supply of money in the economy. Thus additionally, all policies that generate excess expenditures (government fiscal deficits and loose money supply policies) should be eliminated.[21] Initial stabilization policies are primarily policies aimed at eliminating excess demand in the foreign currency market.

The logic of this argument points beyond a one-time drop in the exchange rate to the institution of *flexible* exchange rates, or barring that (given exchange rate volatility), a move to a pegged exchange rate with strict controls on inflation and money creation. Further, since the monetary approach argues that international money and capital flows (as individuals adjust their portfolios and money holdings) is a key adjustment mechanism in restoring balance, opening up LDC markets to allow capital mobility is a longer term goal. These policies should eliminate by definition not only existing payments imbalances, but any *possibility* of a payments gap.

In deploying the Walrasian assumptions about the macroeconomy, individualists also deploy the evaluative criteria of Walrasian economics, to assess their policies of devaluation—not only for its ability to eliminate payments deficits in this one market, but for its impact on the macroeconomic variables of employment and growth in LDCs.[22] In free market Walrasian equilibrium, one should have efficiency, full employment, and optimal growth. The CDD is simply one part of the larger marginalist-monetarist analysis of the problems facing LDC economies.

The key "policy" that emerges is to track down all those things that could be preventing flexible price adjustment in free markets in *any* key sector of the LDC economy. That is, to identify the *structure* (the state intervention) that prevents the individualist outcomes in markets from being attained. Therefore, after first ensuring that distortions from equilibrium brought about by overvalued exchange rates are eliminated (devaluation, fiscal and monetary austerity, and an ultimate move to an exchange rate regime with capital mobility), the next step is to eradicate any other market interventions. Devaluations, like most marginalist-monetarist policies, are best understood not as "policies," but "anti-policies"—elimination of past interventions and getting the "right" market prices in place, rather than new policies for intervening in the economy. As noted in chapter three, individualists are not that far from ISI structuralists when it comes to understanding LDC difference—structure is the source of deviance, and it is identified in order to be removed.

The assumptions required for this type of Walrasian system to work (whether for DCs or LDCs) are phenomenally restrictive.[23] Apart from all the assumptions needed for the specification of utility maximizing agents and profit maximizing firms responding to price signals (technology and utility functions of the right shapes, infinitely large numbers of very small market participants), one needs a structural mechanism like the auctioneer that can *coordinate* price movements in *all* markets to "move" to equilibrium (and further existence and stability conditions). Thus, if devaluation proponents are right that imbalances are a sign of "out-of-equilibrium" trading, then there is no way to guarantee that an economy whose adjustment path *includes* actually-concluded out-of-equilibrium trades will move to the efficient Walrasian market equilibrium. This is a problem for which no proponent of devaluation (and no user of Walrasian Equilibrium in general) has been able to provide a satisfactory resolution. If the mechanisms by which coordinated decision-making by microrational agents in money economies are absent, then one needs to specify agent behavior differently— it is from this perspective that the structuralists in the CDD make their assessments of the impact of exchange rates.

The CDD, as understood by individualists, is a debate about two issues:

a) Can a devaluation clear a payments imbalance?

b) Will it create stagflation and worsening income distributions?

Since individualists understand all BOP deficits to reflect a non-equilibrium position, and since in the long run equilibrium the economy will be at a full employment Pareto Optimal outcome, they understand the debate to be about the *path taken to the new equilibrium*. Thus, the key issue in answering this question for them is whether the *direction* of the adjustments will be toward equilibrium. Devaluation will make exports cheaper and imports dearer, leading to increased production of export revenue generating goods and a reduction of imported consumables, and increased foreign investment, only if the agent responses to price changes are all in the right direction. That is, the "shapes" of curves should be right—agents' (notional) responses to price changes in flex-price systems should be in overall directions that are imbalance correcting rather than imbalance intensifying. In formal terms, the stability conditions need to be met. This aspect of the devaluation debate *has* been formalized in the Marshall-Lerner conditions, where elasticities of agent response to price changes need to be appropriately large to ensure that the devaluation will close the foreign exchange gap. The structuralist position is usually understood as invoking arbitrary rigidities that violate the stability and adjustment conditions (fixed prices being represented as the extreme case of elasticity of response at zero).[24]

To summarize, the individualist analysis answers the three main questions posed above as follows:

> 1. *Conception of Payments Crisis:* A payments crisis reflects an out-of-equilibrium excess demand for foreign exchange.
>
> 2. *Diagnosis:* This excess demand comes from a) an excess supply of money in the economy, leading to too high a level of domestic expenditure, b) persistent interventions in relative prices leading to skewed demand for imports and too low a level of exports, and c) interventions that do not allow exchange rates and domestic prices to adjust to a new equilibrium.
>
> 3. *Policy:* The immediate policy is to correct the imbalance by reducing excess demand and allowing the price of foreign exchange to rise via a devaluation. The longer term policy is to promote flexible real exchange rates, eliminate all government interventions, and reduce the discretionary policies of governments that can lead to such crises.

Additionally, the individualist position critiques the structuralist models by reinterpreting them from the individualist assumptions of agent behavior, as primarily involving a lack of a clear specification of individual behavior in LDC economies, and arbitrarily low elasticities of adjustment.

Structuralists in the CDD

The structuralist approaches that criticize devaluations also operate within equilibrium frameworks. But structuralists do not define equilibrium as "supply equals demand" in all markets, nor do they rely on a drive for individual utility or profit maximization pushing the economy toward market clearing behavior through price competition. Instead, the economy is first specified as characterized by certain underlying rules or relationships. The structural rules in these models are chosen for a) their description of the basic behavioral relationships governing economic behavior, and b) in this debate, specific rules that characterize LDC economies. Equilibrium here is defined as a state in which all these structural rules and constraints are met (if each rule is specified by a behavioral equation, equilibrium is simply a state where all the equations are satisfied).

Structuralist models use rules to specify the behavior that underlies:

> 1) *the various economic activities in the BOP:* Import levels are determined by the propensity to consume foreign goods, and by the need for imported inputs in production; exports are determined by the similar consumption and production needs of the foreign economy; the ability of direct foreign investment (DFI) to generate exchange and growth in the long run depends on the extent to which profits are repatriated; and interest payments are determined by the level of foreign debt and international interest rates.

> 2) *the various internal relationships in the economy for wages, employment, pricing, investment, and production, by which the impact of policies will work their way through the macroeconomy, and which in turn will affect the behavior of the activities reflected in the BOP:* The ability to borrow abroad will determine the extent to which one can ease constraints on internal production by making imported inputs available; total income (and hence equilibrium imports and exports) will be determined by total absorption; and the effect of devaluations will be felt through price increases affecting income distribution and consumption on the demand side, or input constraints creating supply reductions and reduced investments on the supply side.

A structuralist equilibrium may then be characterized by excess demand for foreign exchange at the going exchange rate, and is likely to entail a current account deficit, since structuralists tend to emphasize a need for foreign savings in LDCs.

As discussed above, there are a large number of structuralist models, each having its own technical specification and parametric value for the structural rules and behavioral characteristics. But there are some key assumptions that the New Structuralist models have in common. In particular, there are four rules usually deployed in these models:

> i) Money wages are fixed by convention and labor markets do not clear;

> ii) Prices are determined by markup pricing, output responses are based on quantity responses (markets are demand or input constrained);

> iii) Demand behavior of labor is different from that of capitalists. Labor tends to consume a larger proportion of its income (i.e., labor has a higher mpc); and

> iv) Production is determined by a given structure of relationships between inputs and outputs (the fourth assumption, particularly, about the

nature of production technologies and shortages, is one the key factors governing low productivity and inadequate employment in LDCs).

The operation of economic behavior in *all* markets is specified on this basis, with the structural behavioral rules that govern labor market relationships and production relationships finding their concomitant expressions in the behavioral rules governing goods, money and international markets. Thus, what emerges is not a short run model of the economy with arbitrary rigidities in arbitrary markets, devoid of a careful specification of agent behavior. From this perspective, what emerges is an *equilibrium* description of systemic outcomes governed by "structural rules." These rules *are* the specification of agent behavior. *Equilibrium is when all the rules hold.* The rules tell us how agents will behave in their economic relationships—as consumers, as producers, as investors, as workers. For a structuralist, these rules are the basic economic relationships that the economist seeks to uncover, based on the economic realities of an economy.[25] The fixed price system emerges as a fully specified model of agent behavior in an economy governed by structural relationships.

The main assumption used by structuralists to describe LDCs, and the one to come under strongest attack by marginalists, is their use of production structures (fixed price system with low substitutability in production). The structuralist argument is that the *characteristic* of LDCs is that they do not have a high productivity/efficient substitutability production structure. The characteristic of an LDC is to have unemployment, low productivity, and production rigidities. Quite simply, behavior is not governed by marginalism, and there is no structural mechanism to generate marginal movements in production. It is necessary to undertake investment, especially in infrastructure, to eliminate this structural characteristic. Ultimately, without the type of investment necessary for *changing* economic structures, none of the problems facing LDCs can be "solved." Thus structuralists, like individualists, see structure as the mode for identifying LDC difference— except that where the individualists saw the state as source of difference, structuralists locate the source of difference in the behavioral characteristics of LDC economies.

Thus, structuralists argue that it is entirely appropriate that this investment be financed—by borrowing if necessary. But who undertakes the investment by which difference is converted into sameness? The entrepreneur, who presumably will suddenly be able to act free of the various structures describing the LDC economy. This ability of the entrepreneur to break free of the LDC structures is a moment of collapse into individualism. The BOP emerges as a constraint to necessary investment when necessary imports are unavailable due to foreign exchange shortages. The specific economic events that trigger such a crisis can be exogenous, unpredictable, and unlikely to recur (oil shocks, sudden rises in international interest rates due to DC economic policies, collapses in the price of one's exports, world recession affecting LDC exports disproportionately). Even if such crises are the result of government fraud and mismanagement, that simply makes clear the need for better governance, and does not logically imply the need to abandon investment for development.

According to some structuralist analyses, a payments crisis appears when international agencies and DC governments create forced schedules that place repayment of loans and interest above the use of foreign exchange for necessary investment and imports. Devaluations do not help address the main reasons for a BOP shortfall (the necessity for imported inputs and foreign borrowing to finance development). Instead, devaluation as a policy for LDCs leads to a new equilibrium where economic conditions are worse. Given the structure of production, changing the price of imported inputs does not lead to the movement to domestic input substitutes that can lead to reduced import bills, envisioned by the IMF. Since exporting ability is determined by structures governing access to foreign markets and demand for domestic output abroad, there is no reason to assume that exports will automatically increase to generate more revenue, since the devaluation does nothing to change the basic behavioral rules of consumers abroad. Instead, as imported inputs become dearer, capitalists raise prices, based on their markup on costs. As prices increase, in the face of unemployment, labor cannot gain increased nominal wages proportionately to the price increase. Thus real wages decline, and there is in effect a redistribution of income from labor to capital caused by the devaluation. Since capitalists do not consume as much as labor, there is a net decrease in demand, and hence a contraction in economic output. Thus, devaluation causes stagflation (see Krugman and Taylor 1978 for the formal model that set off the new structuralist critique of devaluation).

Additionally, since the main aim of policy should be to promote investment that eases the structural constraints facing LDCs, foreign exchange shortages and reduced income levels mean even fewer resources available for financing development. Further, the expenditure-reducing policies (elimination of fiscal deficit and loose monetary policies) promoted by the monetary approach to the BOP actually reduce the finances available for infrastructure building and public investment. Thus, in addition to the short term contractions, long term growth is impaired as investment is reduced.

Primarily, the structuralist models involve *equilibrium* outcomes, equilibrium simply being a situation where structural rules are met by the internal adjustments of savings, employment, and production in the economy. There is no reason why an equilibrium should involve market clearing solutions. It is precisely because structural equilibria do not automatically generate full employment with optimum growth that there is a role for government policy in these models. The key argument with foreign exchange constraints in these models is that crises occur when a shortfall either pushes an economy to a lower equilibrium than the current one (the contractionary effects), or prevents the economy from reaching a potentially higher equilibrium (the case for policies that can ease this constraint either through borrowing or international aid).

To summarize, for structuralists too, we find answers to the three main questions posed above:

1. *Conception of Payments Crisis:* A payments imbalance reflects an excess of activities that require foreign exchange (imported inputs), over activities that generate foreign exchange (transfers from emigrants, borrowing, exports, DFI). Such an "imbalance" can occur in equilibrium, since all equilibrium requires is that all the behavioral categories be met—it does not require market clearing. It becomes a crisis in situations where the domestic rules of the economy come into conflict with foreign rules—for example, when a country is faced with a mandate to pay large amounts of foreign exchange for debt servicing and imports, without being able to receive foreign exchange through new loans and grants, and debt rescheduling.

2. *Diagnosis:* A payments crisis emerges when an LDC is unable to meet its short term bills *and* is unable to find ways to overcome the shortfall. This can happen for a variety of reasons, from sudden increases in external interest rates on past debts, to sudden decreases in export prices and markets, or sudden increases in import costs. This may also be because of bad government *implementation* of development policies, but it in no way indicates that development itself is a flawed project; it simply indicates the need for better implementation. What then emerges is a need for adjusting one or more of the rules in place, so as to ease the constraint and avert the crisis.

3. *Policy:* It is entirely appropriate for a developing economy to undertake active policies to overcome the productivity constraints that characterize it. Such activity takes time, and needs financing. If foreign exchange is a constraint on such activity, it should be eased. Most importantly, the necessary savings to finance development investment have to come either from foreign or local savings. In countries where domestic resources are short, money diverted to repay enormous debt servicing burdens (most of which emerged due to external circumstances in

LDCs) is simply money diverted from sane policies for promoting growth and productivity.

Summary

These points emerge from the foregoing discussion:

1. *Conception of Payments Imbalance:* For individualists, a shortage of foreign exchange shows that the exchange rate is wrong and indicates that the economy is out of equilibrium. It is signaled by the existence of excess demand in foreign exchange markets. Ideally, the foreign exchange market should balance trade (which is autonomous) plus autonomous capital flows, leaving only a very small role for government reserves and borrowing. For structuralists, there is no reason for markets to clear. Payments imbalances can occur in equilibrium. They become a problem only when reserve shortages and lack of access to foreign exchange (usually due to a conflict between the rules governing the ability of a domestic economy to move to a higher equilibrium, and the external rules governing foreign exchange access) push the economy to a low-employment low-growth equilibrium or prevent it from attaining a high-employment high-growth one. Government policy is thus seen as affecting most items in the BOP, and a crisis as emerging when an external terms-of-trade or borrowing shock reduces the state's ability to finance growth.

2. *Diagnosis:* For individualists, the payments imbalance must have occurred due to interventions that prevent the market from clearing. For structuralists, the imbalance becomes a crisis when the inability to find the necessary exchange for financing economic activity can prevent attainment of a higher level of equilibrium employment and growth, or push the economy to an even lower level of equilibrium employment and growth.

3. *Policy:* For individualists, the policy recommendation is to restore equilibrium—through corrective devaluations and fiscal and monetary austerity measures to reduce expenditures in the short to medium term, and policies to eliminate all market interventions in the long run. For structuralists, the key policy is to ensure that foreign exchange shortages do not become a binding constraint—by changing the external rules that govern access to foreign exchange (increased aid, debt burden reductions, more access to DC markets for LDC exports, better terms for loans). This will ensure that LDC governments can undertake policies to change their own economies, particularly their production structures, and growth and employment levels, and move to a higher output-higher employment equilibrium in the long run.

Thus, both structuralists and individualists have models that describe LDC economies, define BOP crises, diagnose their proximate causes, and prescribe appropriate policies. Looked at in this manner, the CDD becomes a debate about the correct ontology for an LDC model.

COMMONALITIES AND DIFFERENCES
BETWEEN THE TWO PERSPECTIVES

While both approaches have models based on very different ontological positions, they share some commonalities, and often collapse into their opposite. Here I examine the key commonalities and differences between the two perspectives first in terms of ontological priors, and then in terms of shared Cartesianism, and discuss why despite the commonalities the CDD remains unresolvable. I conclude the chapter in the next section, "Conclusion: Ahistorical Deviance in Development Ontology and Policy," by showing why the contours of the current debate are limiting, and show the need for an alternative theory of LDC economies.

LDC Difference, Ontological Priors, and the
Problem of Empirical Adjudication

In this section, I show that the CDD, because it is at heart a debate about ontological priors, is incapable of being empirically adjudicated. I first examine the commonalities and differences between individualists and structuralists in the implicit goals they set up for policy in LDCs, then examine the role of ontological assumptions in setting the contours within which the CDD operates, and end this section by showing why the underlying ontic characteristic of the debate has left it incapable of being empirically adjudicated for these past three decades or more.

Commonalities and Differences in the Definition of Development

Both the New Structuralists and the Neoliberals share a definition of development economics. For both, the project of development involves identifying the structures that generate LDC difference. Both the Neoliberals and the New Structuralists place growth and industrialization as the key definition of development, and within their own ontologies identify policies that can promote such growth and industrialization. Both see the entrepreneur and investor as the source of salvation for LDCs, and locate him or her as the agent who can (with some help from the state) create LDC sameness.

This creates a spurious sense of common goals and common yardsticks between the New Structuralists and the Neoliberals, and generates a hunt for empirical adjudication of the debate—after all, though the definitions of difference may vary, presumably the goal of sameness-to-come is shared.

The goal can thus be used as a yardstick to assess which LDCs have managed to generate sameness or have managed to bridge the gap between difference and sameness more effectively, to see whose policies make more sense in the "real world."

But the ontological assumptions mean that the goals are not actually the same for the two participants in the debate. As noted in chapter 3, the neoliberal perspective has subtly redefined deviance to mean "deviance from possible efficient equilibrium outcome" rather than "deviance from actually extant DC economies." Similarly, I show here that the move from the original framework of Lewis, Hirschman, and other supporters of ISI to the Cantabrigian framework of imperfect markets and Neo-Ricardian economics has had the effect of changing the goal and criteria of assessment for the New Structuralists.[26]

The original "structuralist-monetarist" debates, as noted in chapter 3, marked the moment when DC debates about the operation of markets spilt over into, and reformulated, the original vision of the Latin American debaters. But this spill-over of the Cambridge-Chicago debates has had the impact of redefining the field of development economics, even though the participants of these debates remain unaware of this redefinition. The original definitions of development, as shown in chapter 3, divided the world into two "camps"—structure defined LDC deviance, and individualism defined the possibility of sameness to come. But Cantabrigian macroeconomics argued that the DC was not marked by individualism, but by structure. The structures identified by Cantabrigian economists in LDCs to define LDC *difference* closely resemble the structures identified by them as describing the DCs whom the LDCs hope to emulate.

Thus, it is no longer clear how LDCs deviate from DCs, since DCs too are marked by structure. What then defines LDC deviance, and how does one define the goal of development and of sameness-to-come? The difference between DCs and LDCs is to be found not in the abstract structural rules governing LDCs—they are the same rules of sticky prices, of marginal propensities, and of mark-up pricing—but the parametric values of the structural functions. The key inadequate parametric value is savings and investment. Thus for New Structuralists, the definition of LDC deviance is no longer deviance from DC in some fundamental sense, but simply deviance from a high growth path generated by investment because of low savings propensities.

This is not any different from the earlier ISI structuralists (and hence, the New Structuralists see a continuity between themselves and the older ISI tradition). What *is* different is the goal. The goal is no longer one of replacing structure with agent, but of replacing bad structure with good structure. The good structure is not only brought about by the state, the good structure, which overcomes faulty structures in *both* DCs and LDCs *is the state*. Thus, the moment of redefining the goal for the New Structuralists has the peculiar result of bringing them closer to the Individualists—both end up relying on the state to "fix" the inadequate market structures, whether it be by the right sequence of reforms to replace the faulty auctioneer, or by fixing market imperfections and generating growth and industrialization. The three key differences are that:

a) In one story the state was also the source of difference while in the other story parametric differences in the value of behavioral functions (as opposed to some larger logic of deeper differences) defines the source of difference.

b) In one story the state as savior is temporary, while the other sees the state continuing to act as savior even after difference is eliminated.

c) The goal of the state is always to unleash the entrepreneur. But where the unleashed entrepreneur is known via efficiency and maximization in one story, the unleashed entrepreneur is known by industrialization, savings propensities, and growth rates in the other story.

This peculiar set of commonalities and differences has three consequences:

a) It provides the common ground by which each theory can comprehend the arguments of the other and take them seriously. Thus, Neoliberals and New Structuralists can talk to each other, and try to assess the logic of each others' positions. Their models have enough in common[27] that they understand each other. Thus, each sees the other as the key alternative contender in the field, and perspectives whose goals and approach do not fit in with these common assumptions are written out of the debate.

b) Each draws on the other to shore up its arguments at key moments of collapse. The common commitment to equilibrium and common partitioning of the macroeconomy into real, financial and labor markets which cohere allows each to draw on its opposite at key moments. Though the two theories depend on each other for logical coherence, and each attacks the others assumptions, neither recognizes the swings between the two ontologies, since the shared equilibrium framework allows such swings between the two.

c) The ontological differences are, however, too large to be bridged by the commonalities. Their differences are more fundamental than they themselves realize, and the differences between them cannot be resolved by use of the common equilibrium framework.

The net result of this is that the Neoliberal-New Structuralist debate remains fundamentally unresolvable, but becomes the main theoretical terrain within development economics for any discussion of the issues facing LDC economies. The mutuality and tension between these two overarching ontologies creates a proclivity for each to fall into its opposite, and for the field of development itself to swing from one pole of the structure-agent dichotomy into the other in an effort to provide coherence, closure and self-regulation in analysis (through the equilibrium models) *even* as it leaves a space for change, disarticulation, and incomplete closure (by its commitment to the development project, which requires a movement from difference to sameness and hence requires some degree of disarticulation).

In particular, the move from difference to sameness forces the individualist to fall into structure and rely on the state, and similarly, the move from difference to sameness forces the structuralists to fall into individualism and call on the entrepreneur. The symbiotic relationship between individualist-entrepreneur and structuralist-state remains unexamined for both theories (to interrogate this relationship too closely would open up the issue of class). Both assume that this symbiotic relationship will generate the *national* good, and fail to interrogate the class-dynamics of such a reliance on the state-entrepreneur nexus for development policies.

Ontological Priors and Development Goals

But though the seemingly common goal of promoting the entrepreneur's interest and generating growth and industrialization provides commonality, the two groups actually do not assess the location of sameness-to-come identically. Each ontology has assessed the ontological contours of the goal of development differently, and hence each looks for different things when assessing the success or failure of development. The goals have been redefined from the "absolute difference" between DC and LDC to the *counterfactual*. For individualists, the actual assessment of development and sameness comes from the counterfactual of *potential efficiency* in free markets—no matter what the level of growth, the potential loss of efficiency due to a deviation from free markets always means that the economy is not fully developed, since it could have done better. For structuralists, the counterfactual is the *potential level of growth and investment* the economy has foregone through neoliberal policies and the elimination of state policies to promote investment. No amount of future growth makes up for the permanently lost level of savings and concomitant investment that the period of adjustment caused the LDC to lose, and no amount of free-market efficiency can compensate for the permanent losses in income levels that the failure to move to a "good structure" of higher parametric values for savings and investment or better production structures via government policy has entailed.

This difference in the mode of assessing the policies is linked to the ontological differences between the two groups: the structuralist ontology does not have micro-rational individuals. Efficiency in the Pareto Optimal sense is irrelevant since the marginal calculating individual does not exist in either DC or LDC. Instead, national growth and output levels are what count. For individualists, the existence of microrational behavior and pre-formed individuals means that the only viable and logically sustainable mode of evaluating outcomes is via Pareto efficiency. Thus the two groups actually have rather different goals in mind for "sameness-to-come," and hence assess the impact of policy on LDCs differently.

This is seen in the way in which neoliberals have attacked the ISI state. Bhagwati, Krueger, and others have explicitly calculated the impact of ISI on LDCs not in terms of the actual growth experience of LDCs, but in terms of the lost *potential* efficiency due to state intervention in markets. Similarly, Kaldor, in discussing Monetarism in the U.K. and devaluation in India, argues that no amount of future growth makes up for the permanently lost growth potential of the economies facing such policies. Thus, an economic contraction for New Structuralists signals a serious problem that no future growth can compensate for.

Incommensurate Goals and Empirical Adjudication in the CDD

The surface similarity in goals has led to a wide variety of empirical efforts to adjudicate the CDD (see Agénor and Montiel 1996 for a very thorough introduction to the empirical literature assessing the CDD). But despite the best efforts at adjudication, the debate has remained unresolved—in some cases devaluations have precipitated a crisis, in others they have not. Further, where devaluations have precipitated a crisis, they have been followed by a recovery.

Individualists point to countries which did not face a crisis following devaluation to argue that there is no inherent reason for devaluations to cause contractions. Further, in the cases where devaluations did cause a crisis, they point to the eventual recovery. For individualists, while there was a short crisis for many countries (because of the "wrong sequence" in reforms, because of lack of credibility by the state, or because of inadequate reforms), *eventually* the policy paid off with growth. And, even in countries that did face post-devaluation crises, the situation would have been much worse if the devaluation had not been put in place.

Structuralists, however, disagree. They point to countries which did face a post-devaluation contraction to prove their point. Subsequent recovery makes no difference to the structuralists, since they point out that after a contraction, recovery will definitionally take place. The recovery does not compensate for the permanent loss of growth potential that the crisis period created, since the lost investment means that the economy will always have a lower level of development that it could have reached without the devaluation. Those countries which have not had a crisis following devaluation are explained by reference to the ancillary policies of the state or by pointing out that the specific parameters of some key components in the contractionary devaluation story (the level of wages, the amount of imported inputs, the extent of redistribution) were high enough or low enough in these countries to ensure that a contraction did not occur. But this is nothing more than a confirmation of the New Structuralist ontology since it explains which countries did face a contraction and which did not. Even in these cases which did not face a contraction, structuralists argue that the output produced was still *relatively* smaller than would have been the case without devaluation.

Since in all cases there is always some form of state policy that goes along with the devaluation and always some form of state regulation, it is always possible for structuralists to point to it as the reason for recovery and for what little growth is taking place, and for individualists to point to it as the reason for low growth. Despite ten years of effort at empirical adjudication and a variety of econometric tests, the debate remains unresolved. Empirical adjudication in the debate relies on what the *counterfactual result would have been* if the devaluation had not taken place. But the counterfactual generated will depend on the model used, and the criteria of evaluation used. Figure 5.1 provides a graphical representation of the problem with using the counterfactual in the empirical debates.

The ability to pinpoint whether an actual devaluation in the real world resulted in contraction or not is practically nil, since in effect, this exercise involves determining whether the contraction was the result of the devaluation or occurred for some other reason, or determining whether the lack of a contraction was a signal of the efficacy of devaluation or whether some other factor overwhelmed the contractionary effect of the devaluation to generate growth. In either case, the devaluation despite the contraction has prevented a possibly worse outcome (for individualists), or the devaluation despite the lack of contraction has in effect prevented the possibly better outcome (for the New Structuralist). This type of reasoning is fundamentally non-testable, depending as it does on the ontology on which one bases one's interpretation of the empirical data and based on which one generates one's criteria for assessing the impact of policy.

The graphs below show two cases—countries which faced a post-devaluation contraction, and countries which did not. In both cases, the efficacy of the policy or lack thereof is assessed by comparing the actual outcome in the economy to the counterfactual outcome of "what might have been" without the devaluation.

A: Contractionary Devaluation

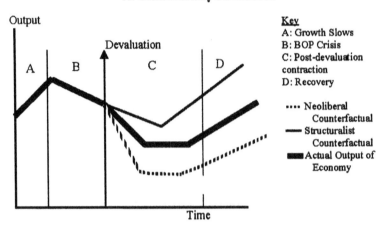

B: Devaluation Without Contraction

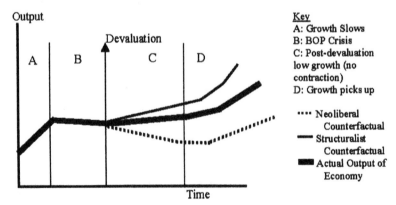

Figure 5.1 Empirical Adjudication and the Counterfactual

Cartesianism

In addition to their conception of development as elimination of LDC difference and of "bad structure," and their definition of development in terms of *national* well-being (whether national well-being is defined as efficiency and growth, or industrial investment and growth), both New Structuralists and Individualists share a common commitment to Cartesianism. As noted in chapter 2, Cartesianism refers to a specific conception of the social totality. The Cartesian totality is specified as a plane or space. The plane or space is defined by its dimensions and parts, and these parts *completely* capture and *make up* the totality. The parts are *logically prior* to the whole. One can therefore study the whole by studying its parts. Metaphorically, Cartesianism can be seen as a "mechanistic" mode of analysis. This mechanism is drawn from the analogy of studying machines, where each part can be "removed" from the totality, and its operation and behavior studied independently. This study of the different parts is the same thing as the study of the whole, since by understanding these parts, one understands the operation of the whole machine.

Both individualists and New Structuralists use Cartesianism. For Individualists, the "parts" which form the Cartesian totality are priorly specified individuals, with one key additional part—the auctioneer—ensuring that the parts "mesh." For structuralists, the parts that constitute the Cartesian plane are their structural rules governing agent behavior. The requirement of Cartesian equilibrium is met by ensuring that the rules are specified in a manner that ensures that all aspects of agent behavior are captured by the structural rules (full articulation), and the structural rules are carefully formulated to be non-contradictory (thus the structure is carefully specified so that the rules are self-reproducing and closed) and thus to generate equilibrium.

The requirements of Cartesianism have generated similarities between structuralists and individualists. Both agree that only a fully specified equilibrium formulation counts as a "proper" economic model—a model which explodes, or does not have full articulation and closure, is one that has "left out" some key aspects of economic behavior and hence does not count. Thus we find individualists who prefer to eschew full individualism and call on the structure of the auctioneer or the state or the "adjustment speed" of a market rather than forego closure.[28] Similarly, we see structuralists who fall into individualism in financial markets, or on the long-run ability of the entrepreneur to overcome structure and act as an individualist.[29]

The common commitment to Cartesianism makes these two vastly different ontologies capable of "talking" to each other, and generates a spurious sense of commonality. The common Cartesianism has generated an agreement about what a "proper" macroeconomic model contains. Both sides specify a goods market, a money market and a labor market (each of which can be carefully identified and distinguished from other markets) as the key series of markets which any economist should have. They agree that the exchange rate is the price of foreign exchange, that the wage rate is the price of labor, that the Money Supply is exogenous, and that the state and state policy are outside the economy "proper." Both agree that in the end the "real sector" determines outcomes and growth.

This set of commonalities generates a peculiar conversation. Each side can easily identify the labor market, the goods market, and the money market in their opponent's model. They then each critique the behavioral specification of the agents in each of these markets as deployed by their opponent, and each offers their own fully specified and closed model as the correct theory. Each then promptly falls into their opposite when trying to define LDC difference or the move from difference to sameness in such a carefully specified and fully closed model, in effect making all the assumptions about agent behavior that they had just accused their opponent of making in order to generate their results.

In both theories, the maintenance of closure and of full articulation creates intellectual problems—how is one to specify the exchange rate in such a world? For individualists, this requirement either makes policy irrelevant and undercuts the basis for the very policies they seek to put in place, or else it requires calling on structure and the state. For structuralists, the requirement of closure in the CDD either requires a collapse into an individualist financial market, or it requires endogenization of state policy and an extraordinarily unsustainable outcome postulated as "equilibrium." Similarly, how is one to postulate both LDC difference and the possibility of sameness-to-come in a closed and fully articulated Cartesian world? Both fall into their opposite when trying to describe how timeless and seamless Cartesian equilibrium can be deployed to describe a changing LDC. In the end, both sides prefer to continue their Cartesian debate, to ignore all alternative policies, and to overlook the intellectual problems with their project of as Cartesian theory of development, rather than eschew the Cartesian world of mathematical fetishism.

CONCLUSION: AHISTORICAL DEVIANCE IN DEVELOPMENT ONTOLOGY AND POLICY

The above discussion of the CDD has shown that:

> a) New Structuralists and Individualists share common perceptions of development as a project. The commonality emerges from their perception of LDC deviance as explained by "bad structure," and their assumption that development is about the recreating of the West in the non-West. Both share a commitment to a notion of national well-being,

both elide class, and both depend on the LDC entrepreneur to generate the hoped-for sameness. Thus, both see anything that impedes the ability of the LDC entrepreneur to undertake investment as "bad," and both proffer policies aimed at sweetening the pot for the LDC investor and freeing him or her from the structures which constrain his/her actions.

b) New Structuralists and Individualists share a common commitment to Cartesianism, and do not accept any open-ended theory of historically determined outcomes, or of economies which are not fully articulated, closed and self-reproducing. Each sees state policy as exogenous, and prefers to fall into its opposite rather than contemplate open-endedness or endogenized state policy.

c) However, the commonalities hide some differences—both have radically different conceptions of economic subjectivity, and hence the mechanism by which each generates Cartesian Equilibrium differs markedly (one generates closure via the auctioneer or the state, the other generates closure via behavioral rules or the state).

d) Both also have radically different goals in mind for development, since though both agree that development is about LDC deviance, they do not agree on the nature of the economy the LDC deviates *from*. One sees the DC which marks the goal as governed by individualist behavior, and the other sees the DC which marks the goal as governed by the "good structure" of the state.

e) The differences generate an unresolvable debate, with the commonalities ensuring that each falls into its opponent's ontology at crucial moments to create "closure," and to describe the possibility of a move from LDC difference to LDC sameness. This dynamic of unresolvable ontological difference superimposed on commonality, along with the intellectually incommensurate commitment to *both* the definition of development as a movement from sameness to difference *and* the deployment of closed, fully articulated Cartesian models, generates a tendency for swings from one perspective to the other. It also means that the Cartesianism that underlies the debate becomes the only terrain on which LDC policy options is debated, and creates a spurious sense of "diversity" of opinions. The actuality is that the enforcement of Cartesianism forecloses alternate perspectives and elides any discussion of history and class struggle.

What lessons does the exploration of ontology in debates about development policy have for contemporary theory? Beneath the varied disputes, we see approaches that conceptualize development primarily through the lens of deviance. These perspectives all elide history, postulate a singular national weal, elide class, and make State policy for supporting the LDC entrepreneur the central focus of their analysis. The next chapter concludes the book by exploring the implications of this for how we conduct economic analysis.

Chapter Six
Ontologies of Deviance

Our exploration of structuralist and individualist ontologies in economic analysis shows that current debates about the type of macroeconomic policy to follow in developing countries (or, for that matter, developed ones, given that development discourse is constituted via the non-West's difference from the West) remains unresolvable. This is because the debate is, at root, about the ontological priors of economic analysis. And ontological priors, by the way they set up their own discursive terrains and objects and logics of analysis, are not subject to proof in the positivist sense of that term. They can, at most, be verified—or going further, made actual through the material effects of the actions and policies their theories generate. I conclude by first providing a short discussion of the current state of the CDD, and then providing a broader discussion of the implications of this book's analysis for the project of doing economics.

THE CONTRACTIONARY DEVALUATION DEBATE TODAY

Though there has been no 'resolution' of the CDD there is a rough consensus about whether devaluations cause contractions. The general answer—accepted now by all sides, even if their comprehension of what this implies remains different—is that yes, devaluations do cause contractions. There is no consensus on whether the contraction is stagflationary—that is, on whether devaluations also cause inflation.

But this 'consensus' masks unresolved tensions. Though most scholars now presume that a devaluation will be followed by some contraction in economic output in the short run, individualists continue to see devaluations as corrective, necessary short term adjustments to ensure long term growth. Structuralists continue to see the post-devaluation contractions as resulting from underlying structures of the economy. The agreement that devaluations cause contractions, therefore, should not be seen as a victory for structuralist perspectives—indeed, the agreement about contractionary devaluation takes place at a time when neoliberal perspectives, though embattled at the political and popular level, remain dominant within economic analysis and policy-making.

Moreover, the locus of dispute about development ontology in the arena of international finance has shifted and is now centered on the term "globalization," rather than the term structural adjustment. In this new discourse, the exchange rate is no longer viewed as an active policy tool for development in the way it was during the height of the CDD. Rather, States are seen as having at most imperfect control over exchange rates, being forced to adjust their exchange rates to 'clear' the foreign exchange market and bring domestic and foreign prices and interest rates in line. The exchange rate is seen as determined by "market fundamentals."

The shift in comprehending devaluations as an active policy tool by the State marks a victory for individualist perspectives—the State is now endogenized to the point where it can no longer control market outcomes. Note however, that this endogenization of the State is not the result of a serious new theory of the State in economics. The State actually remains exogenous—rather, the sphere of intervention of the exogenous State has been reduced. The underlying naturalization of the modern State as a pre-given extra-economic unit remains intact within both structuralist and individualist analyses, and there remains little discussion about the actual formation of actual States, or of the projects and class dynamics of State interests in the constitution of economic policy. Development continues to be defined in terms of the structure of deviance from or convergence with the West, as before, and the modernist exogenous State remains untouched.

TOWARD AN ALTERNATIVE

The purpose of this book was to provide a close ontological reading of development economics, and of a specific policy debate within that field. What the discussion shows is that structuralist and individualist approaches operate within a shared Cartesian field, using approaches that exogenize the State and exclude the issue of State formation and politics. This exogenous State is enabled by the disciplinary divisions in the social sciences that leave serious study of the State to political science, even as political scientists defer on issues of economy to economists (see Zein-Elabdin 2004). This division of knowledge both reflects and reinforces the underlying modernist ontology that that both structuralists and individualists share, leaving the underlying conception of the deviant non-West intact.

Therefore responding to the currently ascendant neoliberal vision requires more than simple opposition to individualist social science. An alternative approach that takes class into consideration, and that provides a more robust analysis of State-formation and State-based projects in concrete historical terms, is necessary. Most importantly, we need to squarely confront and challenge the underlying understanding of the non-West as deviant, and develop alternative social science that does not rest on this normal|deviant, West|nonWest dichhotomy. That is beyond the scope of this book, but I invite readers to explore the new forms of analysis that have been emerging in the past two decades in postcolonial, feminist, Marxist, and Institutionalist scholarship (Zein-Elabdin and Charusheela 2004).

Notes

NOTES TO CHAPTER ONE

1. Terminology is always difficult. For reasons of convention, and not because I view these as pre-performed or self-evident units, I use the terms Third World and Less Developed countries to mark those nations which have been the object of development analysis and policy since WW2. The terms West, developed, and industrialized are used to denote the former colonial powers of Western Europe and their settler colonies in Australia and North America.

2. Cullenberg (1989) examined the debate over the falling rate of profit in Marxian economics using a taxonomy of Hegelian versus Cartesian approaches to the totality. In the debate examined here, both participants use a Cartesian framework. Thus, I extend his analysis to the different approaches that can emerge within Cartesianism, specifically, Individualism and Structuralism.

3. In an ironic turn of language, the view based on individualism refers to its policy packages as structural adjustment policies, while the opponents of structural adjustment are structuralists.

4. The appendix to Fund-Supported Programs, Fiscal Policy, and Income Distribution (International Monetary Fund 1986) provides data for 28 countries recommended structural adjustment policies, with details of the specific policy package for each. A detailed examination of each element of such a package is beyond the scope of this book, and I will focus primarily on exchange rate policies.

5. The Structural Adjustment packages consist of two types of policies. The first set of policies deployed by the IMF is called Stabilization policies. These are aimed at reducing the immediate causes for the payments crisis identified by the IMF, and have as their aim eliminating inflation and overvalued domestic currencies. Stabilization usually includes the three policies of devaluation, monetary austerity, and fiscal austerity. The other set of policies is described in the next footnote.

6. The second part of structural adjustment is a series of policies called Liberalization policies. This is a set of policies aimed at eliminating the types of interventions that the IMF believes is the underlying cause for payments imbalances and lack of growth in LDCs. This includes the elimination of

trade barriers, price and wage controls, and interventions aimed at fostering specific sectors of the economy. In addition, liberalization policies often include policies aimed at privatization of public sector enterprises and nationalized sectors of the economy.

7. The number of attempts to settle the dispute empirically is extraordinarily large, and spans at least three decades. See Agénor 1991; Branson 1986; Cooper 1971a; Díaz-Alejandro 1966; Donovan 1981, 1982; Doroodian 1993; Edwards 1986 and 1989b; Gylfason 1987; Gylfason and Schmid 1983; Gylfason and Risager 1984; Kamas 1992; Kamin 1988; Khan 1990b; Killick et al. 1992; Meller and Solimano 1987; Nunnenkamp and Schweickert 1990; Sheehey 1986; Solimano 1986. Agénor and Montiel (1996, pp. 248-255) provide a very comprehensive overview of the empirical literature on contractionary devaluation.

NOTES TO CHAPTER TWO

1. Resnick and Wolff (1987a) develop the concepts of structuralist and individualist ontologies for differentiating economic theories.

2. Burczak (1994) extends this distinction between essentialist and non-essentialist theories to Hayek.

3. There are non-Cartesian approaches to economy, and not all forms of individualism and structuralism are Cartesian: e.g. Locke's (1980) defense of private property in his *Second Treatise* is based on a non-Cartesian individualism. Within structuralism, Hegelianism can be viewed as non-Cartesian.

4. Since individualist ontologies reduce the social whole to underlying human being/human nature, they are often termed "humanist" (this is the sense in which Foucauldian scholarship critiques economics' humanism).

5. Smith himself did not use methodological individualism, but it is this reading of Smith that much of the economics profession has in mind when they refer to him.

6. There are many varieties of individualism e.g. moral individualism, as with Locke, where the order of social interaction and the morality of property are based on the universal human nature created by God, so that properties of agents are reflections of God's authority. While economics has retained the conceptions of the universal property rights bearing rational agent of liberal thought, it has eschewed the moral arguments of earlier liberal writings in favor of a scientific/Cartesian approach.

7. For examples of non-mainstream structuralist approaches within economics, see Amin 1974a, 1974b, 1976, 1977, 1978; Baran 1952; Cockcroft et al. 1972; dos Santos 1970; Emmanuel 1972; Frank 1969, 1970, 1972, 1978, 1979, 1981, 1984; Hopkins and Wallerstein 1980; Hopkins et al. 1982; Palma 1978; Shaikh 1979; Sweezy 1972; Wallerstein 1976, 1979, 1980, 1983, 1989. The structuralist approaches in mainstream macroeconomics will be explored in detail below.

8. Since linguistics is the area of analysis where the structuralist method was first deployed, key works of structuralist analysis are usually traced to this discipline: in addition to de Saussure's analysis of language, Chomsky's

analysis of grammar and Jakobson's analysis of sound phonemes are among the main contributions to the area. Outside linguistics, structuralism's influences are many, and range from Husserl's work on phenomenology and Hjelmslev in semiotics, to the literary criticism of Bakhtin. Structuralism can be found in a variety of fields, from mathematics and natural sciences to literature and the social sciences. Sturrock (1986) provides a synopsis of the works of key authors within the structuralist tradition; de George and de George (1972) and Lane (1970) collect writings within the tradition. Piaget (1971) presents a rigorous introduction to the structuralist approach.

9. The book was actually created by two of Saussure's colleagues, Bally and Sechehaye, drawing on student lecture notes.

10. The example of the meaning of color is often used to explain Saussure's framework. Here, I draw from Culler's (1986) exposition.

11. This example is drawn from Culler (1986, pp. 33-34).

12. One issue left unaddressed by Saussure, which becomes key for the poststructuralist tradition, is articulation: how individuals, who only experience parole or speech acts, which form a small subset of the total possibilities of a language system, come to know the system of rules governing Language. Saussure himself never discussed how articulation occurred. Some structuralists solve the problem of articulation by reducing structure to underlying human agents e.g. Chomsky (1975), who argues that words have meaning in terms of their location and relationship to the words that surround them in a sentence. Underlying the visible or surface structures of languages is a "deep structure," or underlying set of rules governing all language.

Chomsky's analysis, however, does not open itself to poststructuralist inquiry as does Saussure's, since Chomsky solves the problem of articulation—of how an individual learns the entirety of a language's rules, while being exposed to only a part of the whole language system through speech acts—by arguing that the capacity for language is "hard-wired" in the human brain. This form of analysis is also prevalent in Gestalt psychology.

13. An additional implication of Saussurean structuralism is that words, and therefore meaning and ideas, and hence perhaps even knowledge and truth, are always within language, never external to it. Thus what we know, what we think, and what we can conceive, may be determined by the language system, instead of being part of an externally sanctioned "truth." The application of structuralism to language, and hence to the very fabric of meaning, leads to a disintegration of any purely external notion of truth. The implications of this are picked up by the poststructuralist tradition, most importantly by Derrida.

14. Lévi-Strauss was exposed to linguistic structuralism through his contact with Jakobson, whose field was phonology. Jakobson's work on sound systems as a system of voiced and unvoiced differences in sounds not only informed Lévi-Straussian structuralism, but was also a reference point for Barthes (1974).

15. I diverge from Piaget's delineation of what is to be considered structuralist. Piaget is insistent that "true" structuralism must adopt the structuralist method in purely empiricist terms. He would exclude Husserl's influence via

phenomenology as idealist (based in the mind) and therefore not "true" structuralism. Further, Piaget locates many neoclassical theories, especially Walras, within the structuralist tradition. I differ, for reasons explained in this chapter.

16. Hegelianism, for example, as described by Cullenberg (1989) is a structural system that involves a temporal transformational law.

17. The IS-LM interpretation of Keynes' work is based on Hicks' (1937) paper "Mr. Keynes and the Classics." Since this paper is an attempt to cast Keynes' analysis in the standard equilibrium framework of Walrasian economics, the approach it gave rise to is also called the neoclassical-Keynesian synthesis.

18. One problem within the mainstream Keynesian tradition is the lack of a clear articulated structural rule governing Investment decisions. The partially disarticulated investor is the cause of Keynesian crises and fluctuations. If the investor were fully articulated, then, having once reached full employment via state policy, no further policy would be needed as the system would reproduce the new full-employment equilibrium.

    I think it is this moment of dis-articulation in the Keynesian framework that the Post Keynesians pursue (see Davidson 1972, 1982; Leijonhufvud 1966; Minsky 1982, 1986; and Vickers 1978, 1985, 1987 for just a few examples of the diverse Post Keynesian tradition). It is also, I think, this possibility of disarticulation in investment behavior that informs the work of the Austrian school (see Hayek 1944; see also Burczak 1994 on Hayek). Thus, in both these traditions the possibility of systemic disarticulation revolves around the uncertainty contained in one specific set of decisions: investment decisions. There is no corresponding disarticulation for other agent behaviors (consumption remains articulated, as does the work decision). However, even this carefully delimited moment of disarticulation is enough to cause a collapse into individualism, into contradiction, into systemic non-reproduction.

    In development economics there is no Post Keynesian or Austrian strain of open-ended crises due to disarticulated investment behavior. The idea of a disarticulated investor has been used only in very recent work—none of which has had much bearing on the CDD. In fact, in the CDD and development economics in general, the possibility of open-endedness or of sustained implosions and instability due to disarticulation is exorcised by the systematic insistence on equilibrium by all debaters. Disarticulation would make policy unpredictable and chaotic in its effects—something that development economics, given its origins as a field explicitly devoted to policy recommendations, cannot countenance.

19. Liquidity preference, like investment, is not well-specified or fully articulated, and forms a moment of collapse for structuralist IS-LM Keynesianism. This too is then re-specified as disarticulated and chaotic, and forms one of the moments where Post Keynesians diverge from IS-LM Keynesians. It is also a location for individualist critique: monetarists, in particular, re-specify the IS-LM Keynesian specifications of money demand along individualist lines, and strongly criticize the ill-specified IS-LM notion of liquidity preference (see Friedman 1953, 1959, 1963, 1968, 1969, 1971).

20. I am indebted to Steven Cullenberg for insights about how the Cartesian method operates as a way to describe/formalize ontological reductionism.
21. Saussure never used the word "structure," and instead used the word "system" throughout his work.
22. Since this text was written before Donald became Deirdre, I retain the use of 'he' as a reflection of both the time of McCloskey's writing and my own.
23. McCloskey himself does not view this in terms of the ontological fissure, but rather sees it as yet another way in which to see not only economics as a field, but the economy itself, as a means of communicative language. He argues that the price system should be understood as a mechanism of communication. McCloskey implies that the market should be seen in the liberal sense of a marketplace of ideas, or as a free exchange of information.
24. This point is taken up by materialist/Marxist analysts of the formation of social subjects. Here, the signified is not prior to the signifier. Thus, the concept or meaning signified does not take precedence over the process of "naming," or the creation of a signifier. The signifier could by the process of naming and association, create the concept being signified. This implies that human subjectivity is material, in that it is materially created by the very words and signs that then create the available concepts or signifieds by which the subject sees the world. See for example Coward and Ellis (1977).
25. The Saussurean system has a richness and additional level of play that is absent in the Walrasian vision. In the Saussurean system, the communicative sign consists of two elements: the signifier, or verbal/symbolic sound or icon, which is the material manifestation of the sign, and the signified, or the concept/idea that the signifier indicates. The word/sign always consists of both these parts, and they are simultaneous: one does not appear independent of the other. These two aspects are linked dialectically, so that it is not just the signified, or "underlying" concept that shapes the expression/sound/signifier. Instead, signifiers themselves refer to other signifiers, and so one has the postulate that the signifier can shape signifieds: the material expression can craft the conceptual frame. This leads one to see that it is not simply the agents who by prior concepts then create signifiers to form language. The signifiers themselves shape the conceptual frame, and so can interactively create the conceptual world of the agent: language can shape the mind.

    This insight was key to the subsequent Marxist engagement with structuralism, since it opens the door for a materialist understanding of the creation of agency via language. As Coward and Ellis (1977, p.3) note, structural linguistics insisted on analyzing the relationship between the means of expression and the concept as one of simultaneity. Thus, they say, "This separation [between signifiers and signifieds], glimpsed by Saussure, made possible a study of the relations entered into by the signifiers themselves in the production of meaning. This analysis of the proper relations of the signifier led to the conclusion that 'no meaning is sustained by anything other than reference to other meaning' (Lacan, *Ecrits*, p. 498)." They go on to discuss how this insight shatters the humanist essences of idealism, and shows how the humanist subject is created via the material acts of language, an insight key to any Marxist theory of subjectivity.

26.   Disarticulation refers to the possibility that the structure may not be "articulated." That is, for a structure to be self-regulating and self-reproducing, there must be some means by which the agent/speaker learns and internalizes the underlying rules that govern the structure. The agent, after all, does not come to encounter each and every possible act that can emerge within the structure. She encounters but a small subset of the whole in her acquisition of language, and in her interactions within the structure. Unless the agent is "preformed," fully knowing the structure, what enables the agent to know the whole? Secondly, if the agent does not know the whole, what then coordinates the actions of different agents so that the outcome is the self-reproducing whole, instead of a disintegrating and chaotic whole? This is a problem for structuralism and the point where it often dissolves into individualism.

27.   The mathematical expression of this structural law is to be found in "Walras' Law": that the excess demands in all markets will sum to zero when the system is "out of equilibrium." Walras' law makes no sense if we are in a world with only one person/atom, since there is no such thing as excess demand in such a world. Excess demand only arises when there is more than one person: it is an expression of the need for coordination between agents-that is, it is a relational, and not an individual concept. For the law to work, not only must the excess demands reflect the underlying agent (the individualist reduction), the price system must operate in a fashion that coordinates all these individual desires (the structuralist collapse). The "auctioneer" provides the coordination needed for structural coherence.

Some committed individualist neoclassical theorists recognize this moment of collapse e.g. Hahn 1987, pp. 136-138. See Amariglio, Resnick and Wolff, 1990, for a detailed discussion of how the contradictory desires for full articulation and microrational universalist individualism shape the discursive terrain of economics.

Most economists working within the individualist tradition are supremely unconscious of the problems Hahn recognizes: they often will simply posit: by Walras' law, we know that the excess demands sum to zero, and so can drop one equation from the system. This dropping of one equation from an overdetermined (in the mathematical sense) system is the equivalent of positing closure and articulation by invoking a structural rule.

28.   This vision of the state is changing, with the "New Political Economy" of Buchanan, and the Rent-Seeking literature associated with Bhagwati and Krueger, where the state's activities are seen simply as the outcome of rational pre-specified actors in the Government (see Bhagwati 1991; Buchanan 1986; Buchanan, Tollison and Tullock 1980; Krueger 1974, 1993; Krueger ed. 1996; Krueger and Jones 1990).

29.   Orthodox theorists may be willing to discuss the possibility of dynamic disequilibrium, or to postulate, via game theoretic formulations, alternative mechanisms that do not lead to social harmony. But the rational agent who is specified and prior to social interaction is non-negotiable.

30.   It might be argued that the properties of the agents themselves, such as desire, ownership, and so on, are structural laws that govern agent behavior. This formulation is not useful, since then any positing of agents at all, or any

attempt to describe parts, is automatically structuralist. The distinction between individualism/atomism and structuralism would lose all meaning.

Structural laws, properly speaking, is a term that is usefully reserved for laws which are applicable to the whole, which are themselves structuring of the parts, and which are not seen as innate and intrinsic characteristics of any one part, but meaningful only in the context of the whole.

Desire/utility, reason/ knowledge and rationality/maximization which describe the underlying agent are on the other hand understood as innate, and not dependent on the social whole. The agent is unchanged whether participating within the structure or not. Thus the Walrasian framework is individualist. The auctioneer, however, is appropriately seen as a structural law, since it is not the innate property of any one individual, and makes sense only in the context of the social whole.

31. I am not referring to individual behavior in the sense that structuralists describe/analyze individuals. Structuralists do analyze human behavior, by defining the structures in which agents are enmeshed. I refe here specifically to the type of collapse into individualism that I identified above: a collapse that requires structuralists to rely on the innate, pre-structural characteristics of human agents to close their models of the whole.

32. This historical constraint is especially found in development economics. A historical explanation of the origins of the structures leading to LDC underdevelopment would have to look explicitly for the roots of underdevelopment in the colonial history of LDC economies or at the history of class conflict in the developing world. But development in the mainstream of the profession has tended to avoided that: development and modernization were ways to resolve the problem of the decolonized world without addressing the ethical debts of colonial history (see Escobar 1995).

33. The Hegelian totality described by Cullenberg (1989) is a form of structuralism that posits just such a rule: a "metastructure" of change, which is the telos of history, and which governs, in fact, impels the structure to change in predetermined directions.

34. This implicit "conjuring up" of their opposite by each ontology to shore up their argument can be viewed as an example of Althusser's (1971, 1979) notion of the "effectivity" or presence of that which is "absent" in a theory. Here, each ontology depends on that which is absent in its theory for its very postulates and its efforts to promote closure, even as any recognition of this "absent presence" undermines the theory.

35. For IS-LM, unemployment in equilibrium does not mean that system is unclosed. The system is closed and will reproduce itself. There is no particular reason for the closed system in its self-regulating state to produce full employment. In fact, this is only a requirement if you define self-regulation as a state of full employment, and believe that persistent unemployment is unsustainable.

36. The Cartesian totality was developed by Cullenberg in his discussion of the debate on the tendency for the rate of profit to fall in Marxian economics, and contrasted with the Hegelian totality. The Hegelian totality starts, not with the priorly specified individuals, or the regularities or structures comprising the whole, but the laws of motion governing the movement of

the totality. These underlying laws of motion drive the changes in the totality, and specify the direction and motives which guide such changes. Thus while they are, in some sense, structural laws, they differ markedly in their nature from the type of synchronic structuralism described here.

37. The Cartesian mode of analysis also shows up in the pedagogy of economics. The 2x2 economy of the individualist story is built up by starting with two individuals in a barter economy, the simplest form of interaction, and then extended, without any change in the logic, to more inputs, more goods, and more individuals. The structuralist story too starts with the "first piece" of its social totality: the goods market. Having specified the operation of the Keynesian demand model in the goods market, one then extends the model without in any way having to change the rules discovered as governing consumption behavior, to add the rules governing the money market. In each case, Cartesianism allows a move from the simple in which adding new parts leaves previous parts unchanged. This standardized method of teaching may have much to do with the insistence on a Cartesian language by most economists, and their sense of bewilderment, or presumption of a 'lack of rigor' when confronted with non-Cartesian logic in analysis.

38. I use the terms "entry point" and "logic of analysis" in the sense described by Resnick and Wolff (1987b).

NOTES TO CHAPTER THREE

1. This paradigm shift occurred in a larger context. Toye (1987) and Hirschman (1981, 1986) are good places to see how structuralists view the shift. Arndt (1987) discusses it from the perspective of the individualists. Ruccio (1991) and Escobar (1995) provide analyses from perspectives that take ontological issues seriously.

2. Often, this second school of thought is referred to as EPI (Export Promoting Industrialization), but this characterization is inexact for a number of reasons, especially if it is meant to point to the East Asian economies (Amsden 1989; Amsden et al. 1992; Taylor and Shapiro 1992).

3. There remain areas of debate within both theoretical paradigms. Individualists dispute questions such as the sequence of liberalization policies, while structuralists may disagree over whether the foreign exchange constraint or savings constraint is binding.

4. Textbooks and readers help to identify the contours of a field, since they self-consciously seek to present the field to students/practitioners. Meier and Baldwin's text became Meier's text over time, and had long been the standard text in economic development, with Todaro's text replacing Meier's as the profession's standard text in the past 20 years or so. Okun and Richardson were respected practitioners in the field, and their reader covered all the key areas and readings that constituted the field. In the discussion that follows, I will be using these two texts as the "frame," but will draw on general readings in the field as appropriate for each area discussed.

5. This mode of thought remains central to the task of development economics. Hirschman notes in his ruminations on the early development of the field:

> Nor does it come to me as a disappointment that I must give up the pretense of having discovered the distinguishing characteristic of underdeveloped societies . . . (In order not to be misunderstood I must emphasize that I do not renounce my basic idea . . . but only the claim that with it I had hit upon the distinguishing characteristic of a certain group of economically less developed countries.) (Hirschman 1992, p. 14)

Early pioneers in the field may have given up their claim to have located the source of difference, but difference remains the central concern of development economics today.

6. The conception of primitive accumulation that Marx deploys is rich and historically specific (Marx 1977, *Capital Vol.* I). The description I give here is based on the specific variant of Marx's thought picked up by the mainstream development tradition, and is not meant to represent the full richness of Marxian writings on development.

7. I am explicitly focusing on the variant of classical thought—particularly Marxist thought—that was picked up by mainstream development economists in fabricating their vision of import substituting industrialization.

8. It is at this specific point that the "break" between Marx's own writings on the link between colonialism and capitalism, and the mainstream rendition of Marxian thought is to be found. Marx's own writings on the question of colonialism were extensive. He explicitly links the process of primitive accumulation in the West with the processes of colonization (see Marx 1977, *Capital Volume* I, especially the chapters on primitive accumulation). Further, it is indeed the case that Marx's writings on the impact of colonialism on the colonized had important modernist limits (in particular, his conception of the Asiatic Mode of Production and his understanding of pre-colonial oriental societies as static, and the teleological vision of history found in the Younger Marx), leading him to have a progressivist comprehension of colonialism's impact on the non-West. But while Marx may have seen the emergence of capitalism as a possible source for change and dynamism, this by no means implies that he was unaware of the brutalities, the hypocrisies, and peculiar social dynamics between colonizer and colonized (see Marx 1969).

9. If colonial encounters lay at the heart of the transition to capitalism, then this would also raise the issue of culture and development very differently—an issue that, while not discussed in this book, became part of the vision of the development project. The question of culture loomed large in the initial writings on development. While in today's parlance this has been rephrased as "human capital development" and given a more nuanced and carefully circumscribed meaning of education and skills, in the earlier books and writings it was quite explicitly referred to as "socio-cultural development of values" (both Meier-Baldwin and Okun-Richardson devote considerable space to the question of norms and values and socio-cultural barriers to development). The texts are rife with references to the lack of proper attitudes in the non-West as a retardant to development, and the need for a transformation of subjectivity to take place, so that non-Western subjects start to more closely reflect their western counterparts.

Of course, if the self-constitution of the Western subject emerged as part of the colonial encounter, then this complicates the issue of recreating the native in one's own image. As postcolonial scholars have argued, the conception of universal human qualities within the West emerged at least partly in reference to conceptions of the difference between those in the group which possessed such qualities (white/western) and those outside it (not-white/not-western). If one crafts a notion of the clear difference between oneself and the non-West, then all who are within this conception of self are rethought as equal in some abstract way, but this rests on marking all others as lesser. Similarly, if one's notion of the superiority of one's culture is buttressed by the notion of the inferiority of others, then this act would itself create an ideology, an ethic. We know we understand the value of labor, and are hard working. We know that we are thus because we know that the "native" is not hardworking, is not imbued with a strong work ethic.

10. Equally instructive is the "Introduction" to Singer's book by Paul Hoffman, then Managing Director of the United Nations Special Fund:

    Mankind today is facing its greatest challenge since the dawn of civilization. Two hundred years ago, through a combination of fortuitous circumstances, one nation got on the road to self-sustaining growth, opening up hitherto undreamed-of possibilities of material prosperity—the Industrial Revolution came to England. Within the next century, many other nations followed her example and embarked on the road to industrialization; but large parts of the world remained unaffected. The mid-twentieth century found three-quarters of the world's population living in the conditions of stagnation and poverty which had characterized the lives of their ancestors, while the other quarter lived in an environment of affluence and steady material progress.

    One has the impression that the "fortuitous circumstances" were all benign and had no relationship to the conditions of the three-quarters of the world living in poverty, and that the poverty found in the LDCs was simply something about their failure to follow England's example. The images here reflect the approach to development coming from the classicals that I describe above—development as internally driven, and LDCs' poverty as a result of purely internal factors.

11. Meier and Baldwin are interesting in that they do include (unlike any of the other readings) a substantial discussion of colonialism. This is primarily a detailed discussion of how the industrial revolution actually developed, and why there emerged a Britain-centered world, but despite the level of detail devoted to some aspects of the industrial revolution, class, colonialism, and their effects on colonized economies are all but absent in the *analysis* of development.

12. Note that they use the word "Center" here not in the sense of a dynamic and dualist relationship between center and periphery as developed in dependency theory, but in the sense of whose economy became globally central, and who failed to replicate that but stayed peripheral. This is not about the fabrication of the periphery, but simply uses the term to denote the failure to become central. This is an early version of the "Center-Periphery" distinction, deployed descriptively by Prebisch. Only later does this concept take

on the ideas of a dynamic dualism, and a relationship between the location of the Center and the impoverishment of the Periphery, as developed by Sunkel, Furtado, Frank, and others.

13. Singer (1964) describes the sense of dismay created by the theories of Linear Stages of growth and Balanced growth. On Rostow's theory, he notes:

Yet another reflection, and perhaps also cause, of this change in thought [from pessimism about DC growth prospects to optimism about unlimited DC growth] was the notion of the "take-off into self-sustained growth," most popular in the form put forward by Walt Rostow in his *Stages of Economic Growth* . . . Now let us look at the other side of the coin, namely the change-over . . . [to pessimism about LDC growth prospects] . . . This is particularly clear if we look at the take-off theory proposed by Rostow. According to this theory, the underdeveloped countries stand at the beginning of the runway or are not even on it yet, and a terrific concentrated effort will be required to take them down the runway in exactly the right combination of circumstances and at very high speed so that they may become airborne. More directly, according to Professor Rostow, an underdeveloped country must first create a number of diverse preconditions which include changes in institutions and attitudes, the provision of social and economic overhead capital, raising of agricultural productivity and solution of land-tenure problems, etc. Even the successful solution of these problems will only place the underdeveloped country on the runway; then before takeoff is achieved, it is necessary for an underdeveloped country to increase its rate of net investment roughly from 5 to 10 percent within a comparatively short time, to develop a leading manufacturing sector strategically placed so as to have strong linkage effects on the whole economic system, and simultaneously to create the capacity to transfer this impetus to other leading sectors as soon as the first leading sector begins to slacken. It will be seen that these are very formidable requirements indeed. In fact, one begins to wonder how any country has managed to achieve takeoff. (Singer 1964, pp. 9-10)

14. Singer (1964) reflects on this as follows (p. 8): "On a more purely theoretical plane, the [developed country growth prospects as optimistic] idea of self-sustaining growth was impressed by the growth models of the Harrod-Domar type." He follows this on page 9 with his reflections on Rostow's notion of a take-off into self-sustained growth and the optimism about DC growth prospects it reflected (excerpted in note 13 above). And he goes on to note (p. 9-10): "Now, let us look at the other side of the coin, namely the change-over [to pessimism about LDC growth prospects]. *In some ways this follows directly from the change from pessimism to optimism in views concerning the more developed countries.* This is particularly clear if we look at the take-off theory proposed by Rostow . . . (emphasis added)." And further on page 10: "Similarly, a pessimistic trend of thought concerning the underdeveloped countries can be deduced from the Harrod-Domar model. Given the right kind of parameters—particularly a high rate of pop-

ulation growth—lo and behold! The Harrod-Domar model is converted from a description of cumulative self-sustaining growth into a description of cumulative self-sustaining stagnation." Thus, the stories about optimistic growth prospects for DCs are based on ideas about the existence of practices and institutions and subjects who, freed from the structures of tradition, have unleashed self-sustaining growth. These same stories become a source for pessimism about LDCs, since the very definition of the LDCs' deviation from DCs and the causes for its poverty are the failure of LDCs to put in place these behaviors, freedoms, institutions, that can create self-sustaining growth.

15. Singer (1964) calls this the shift to U-optimism (his term for optimism about LDC growth prospects, which he shares).

16. Population and norms and values remain central concerns, but seem to have left development economics relatively serene. Population control still remains a key area of intervention, and neither the New Structuralists nor the NLs seem to have much disagreement on its necessity. Norms and values, which seem to have been accorded much space in the earlier literature, more or less disappeared from the field, and seem to have been reformulated into education and human capital development, rather than using the language of "attitudes" and "cultural backwardness." In the late 1980s and early 1990s, however, one sees a renewed interest in the question of "norms" and "attitudes," especially in discussions of the role of cultural attitudes towards authority, discipline, thrift, and "entrepreneurial culture" in generating economic success (see Billig 1994). It is in the third area—growth and industrialization—that the fights and polarities in the field have made their appearance.

17. Hla Myint (1958) is also included among scholars who draw, in particular, on the 'vent for surplus'—or 'staples'—theory of the relationship between trade and development. But unlike the neoclassical users of the vent for surplus argument such as Caves, Myint did not argue that by operating as a vent for surplus, trade would necessarily lead to development. Rather, Myint noted that Adam Smith's (1955) original argument that trade could act as a vent for surplus—that is, provide a market outlet for nations with unutilized or 'surplus' resources—provided a simple and compelling explanation of the relationship between trade and development for the early history of the relationship between trade and development in low-population high-land-base LDCs. Further, he distinguished between different types of vent for surplus, some of which could lead to development through utilization of unutilized resources, but others of which could lead to either dependent development and growth, or else simply dependent growth. See Neill (2004) and Kibritçioglu (2004) for further discussion of the vent for surplus theories.

18. This earlier vision of a role for the state in promoting development, though in a pro-trade manner, explains Bauer's appearance in the list of articles on Linear Stages and Balanced growth in the Okun-Richardson reader. Bauer later became one of the most famous proponents of neoliberalism, following the victory of the pro-ISI perspective. He had been in favor of state-led

development, but only in a manner that conformed with free trade. His article (with Yamey) in the Okun-Richardson reader is a dissent on the focus on industrialization as a key to development, though he agrees strongly that growth is the key. His 1957 *The Economics of Underdeveloped Countries* (also with Yamey) spells his vision of a state which promoted development by eliminating old institutions, undertaking agrarian reform, promoting entrepreneurship, and facing up to those who resist change and forcing growth by creating compulsory savings in the face of resistance. Definitely an active state, just one active in different arenas than those which form the ISI vision! The early vision of development with an active state promoting the development agenda of growth, as we will see, resurfaces in the neoliberal vision, for all that the Neoliberal theory and ideology maintains that it is about "dismantling the state."

19. Two additional views, one put forward by Myrdal (that the playing field was not even, and that primary-product exporting LDCs faced instability in their revenues), and by List (the infant industry argument for protection) were also important, and are accorded much space by Arndt (1987) in his historical examination of the field of economic development. But while they may have played a role in the debates, I find that the most ubiquitous references of that time are to Prebisch-Singer.

20. As I argue in the next section, the NL individualist ontology actually does end up advocating a strong role for the state. But while the policies they end up with depend on the state, this emerges because of a moment of collapse into structuralism as their theories try to formulate a coherent vision of change. But the theoretical apparatus deployed is basically the Walrasian vision described in chapter 2, with very little room for a discussion of change or a role for the state within the ontology and theory as set up.

21. As noted in chapter 2, structuralists have usually had a very difficult time handling the concept of the investor. While Post Keynesian theorists of today have used this moment of breakdown to suggest radical instability and to eschew the self-reproducing, self-regulated, fully articulated structuralism of equilibrium theory, mainstream economics has clung to equilibrium in the Neoclassical-Keynesian synthesis. The same types of difficulties found within the mainstream Keynesian tradition in its efforts to formulate closure emerge in the ISI vision when assessing investment decisions.

22. In the individualist re-reading of the Harrod-Domar model, this specific assumption reflects underlying fixed input proportions in the production isoquants with constant returns to scale. This implicit assumption about fixed isoquants prevents the capital-labor ratio, and hence the capital-output ratio, from changing. Solow's reformulation of the Harrod-Domar model to conform with the neoclassical paradigm works by changing this structural law about the nature of technology, and reformulating the fixed isoquants along more standard neoclassical lines (see Solow 1956, 1970).

23. Solow's (1956) revision of the Harrod-Domar model operates by carefully identifying the fixed capital-output ratio as an implicit assumption about the fixed marginal productivity of capital. Hence, the model must have, from a neoclassical perspective, been using production functions with fixed

isoquants and constant returns to scale. Solow reformulated this model to make it more "general"—that is, he replaced the fixed "k" with a variable "k" which reflected the underlying assumptions of neoclassical production functions—with flexible capital-labor ratios and constant returns to scale, the capital output ratio varies as the capital-labor proportions vary. In particular, the reformulated "k" reflected the declining marginal productivity of capital with flexible input proportions. This implied that "k" would change as the capital-labor ratio changed in response to changing market prices. Thus Solow's revision avoided the Harrod-Domar knife-edge, by replacing the fixed isoquants of the Harrod-Domar model with neoclassical marginal assumptions about changes in input ratios.

24. Note that in the original formulation of the Harrod-Domar growth model, the issue at stake was the link between growth and employment. Thus, the problem of a possible mismatch between S and I, and the consequent explosion of the model led to the Harrod-Domar "knife-edge." But the knife-edge aspect did not enter into much of the development debates, since presumably, these were not really demand-constrained economies, but were rather marked by low growth because of supply side factors. Investment would not be lacking once the state stepped in, at issue was why the S was not forthcoming. Further, Solow's revision of the Harrod-Domar model (described above), implied that as investment responded to market forces, the capital-labor ratio, and hence "k," would change and hence the knife edge would be avoided.

25. Infrastructure and technological change were investments and so needed to be financed—changing k in the long run itself needed higher levels of savings.

26. Fei and Ranis (1964) developed the original Lewis model to examine some questions about the terms of trade between agriculture and industry, and the impact of population growth on the industrialization process, which the original model had left unanswered.

27. Lewis' use of marginal analysis in his MPLA = 0 has been read by some (like Findlay 1973), as marking him as a marginalist-individualist in his analysis. However, unless one is ready to specify some rather bizarre innate traits in the preferences of LDC agriculturists, while one may derive a non-market clearing wage within individualist analysis (so that the fixed wage is not a constant institutional wage, or even fixed, but merely an unemployment equilibrium wage), it is nearly impossible to also produce MPLA = 0. Open unemployment can be theorized. The type of hidden unemployment that the various Lewis models also seem to refer to, however, can only be found by looking at structural relationships. It is thus not surprising, I think, that instead of going after the constant wage assumption, many of the key critics of the surplus-labor model (like Schultz 1964) went after the assumption that MPLA = 0. It is this assumption that really breaks down the individualist ontology.

28. There were sociological and cultural studies like Myrdal (1968), but the kinds of issues he addressed have been usually confined to essays, while the hard business of economic modeling concentrates on the fixed subjects of equilibrium analysis.

29. Lewis does not ask what will happen to agricultural wages once all the surplus labor is absorbed by industry. In the Fei and Ranis model, at this point agricultural subjects (suddenly) break free of tradition and exhibit microrational behavior, and start equating wages to marginal productivity.

30. There is an additional question that the Lewis Labor-Surplus model tries to address. As agriculture sends surplus labor to industry in this model, total agrarian output has not changed (since MPLA = 0). But industrialization requires that agriculture not only provide labor to industry, but that it also generate a food surplus, to finance industrialization and feed the urban work-force. Without a growing food-supply, the process can come to a halt. While wages here are tied to the subsistence level and hence do not rise enough to shut off capitalist profits, the problem of rising food production is not adequately answered by Lewis. On pp. 300-301 Lewis addresses the question of necessary increases in food production by arguing that agricultural productivity may be rising. But, how that assumption is to be squared with his earlier assumption that MPLA = 0, he does not tell us. Instead, he argues that historically, it has been state action which prevents agriculturalists from enjoying the higher standards of living implied by the decreased surplus labor, and which has, via taxes and rents, transferred this surplus to industry—income distribution, rather than a rise in total agrarian output, gives us the necessary surplus. The Fei-Ranis (1964) model of labor surplus (pp. 21-23, and Ch. 6) argues that since the agricultural wage is set = APLA, the result of reduced agrarian labor is an increase in agricultural incomes (same output, fewer people). This increase results in savings passed on to the industrial sector, and hence agrarian surpluses which finance industrialization are ensured.

31. This is the key theory within mainstream development that explicitly looked to the history of colonialism to examine the constraints facing LDCs. In addition, some of the original formulators of this position provided a strong role for the internal dynamics of class struggle in formulating their theories. Danby (1992, 2005) examines the class-based theories of Noyola, and Noyola's role in developing the arguments of the earlier Latin American Structuralist Economics (drawing on Kalecki's work).

32. Here, if the third world is marked by poverty, this can be explained by way of the specific tastes for children, leisure, and risk-aversion that mark the decisions of LDC maximizers. This is "poverty" only in the sense of a chosen state—a preference for a lower standard of living with more leisure, lower risks, and more children. Tastes do not provide a rationale for state intervention. The other possible reason is lower levels of resources, and even here, there is no role for policy—left to itself, the economy will slowly accumulate efficient resources and grow. The state itself can do nothing about smaller resource levels, and whatever interventions the state can undertake to improve resource levels, the markets do that and do it better.

33. Arrow-Debreu, Samuelson, Solow, Bhagwati, the early formulations of micro-founded macroeconomics by Friedman, Muth, Lucas and Sargent—all of these theorists were actively creating their theories and defining the shape of neoclassical theory in this period.

34. In the case of the microfoundations of macroeconomics, there was clearly a political agenda for some of the theorists, working to scuttle the Keynesian welfare state. But while this was an important current, it does not, I think, capture the ontological shift—many of those working to define neoclassical science were not working on political battlefields, but on intellectual ones.

35. See Ruccio (1991) for a discussion of some of the other forces that shaped this intellectual battlefield.

36. Like the structuralist ISI theory it opposed, Neoliberalism borrowed heavily from and depended on theories which had been crafted to explain and analyze the West.

37. The term seems to coincide with the IMF's vigorous pursuit of the neoliberal agenda across the globe in the wake of the debt crisis, though as Foxley (1983) notes, neoliberal policy pre-dates the crisis itself.

38. World Bank (1993) and Cardoso and Helwege (1992) also provide a coherent vision of neoliberalism as a field.

39. The progress that the WDR points to is health, education, and growth in average incomes. The greatest excitement is reserved for the growth in average incomes, "a rate of progress that is unprecedented by historical standards." (WDR, p. 1)

40. The East Asian Miracle and the Japan success story have been added to the list of late. While Japan has definitely achieved "sameness," though of a very uneasy type if the questions about the "Japanese style of business" are any indication, East Asia hangs in the balance.

41. Here we find references to the "so-called two gap model" of Chenery, the "bias against exports" promoted by Prebisch and Singer, special attention is given to the influence of the Soviet model and the Keynesian revolution in creating notions of the "brightest and the best" and the state as the "commanding heights" of the economy (the words are put in quotes in the original text of the WDR). The tone is a combination of hostile astonishment and bemused condescension over past ignorance.

42. Note that this is difference in outcome (for example, difference in products produced due to specialization), but not difference in subjectivity.

43. Viner is pessimistic about the possibility of state-led development, but he is equally pessimistic of any quick solution to the question of poverty. In the early 1950s, he is the free-market equivalent of the pessimism of the early growth theorists. Bauer in his early writings did not have the tone of ringing optimism one finds in the NL vision today. He heaps scorn on the dirigiste ISI theorists, but does not claim that the LDCs will grow at fast rates under the free-market. Like Viner, his main conclusion then was that there is no quick solution, and that the free market will provide the best outcome. If the outcome is slow and it looks like development will take a century or more, then we have to accept that as the best that can be done.

    The current NL vision, however, is one of unbridled optimism. Not only will the market succeed, the market will succeed quickly. This vision has emerged because of the high growth rates of the East Asian NICs. If the NICs had not come on the scene at the same time that the debt crisis hurt the countries practicing ISI, the NL vision would not have succeeded in capturing the development agenda so completely.

44. In the context of the cold war, Bauer and Yamey are providing an unabashed conflation of markets and democracy, with freedom being defined primarily as the Lockean notion of freedom to own and dispose property in civil society. The success of the NICs has seen the sudden elimination of the idea of democracy from this definition, with the focus carefully restricted not to larger choices and options (which may lead towards Amartya Sen's notion of entitlements and basic human needs) but to economic growth. The NICs were not famous for their democratically decentralized economic and social institutions. However, as the NICs in more recent years have been very slowly flirting with political reform, we see the re-emergence of this peculiar conflation between markets and freedom.

45. They argue that the state should have an effective monopoly on violence, and should use this according to well-defined rules. They do not explain the rules; however, they provide an example: They decry how in some developing countries the state cannot safeguard property or lives. Property is clear, but what of lives? It turns out they don't mean lives lost to poverty or malnutrition or terrible conditions of labor, or environmental degradation and other such free choices. They are upset that in Lagos, in 1950, the government was unable to prevent physical maltreatment of people who wanted to work during a partial strike. Thus, the rule to be used by the state in deploying violence is one of safeguarding private property along Lockean lines.

46. This insight is then developed by Bhagwati and Srinivasan (1969) in their "theory of the second best." In all cases, if one does have to intervene in the economy, a policy of direct intervention at the point of resources or incomes is preferable to any policy that intervenes at the level of relative prices.

47. There are elements of Bauer's vision that come very close to Nietzsche. Those who win, do so because they are strong, entrepreneurial, hard working, innovative, and capable of being motivated to ruthlessly reach their ends. Trapped in a slave mentality and obsessed with colonialism, the LDC is responsible for its own condition.

48. Their discussion is disingenuous: On p. 180, they say: "All economic change creates advantageous opportunities for those who are adaptable or enterprising, and the possibility of loss, either absolutely or relatively . . . for those who are not successful in reshaping their activities to suit a changing environment." They propose liberal measures to cushion the effect of change, and political and economic education. Presumably the resistance to change coming from those who lose communal property rights is a "law and order" issue, since it is not discussed. But one can see why the later NLs seem to feel that perhaps, a "strong state" may not be a bad idea in overcoming "resistance to change."

49. When the Cantabrigian economists did present Latin American work, they chose to present the relatively conservative writings of such figures as Sunkel (1958). They acknowledged the importance of Noyola as the original source for the Structuralist arguments, but they never translated Noyola, whose works remain unknown to most of the Anglo-Saxon world to this day. By

the early 1960s, Seers' Cantabrigian imperfect competition had completely taken over Structuralism. In the 1963 conference that brought together Anglo-Saxon and Latin American participants of the Structuralist-monetarist debates (Baer and Kerstenetsky eds. 1964), Arthur Lewis jokes that "whenever I try to characterize the views of a typical Latin American, that typical Latin American turns out to be Mr. Dudley Seers."

50. The Neoliberals of the 1980s took the argument a little further than the monetarists of the 1960s, however, and took it upon themselves to discover the roots of this Structuralist perspective. Because of the role that Cantabrigian economists had played in re-interpreting Structuralism via their own theories, Little (1982) located the roots of the theoretical arguments of Structuralists in Cambridge, particularly in the post-WWII planning debates in Britain.

51. Just as the Latin American Structuralists were reduced to Cartesian Cantabrigian economics, Seers and other Anglo-Saxon champions of the Structuralists mapped "Chicago school microfounded monetarism" onto the Latin American monetarists. Seers (1962a and 1962b) especially uses his writings to heap scorn on "monetarists," though the monetarists he repeatedly refers to and sneers at are not the Latin American writers like Campos, but the Hayek-Friedman tradition found in Chicago.

52. There were, of course, other alternative structures ready to be identified and dismantled: class structures, structures that allowed capital flight, first-world-third-world relationships, the development and maintenance of a fat-cat entrepreneurial, bureaucratic and developmentalist NGO sector that required vast amounts of borrowing to uphold its existence and finance its spending needs, all of these could easily have been identified as the source of the failure of development.

53. Examining the path that the NICs took entailed, just as with the previous story of western development, an examination of how they developed via primarily internal resource mobilization. Of course, for Japan earlier, the source for resources had been the US, followed by a strong Japanese State. For most of the NICs, the source for resources had also not been primarily internal—almost all the NICs were net debtors to the rest of the world in the 60s and early 70s. But this would be conveniently recast as "Direct Foreign Investment" in the new story. Further, the NICs were nice, because they finally laid the ghost of colonialism to rest, and proved Bauer's point that if the LDCs just gave up their "DC envy" and fixation on colonial history and got on with their lives, then perhaps they would get somewhere.

54. Note that the focus on "human capital investment" and education, and on population, are reformulations of the original "values and norms" and "population" planks of ISI.

55. Though the "investing in people" section makes much of income security and "safety nets," the WDR is clear that all such policies of income security, nutritional and health security, must be financed through taxation, must be cheap, and must primarily be about using minimal resources for maximum effect via NGOs and other organizations that effectively replace the state as the primary providers of such social security.

56. The WDR does accept a role for industrial regulation in the area of health standards, environmental protection, worker safety, and elimination of monopoly practices. However, it gives no examples at all of such regulation, and concentrates on "bad" regulation.

57. Though poverty would—note the careful distinction made between poverty and underdevelopment by Viner. Poverty alone is not a sign of underdevelopment if the poverty takes place at an "efficient" level of production. What marks underdevelopment is the existence of a potential rise in standards of living which has not been taken advantage of.

58. Here too, the NLs must be implicitly calling on structure. If individuals have perfect information, and their time-preference is to be the key indicator of "correct market prices," then presumably the resisting individuals have undertaken the appropriate marginal discounting and efficiently decided that bread today is better than jam tomorrow. Why then call on the State? Why not abide by the clearly signaled rate of time-preference? On the issue of mass resistance, NLs adopt the tone taken by the ISI theorists—the natives for some reason, despite their marginal individualist preformed rationality in every other sphere of life, fail to act rationally here.

NOTES TO CHAPTER FOUR

1. Equilibrium prices emerge when all structural rules governing agent behavior are met for structuralists, and when full market coordination ensures that individualist decisions mesh for individualists.

2. Converting an accounting balance into a theory of equilibrium involves positing that the balance attained is one of systemic closure, and is part of a self-reproducing and self-regulating state. This requires assumptions about the behavioral characteristics governing agent decisions for the different variables in the account, and identifying which variables adjust to bring balance in the system.

3. This accounting identity and examples of balancing the accounts is adapted from Kindleberger (1987). Dornbusch (1980, Part 1) provides both a basic introduction to the BOP, and describes the relationship of the BOP Account to the National Income Accounts of an open economy.

4. Since capital exports use revenues, they are subtracted in the identity; capital imports generate revenues, and bear an implicit negative sign, so that they would be added as a source of foreign exchange.

5. Again, note that since an increase in official reserves is a use of foreign exchange, it is subtracted. Net decreases in reserves have an implicit negative sign, and so would be added as a source of foreign exchange.

6. This is Nurkse's "Basic Balance," described in Kindleberger (1987).

7. Kindleberger (1965b).

8. It was this mechanism of specie-flow and the quantity theory of money that Ricardo used in his statement of the original theory of comparative advantage. Shaikh (1979) shows that in order to generate Ricardo's theory of comparative advantage, one needs both Ricardo's model of comparative costs and his analysis of the specie-flow mechanism. Neoclassical "Ricardian"

comparative advantage lacks Ricardo's theory of monetary flows and price levels. As I show in the section discussing the Monetarist and Rational Expectations approaches, supply adjustment mechanisms and theories of financial flows and price and output determination replace Ricardo's gold-specie flow mechanism in today's individualist approaches to the BOP.

9. Triffin (1964) takes issue with the textbook description of the Gold Standard. He argues that historically, the rules of the game were not followed by central banks. Instead, adjustment came from deteriorations in the terms of trade and exchange rates of colonies.

10. Since the implicit presumption here is of "money as a veil," the closest one can come to specifying a demand for money within this model is transactions demand. However, since transactions demand here does not affect any real variables, but only affects the price levels, I assume that the demand for money balances must be described by the classical quantity theory.

11. The "correct exchange rate" in this story is definitionally the correct real exchange rate which given the purchasing powers of the two numéraires ensures that markets clear and numéraire conversion takes place at the correct level and hence generates the correct relative prices for the underlying real variables in the demand and supply for international goods and services.

12. While the discussion is conducted in terms of a "partial equilibrium" story about whether the foreign exchange market clears, the discussants are aware that the issues are not simply those of partial equilibrium, but of general equilibrium. The reason for this is that ultimately, the demand and supply of foreign exchange are derived demands, reflecting the real demand and supply for goods and services across borders. The elasticities of response to changes in the price for foreign exchange ultimately are reflections of the underlying real demands for goods and services across borders, given the changing relative prices the agents face as the exchange rate changes.

13. Note that here, since the demand and supply of foreign exchange have been viewed as "derived demands," and the underlying demand and supply of goods and inputs that lie beneath these curves are based on relative prices alone (since money is a veil here), it follows that the elasticities of demand and supply here can be seen as reflections of the underlying shapes of the utility curves. Thus, the elasticities and adjustment mechanism could be rooted in the underlying preferences for imported and exported goods on the part of individuals. Viewed this way, the Marshall-Lerner conditions are nothing more than a reformulation of the Hicksian conditions of "gross substitutability." In other words, they can be seen as the conditions that tell us about the required types of utility curves (where income effects do not outweigh substitution effects giving us curves with the "wrong" elasticities) needed to generate stability.

14. Foreign spending rises because foreigners start dishoarding. In effect, the devaluation causes them to face a sudden excess of money holdings in their asset portfolio which they then discard as they move out of money and into goods on the margin. The sudden excess in their money holdings emerges when the devaluation causes an increase in the real relative value of their

money holdings. It is the real value of money holdings which enters their utility functions and determines their decisions to hold money balances.

15. If the market is issuing private bonds which reflect the risk-return profile of the credit flows across borders, that is one thing. But when the state issues bonds to international investors, the market mechanisms of assessing the risks of the flow of debt breaks because of the state guarantee. By issuing government-backed securities, the state creates a flow excess supply of financial instruments to finance trade imbalances. Thus, monetarists are especially fearful of the state itself undertaking the flow excess supply of financial instruments to pay for imports, since this prevents the normal mechanism of credit squeeze from correcting the imbalance.

16. Note that both i) perfect knowledge of the future allowing individuals to make the right decisions, and ii) instantaneous and complete price adjustment in the asset market to ensure there is no excess supply are parts of this argument. Assume for example that for some reason one of the prices (say the price level in the economy) changes a bit slower than the instantaneous adjustment in the asset market. The individuals with perfect knowledge know the new equilibrium, and the path that prices will take to adjust to the new equilibrium.

The interest rate will adjust to ensure that the asset market clears in both the short and long run. But in the short run one can get occasional "overshooting," a too fast adjustment in the nominal interest rate, increasing the real rate momentarily. This does not mean that a trade deficit will appear, though the interest rate is a bit high. It does mean a momentary reduction in real demand, reducing employment. That is, the interest rate will occasionally appear to be higher than the long run interest rate as the economy approaches equilibrium.

This "over-adjustment" is a compensation in the perfectly adjusting market to the known slowness in some other market. The perfectly adjusting market will never for a moment have an excess demand since it is compensating for the other market's lack of adjustment. It will be in the market that is slow to adjust (the output market) that an excess demand may show up, with a concomitant excess supply in the labor market. This will clear up as individuals compensate for the momentary rise in real rates, however, since they know the path being taken to the new equilibrium. Dornbusch (1980) describes a series of such overshooting models.

17. Credibility of state policy becomes the key to the success of the reforms. Credibility involves sending the appropriate signals of resolve, firmness, and commitment to the liberalization process. The key aspect of credibility is that the state convey to agents that the reforms are irreversible.

18. For neoliberals, state guaranteed debt in financial markets is a problem because normal channels by which the market allocates credit based on risk-return assessments are circumvented. Such debt also circumvents the normal credit-squeeze via rising interest rates that will put an end to the payments disequilibrium, since international investors will keep channeling resources to the state regardless of the actual risk-return profile of the activities financed.

19. If the state continues to intervene in markets after the stabilization, then any time the economy moves out of equilibrium, the market will be unable to move the economy back on track. This could cause a reemergence of the long-term BOP crises. The only long-run solution is to ensure that the mechanisms by which automatic adjustment to Walrasian equilibrium emerges are put in place.

20. The need for a stable numèraire conversion has resulted in a debate about the appropriate role for the state in the move to the new equilibrium under neoliberal policy reform. Some neoliberals would prefer floating exchange rates so that there is no way in which the state could possibly prevent correct numèraire conversion. Others believe that since the exchange rate affects relative prices in too many markets, ideally it should be stable for fear of any large-scale disequilibrating movements in relative prices. They thus prefer fixed exchange rates, with the state following some form of money supply rule in a quick move to liberalization. A final group argues that even in long run equilibrium there may be some role for the state to defend the currency. This position emerges in the "sequencing" literature, discussed in the next chapter.

21. Note that Dornbusch's (1980) models use elasticities to describe the response of spending categories to relative price changes, especially relative price changes between import competing goods (components of C) and imported goods (M). This does not mean that the model is individualist. Elasticities need not derive from an individual maximization process, but could represent broad structural rules governing price formation and response in much the same way that marginal propensities are broad structural rules describing the economy. In fact, given that the Keynesian approach explicitly uses marginal propensities to consume and import in its formulation of demand behavior, and the marginal propensities are not derived from microrational behavior, the introduction of elasticities should be interpreted as structural rules governing agent response to price changes. It would be intellectually almost impossible to reconcile a fully individualist reading of price-elasticities with the use of marginal propensities in the income-expenditure model.

   The Laursen-Metzler analysis and the J-curve, in fact, represent the synthesis between the absorption and elasticity approaches via just such an interpretation—they examine, using elasticities of responses to relative prices and marginal propensities to consume and import, the stability condition for a devaluation to improve the BOP. The elasticities, however, are not actually derived from individuals who maximize—if they were, the externally specified marginal propensities to consume and the demand driven model of output determination would disappear. Rightly speaking then, elasticities in conjunction with an absorption approach are nothing more than additional structural rules describing agent responsiveness to prices. They are not to be confused with the elasticities of neoclassical models which reflect underlying preference orderings and maximization with full market clearing.

   Unfortunately, the economics literature on this subject has assumed, and continues to assume, that an elasticity is a market response to price changes, and hence, an elasticity must assume individual maximizing agents. From there, to critique structuralists for not assuming adequate elasticities, or for arbitrarily postulating too low an elasticity, is a small step! Structuralists themselves have no answer to this charge of arbitrarily postulated low elasticities on intellectual grounds, since they too are trapped by the usual notion of price-responsiveness as primarily a reflection of maximizing behavior.

22. The requirements of maintaining the IS-LM theories of the interaction between goods and money-markets in the domestic economy and also having open financial markets that may be autonomous (and requiring additional rules that specify the choice of assets between the domestic and foreign economy and of liquidity preference across national borders) are quite onerous. If coherence is to be assured, then in addition to the endogenous mechanisms generating goods and money market equilibrium (income adjustment and interest rate adjustment respectively), one would need some mechanism ensuring BOP equilibrium. This means some variable currently exogenous and reflecting either a policy tool or a structural rule would have to be endogenized. IS-LM Keynesians cannot endogenize the structural rules governing economic behavior without giving up their ontological specification of agent behavior. Endogenizing one of the existing policy variables will eliminate their careful specification of the state as exogenous—and they need an exogenous state to describe how the economy can move from one equilibrium to another. The system starts to break down and equilibrium cannot be specified because there are not enough equilibrating mechanisms. In the face of such a breakdown in equilibrium, IS-LM Keynesians have concentrated on the goods markets flows, and assumed that the money market (despite all the rules governing domestic money market behavior) will simply accommodate the goods market.

23. Individualists respond that it is precisely because of the state policies of accommodating payments deficits that are implicit in the structuralist model that there is a payments imbalance and debt crisis in LDCs.

24. The mechanisms, as shown in the section discussing individualist theories, are varied. But in all cases, the fixed exchange rate is sustainable because some other mechanism ensures that through a change in the price level or the interest rate, the real purchasing power of the currencies in global markets are brought in line and the real flows reflect the underlying relative prices of global markets in equilibrium.

25. The only theory for which this is not relevant is the theory of the floating exchange rate in the elasticities approach. Since here there is no story of how an excess demand for foreign exchange may be accommodated (the excess demands are purely notional and never actually met at the out-of-equilibrium price), there is no story of the how the process of financial accommodation may then itself let loose a set of changes in price levels and/or interest rates to automatically bring demand and supply for foreign exchange in line as money flows across borders. Here the adjustment to equilibrium comes from within the exchange rate itself.

26. Even the elasticities approach implicitly draws on a structure—the flawed auctioneer who uses the "wrong" price signal-changing rule—to create the

possible instability in exchange rate markets and the failure to move to equilibrium (equilibrium is still the place where there is no BOP imbalance, and payments deficits can only occur when the market is out of equilibrium). If the auctioneer had used some other price-changing rule, the market could have cleared. In such stories, the role is not for a devaluation, but for the state to step in with the correct equilibrium price when the market cannot ensure a move to the right equilibrium price.

27. Note that unlike the IS-LM theory described in chapter 2, where the equilibrium described was self-reproducing and closed, and the state entered to change the equilibrium, over here the equilibrium itself is not attainable without the state implicitly guaranteeing that accommodation of the BOP deficit will take place. The earlier theory was one where the state was truly exogenous and entered to move the economy from an undesirable to a desirable equilibrium. Here the state has implicitly been endogenized, and the existence of equilibrium (and not merely the level of the equilibrium) depends on the state actively creating and maintaining the equilibrium.

28. If the state is guaranteeing financial accommodation, then note that state behavior has been implicitly endogenized to give us a structural rule governing state policy—the rule the state follows in making policy is to accommodate the imbalance in the current account.

29. If a BOP imbalance in equilibrium implicitly implies a structural rule governing state policy, then a breakdown of accommodation is a breakdown of a structural rule that ensured self-reproduction and closure.

30. Note the subtle distinction here between a BOP crisis and Cartesian equilibrium. Crisis cannot emerge in equilibrium because the autonomous flows cohere definitionally. But even if there is no crisis, it does not imply that one has systemic equilibrium—crisis in the BOP, after all, is defined as the unsustainability of the accommodating flows. Though accommodating flows may be sustainable in the short term, lacking a theory of how or why they are sustainable or how they are determined, one does not a proper theory of equilibrium. To have a proper theory of equilibrium, one should be able to describe exactly where the system would move to if the accommodation did not take place.

31. The problem with the structuralist theory of the BOP is not that they have non-clearing markets per se. A non-clearing labor market poses no problems for the structuralists, for example. Logically, there is no inherent reason for the labor market to clear, and a non-clearing labor market does not require any extra-systemic assumptions to be self-reproducing. But a non-clearing balance of payments, where autonomous flows do not automatically cohere to create balance in equilibrium does require some form of extra-systemic actions for systemic self-reproduction and closure. While a structuralist can quite logically define equilibrium in non-clearing labor markets, he or she cannot logically define a self-reproducing and closed equilibrium in the BOP when the autonomous flows do not cohere (it would be the logical equivalent of trying to describe goods market equilibrium when leakages do not automatically adjust to equal injections). The reason is that there is no inherent reason for labor demand to equal labor

supply, but given the accounting identity underlying the BOP, it is absolutely essential that the equilibrium have some internal mechanism of ensuring that the BOP identity is met and reproduced.

32. As noted, it is very difficult to specify a full system of financial and goods markets flows which are all autonomous and cohere in equilibrium. To do that one would have to either endogenize one of the behavioral parameters which define the structural rules governing agent behavior (something structuralists cannot do, since this would destabilize the ontological essences of their theory) or endogenize the state's policy decisions (again, something structuralists cannot do because they need exogenous state policy to describe how the system can move to a new equilibrium). Mathematically, specifying coherence and retaining the ontological priors of the structuralist models is irreconcilable. The only other route to take— eschewing equilibrium—they are not ready to take since it destabilizes the essence of structural rules governing agent behavior (see chapter 2 on why a lack of articulation and self-regulation/closure destabilizes structuralist essences). De facto, structuralists have endogenized state policy when they define equilibrium with a BOP imbalance. But they are loath to admit this, since then they cannot have an extra-structural agent who can step in and change the equilibrium via policy.

NOTES TO CHAPTER FIVE

1. In theoretical terms, this agreement is odd since the question of whether devaluations do in fact improve the trade balance had been the center of controversy within the field of international finance (see Alexander 1952). But the field of development has by and large accepted the trade balance improving effects of devaluations, and concentrated instead on growth. This concentration on growth in the devaluation debates in LDCs is not surprising if one remembers that growth is the primary focus of development economics.

2. This view is not generally accepted by neoliberals, and has been put forth by a few neoliberals in the "sequencing" debate," and will be taken up in the next section.

3. The number of studies attempting to resolve the CDD empirically via before-and-after, econometric modeling using cross-country data, or macrosimulation approaches, is large: Diaz-Alejandro (1966), Cooper (1971a), Killick et al. (1992), Kamin (1988), Edwards (1986 and 1989b), Donovan (1981 and 1982), Gylfason (1987), Gylfason and Schmidt (1983), Gylfason and Risager (1984), Kamas (1992), Branson (1986), Khan (1990b), Doroodian (1993), Sheehey (1986), Meller and Solimano (1987), Solimano (1986), Gylfason and Radetski (1991), Nunnenkamp and Schweickert (1990). The most influential studies have been those by Diaz-Alejandro, Killick, Edwards (especially Edwards 1986), Khan, Kamin, and Gylfason. Agénor and Montiel (1996) provide an excellent overview of the various empirical studies.

4. Agénor and Montiel (1996) provide a very comprehensive overview of the various empirical studies. Despite their own commitment to neoliberal reform,

Agénor and Montiel (p. 254) end their review by concluding that " . . . so far, evidence concerning the contractionary effect [of a devaluation] on real output is mixed."

5.   See IMF (1977, 1987), Balassa (1987), Khan (1990a), Khan and Knight (1981), Khan and Lizondo (1987), Khan and Montiel (1987), Agénor (1991), Aghevli, Khan and Montiel (1991), Edwards (1984, 1989a, 1993), Edwards and Montiel (1989), Guitian (1981), and Dornbusch (1980).

6.   Despite Edward and Montiel's explicit claims of a carefully specified and fully microfounded model with rational expectations, they have to assume some structure. They cannot postulate the need for a devaluation if in fact all the markets and relevant channels for adjustment were in place: if the mechanisms for instantaneous interest rate adjustment are in place, then why have a corrective devaluation? But this then leaves unresolved the question of what, if the channels of interest rate adjustment are not in place, it means for agents to have rational expectations. On what prices do agents base their rational expectations if the market channels do not exist?

In effect, the simultaneous call on structuralism and individualism is the tactic of describing a structural moment to explain LDC deviance, and deploying an individualist agent to generate the sameness-to-come. The absent channels for adjustment (the effect of state intervention) explain deviance, the microrational agents postulated (even when the mechanisms for their ability to have rational expectations are absent) generate the neat results of a move to efficiency once the state undertakes the corrective devaluation.

7.   Hence, as noted in chapter 4, and in the previous section when describing the general contours of the NL positions within the CDD, even when some neoliberals grant that it is possible that in the short run a devaluation may have a contractionary effect, they see this as the result of the short-run path the economy may take in the move to equilibrium. In the long run, a corrective devaluation (the only devaluation which makes sense in these models) cannot be contractionary and the economy will move to the efficient equilibrium position. This interpretation of the New Structuralist critique also takes care of the problem with empirical adjudication, since an empirically observed short-term economic contraction post-devaluation is merely part of the move to equilibrium, and does not discredit the neoliberal reforms. All the neoliberal models that concede that a devaluation may occasionally create short-term output contractions understand this as a "move to equilibrium" issue (see discussion of "sequencing" in the sub-section "Neoliberal Collapse into Structuralism" in this chapter).

8.   I would argue that the short-run long-run distinction in neoclassical economics boils down to slower "adjustment speeds" in some markets, so that in effect, either the agent is constrained by structural rigidity from responding to prices fully in the short run, or else the auctioneer is slightly flawed. Ultimately, the difference between short-run and long-run for neoclassicals is found in their effort to reconcile possible coordination flaws in their moment of structural collapse and incomplete agent-response to the auctioneers' calls in the short run with their long-run theory of full coordination of microrational behavior. They have to carefully ensure that such structural

constraints, restraints, and flaws in the short run do not in any way destabilize or effect the prior specification of agents in their models.

9. So, for example, if the nominal exchange rate rises, but prices rise even
faster, the real exchange rate has fallen. Thus, in terms of relative prices, imports are cheaper than before, while exports are dearer. But if agents have
"money illusion," and make their demand functions depend on nominal
rather than real values, they respond to the rising nominal exchange rate and
reduce imports and increase exports. The Walrasian specification of individual maximization cannot handle this, and in fact, the neoclassical utility-
maximization theory ensures that demand and supply curves derived from
underlying rational maximizing agents depend on real-relative values, and
not on nominal values.

10. The distance between "adjustment speeds" and "inelastic supplies and arbitrary bottlenecks" is actually very small. The markets identified as having
slow speeds of adjustment are all the same markets identified by the structuralists as having rigidities and supply inelasticities—in the sequencing literature, the goods markets respond quickly on the demand side but not on
the supply side, in the labor market wages do not adjust fast enough, and
the move from import-competing production to export-oriented production
takes a little time. This sounds a lot like sticky prices and supply bottlenecks!

11. Some neoliberals like Lal (1986), Krueger (1985), Agénor (1994, 1995) do
not agree that the problem is lagging response in some markets or a failed
auctioneer. For them, this is inconsistent with the neoliberal view and they
implicitly see it as structure via the back door. Lal (1986, p. 218), commenting on Edwards' arguments in favor of a sequenced program of reform
notes: "I think Edwards' use of the Melvin diagram was useful. It brings out
clearly that the unnecessary switches in resources which so concern Edwards
[the "wrong responses" in some markets which are the result of lagging adjustment speeds in other markets] are due to the assumption that private
agents are myopic . . . it is difficult to believe that a private agent . . . will
not see that the initial real exchange rate is going to be changed." In other
words, why do microrational agents who are fully specified not know that
this is a disequilibrium moment and adjust their responses accordingly?
Why will rational agents exhibit myopia?
For Lal, Krueger and Agénor, the reason for the failures of liberalization and
stabilization in Chile and elsewhere are not to be found with the faulty minimal structure of the auctioneer. Hence, not surprisingly, the failures are
linked to the other faulty structure neoliberals call upon to explain LDC deviance—the state.

12. Agénor and Montiel (1996) also discuss the contractionary devaluation literature. But while they present the structuralist arguments scrupulously,
they "expand" the discussion to make it more "general"—with the unsur-
prising result that if you get rid of the structuralist assumptions and add
some other assumptions and mechanisms to make the model more general
(i.e., less structuralist), the contractionary effects start to disappear.

13. The reason is that while the IS-LM Keynesian approach can handle
money markets in a closed economy by exogenizing the supply of money,

in international markets with the exchange rate affecting behaviors in both the goods market and the money market, international financial flows destabilize the careful specification of the money supply—the result is instability, and structuralists, like the individualists, want closure and equilibrium. Hence, while in a closed economy one can handle an equilibrium formulation of both goods and money markets, one cannot so easily handle such flows in an open economy. The absorption approach thus looks at international interactions only in the goods market via the marginal propensities to import. If the exchange rate further affected liquidity preference and interest rates in the money market, the equilibrium formulation breaks down in simple mathematical terms—not enough endogenous variables to handle the number of structural rules (since one endogenous variable—the exchange rate—has to ensure that both the behavioral specifications of the goods markets flows across borders and the behavioral specifications of the money market flows across borders are met). This is not far from the problem faced by individualists seeking closure and equilibrium in the Cartesian framework—they cannot handle two numèraires.

14. This type of historically determined endogenous state policy will not give equilibrium and closure automatically. The actual policies of accommodation undertaken, and the question of who the state accommodates financially and why, will depend on the historical existence of militant social movements to pressure the state for financial accommodation of consumption needs. Otherwise, though imports for investment may be accommodated, there would be no accommodation of workers needs for imported food, nor any effort to stabilize the price of non-traded consumption goods in short supply via state imports—the marginal propensity to import, and along with it the wage bundle, the real wage, and value of the mark-up become unstable and determined by political struggle. Thus the mark-up, given wage share, and fixed wages for Noyola were not "structural rules governing LDC behavior," but a very contextual and historically specific description of the actual push by mass movements in Latin America in the 50s and 60s to maintain the real purchasing power of workers' incomes. The Latin American state, faced by the conflicting demands of investors and workers, was unable to close the gap without creating inflationary wage-price spirals. The inflationary spirals generated in such economies cannot be "closed" by some "automatic equilibrium." Their resolution is determined via historical struggle, and the state either has to destroy the working class movements, or else the increasing crises and growing mass movements completely revolutionize the economy and change the class relationships in society.

15. That is, endogenizing the labor market without using the neoclassical assumptions about equilibrium market-clearing wages, which would eliminate the Keynesian demand-driven side of the model.

16. This is a sharp contrast to the structures that govern the production side of the informal economy in the New Structuralist models. The informal economy on the production side is also demand constrained, faces production rigidities, has fixed nominal wages and follows mark-up pricing—though it is never explained why absent unionism and activism and given the wide use

of home-based production and the putting out system, the mark-up in the urban informal sector is constant. Nor do the theories explain how informal sector workers lacking formal wage contracts and often paid piece-rates manage to defend their nominal wage.

17. Making sure that productive capital investment is profits-determined and pricing in output markets follows markup rules (rather than the market clearing full financial intermediation rules governing informal finance) is crucial for New Structuralists. If the production side of their model followed the same pricing mechanism as the financial side, then with market clearing prices their Keynesian demand-side specification of the goods market clearing via income-expenditure flows rather than via price adjustments would break down. Further, if savings automatically translate into investment via full financial intermediation, then it is unclear why the equality between income and expenditure comes by output contraction (since all leakages should be transformed into investment via interest rate adjustment). Here, the reason for the continued use of the income-output determination is twofold—while savings will automatically translate into investment in working capital via the financial markets, prices in goods markets cannot adjust (because of mark-up pricing), and investment demand for fixed capital remains dependent on the profit share and not on the interest rate. Wages are fixed and the labor market does not clear, corresponding to an equilibrium non-clearing goods market without market-clearing prices. Fry (1988, pp. 104-105) notes that if prices in the production sector are also governed by market clearing rules, the New Structuralist results disappear under the perfect financial market intermediation they assume, and instead give neoclassical results.

18. See IMF 1977, 1987; Khan 1990a; Edwards 1986, 1989a; Guitian 1976; Johnson 1959, 1977a and 1977b.

19. This policy is the panacea not only for payments crises, but for unemployment, growth, and all other aspects of macroeconomic policy. The problem of using equilibrium to be definitionally market clearing is contested in the debates on labor markets and unemployment in macroeconomics. Sidney Weintraub points out in *Keynes, Keynesians and Monetarists* (Weintraub 1978, page 10) that if one starts by writing "labor supply = labor demand" as a defining moment of equilibrium, it is tautological to assert that there can be no equilibrium unemployment.

20. Individualist devaluation advocates carefully refer to corrective devaluation. This is consistent with the position that devaluation is not a policy aimed at actively intervening in markets, but is simply attempting to undo past policies mistakes.

21. In the monetary approach, loose fiscal and monetary policies create excess demand, and domestic inflation in the short run. Since these are not matched by rising foreign exchange prices due to government interference, this will make the relative price of foreign exchange too cheap, leading to payments deficits. In the long run, unless government interference is sustained, the imbalance should correct itself by money flows across international borders, with money leaving the deficit country and moving to surplus countries. This outflow of funds should raise domestic interest rates, and thus reduce domestic demand (as individuals then choose to hold more money balances

in their portfolios). The process continues till the excess expenditures are eliminated. Thus, since in the monetarist-marginalist approaches, money is neutral in the long run, there is no behavioral reason why economic actors will not reach an optimal market clearing outcome in the long run (and, in the rational expectations approach, in the short run), unless there are persistent interventions in the markets by the government.

22. The evaluative criteria for such policies are the standard Pareto Optimality criteria. Since distributional justice does not form part of these criteria, the theory does not handle income-distribution issues well (income redistributions due to devaluations are a key part of the structuralist critique). In theoretical terms however, the argument is that the gains from the free market policies are large enough to compensate the losers.

23. See Katzner 1988.

24. In assessing structuralism, Little (1982) argues that "the structuralist sees the world as inflexible . . . In economic terms, the supply of most things is inelastic . . . as a result of poverty demand too was inflexible . . . demand for imports would be highly inelastic" (pg. 20).

25. See for example Taylor's introduction to Taylor, ed. 1993.

26. The New Structuralists see continuity between themselves and the earlier ISI tradition. Since they are development economists and do not actually deploy their models to examine the DCs, the implicit change in the goal and criteria of assessment is not one they are conscious off. Nevertheless, the implicit shift in their goal for development has changed their implicit criteria for assessing policies. I show below that this shift then leads to very different ways of assessing success or failure of policy in the CDD, and thus leaves the debate unresolvable.

27. Both perspectives share a commitment to equilibrium. They focus on the same markets—labor markets, goods markets, money markets—and so they can assess each other's equations. They agree that growth and promotion of the LDC entrepreneur should be the focus of development, that the state is an extra-economy force, and that policy is exogenous. Both depend on the state to convert LDC difference into sameness, and both focus on the same sets of policies—interest rate policies, exchange rate policies, monetary and fiscal policies. Neither focuses analysis on other types of state activity like land reform, protection of commons-access for the poor, and so on. Both see the household as primarily a place where consumption decisions take place, and neither examines the links between the domestic non-market economy and the for-market economy. Both see work relations as governed primarily by the return on wages under capitalism, and both see industrialization as benign. Neither looks at the links between economic outcomes and social/political struggles, neither sees class (New Structuralist class is merely an issue of income determination and distribution in equilibrium—class is not a social-historic category). And both understand the primary goal of development as one of eliminating "bad structure" which explains LDC deviance.

28. This would be in contrast to some individualists whose commitment to individualism takes precedence over closure. An example would be the open-ended individualism with fluidity and history sans closure of someone like Hayek.

29. In contrast to those who prefer to postulate a post-structural open-endedness in contradictory, historical structures which do not have full articulation. Examples would be the open-ended post-structuralist moment of historically determined outcomes from class-struggle and social politics with endogenous state policy for someone like Noyola, or the open-ended and fluid discussion of financial markets of either the Post Keynesians or of Marxists drawing on Marx's discussion of finance in *Capital Volume* III (Marx 1977).

Bibliography

Agarwala, A, N. and Singh, S. P. eds. 1963. *The Economics of Underdevelopment*. New York: Oxford University Press

A. Agénor, P.-R. 1991. "Output, Devaluation, and the Real Exchange Rate in Developing Countries." *Weltwirschaftliches Archives*. 127: 18-41.

————. 1994. "Credibility and Exchange Rate Management in Developing Countries." *Journal of Development Economics*, 45 (August): 1–16

————. 1995. "Credibility Effects of Price Controls in Disinflation Programs." *Journal of Macroeconomics*, 17: 161–71.

Agénor, P.-R. and Montiel, P. J. 1996. *Development Macroeconomics*. Princeton NJ: Princeton University Press.

Aghelvi, B. B.; Khan, M. S.; and Montiel, P. J. 1991. *Exchange Rate Policy in Developing Countries: Some Analytical Issues*. IMF occasional paper 78.

Ahluwalia, M. and Lysy, F. 1981. "Employment, Income Distribution, and Programs to Remedy Balance-of-Payments Difficulties." In W. Cline and S. Weintraub eds. *Economic Stabilization in Developing Countries*.

Alexander, S. S. 1952. "Effects of a Devaluation on a Trade Balance." *IMF Staff Papers*. 2 (April): 263-78.

Althusser, L. 1971. *Lenin and Philosophy and Other Essays*. Trans. B. Brewster. London: New Left Books.

————. 1979. *For Marx*. Trans. B. Brewster. London: Verso.

Amariglio, J. L.; Resnick, S. A.; and Wolff, R. D. 1990. "Division and Difference in the 'Discipline' of Economics." *Critical Inquiry*, 17 (1): 108-137.

Amin, S. 1974a. *Accumulation on a World Scale: A Critique of the Theory of Underdevelopment*. Trans. B. Pearce. New York: Monthly Review Press.

————. 1974b. *Neo-Colonialism in West Africa*. Trans. F. McDonagh. New York: Monthly Review Press.

————. 1976. *Unequal Development: An Essay on the Social Formations of Peripheral Capitalism*. Trans. B. Pearce. New York: Monthly Review Press.

————. 1977. *Imperialism and Unequal Development*. New York: Monthly Review Press.

————. 1978. *The Law of Value and Historical Materialism*. Trans. B. Pearce. New York: Monthly Review Press.

Amsden, A. H. 1989. *Asia's Next Giant: South Korea and Late Industrialization*. New York: Oxford University Press.

Amsden, A. H. et al. 1992. *Taiwan's Enterprises in Global Perspective.* Ed., N. T. Wang. Armonk NY: M.E. Sharpe.

Anjaria, S. J.; Iqbal, Z.; Perez, L. L.; and Tseng, W. S. 1981. *Trade Policy Developments in Industrial Countries.* IMF Occasional Papers, no. 5.

Arndt, H. W. 1985. "The Origins of Structuralism." *World Development* 13 (2): 151-159.

—————. 1987. *Economic Development: The History of an Idea.* Chicago: University of Chicago Press.

Arrida, P. "Macroeconomic Issues for Latin America." *Journal of Development Economics.*

Aubrey, H.G. 1955. "Industry investment decisions: a comparative analysis." *Journal of Economic History,* 15 (4): 335–51.

—————. 1956. "Rejoinder." *Journal of Economic History,* 16 (3): 354–5.

Bacha, E. L. 1984. "Growth with Limited Supplies of Foreign Exchange: A Reappraisal of the Two-Gap Model." In L. Taylor, M. Syrquin, and L. Westphal eds. *Economic Structure and Performance: Essays in Honor of Hollis. B. Chenery.* New York: Academic Press.

Bacha, E. L. and Díaz-Alejandro, C. F. 1982. *International Financial Intermediation: A Long and Tropical View.* Essays in International Finance; no. 147. Princeton, N.J.: International Finance Section, Dept. of Economics, Princeton University.

Baer, W. 1962. "The Economics of Prebisch and ECLA." *Economic Development and Cultural Change.* January: 169-182.

—————. 1967. "The Inflation Controversy in Latin America: A Survey." *Latin American Research Review.* Spring: pp. 3-25.

Baer, W. and Kerstenetsky, I. eds. 1964. *Inflation and Growth in Latin America.* Homewood IL: Richard D. Irwin, Inc. (A publication of the Economic Growth Center of Yale University.)

Balassa, B. A. 1964. *Trade Prospects for Developing Countries.* Homewood, IL: R. D. Irwin.

—————. 1981. *The Process of Industrial Development and Alternative Development Strategies.* Essays in International Finance, no. 141.Princeton: International Finance Section, Dept. of Economics, Princeton University.

—————. 1984. "Adjustment Policies in Developing Countries: A Reassessment." *World Development.* 12: 955-72.

—————. 1987. "Effects of Exchange Rate Changes in Developing Countries." *Indian Journal of Economics.* 68: 203-21.

Balassa, B. A. et al. 1982. *Development Strategies in Semi-Industrial Economies.* Baltimore: Published for the World Bank by the Johns Hopkins University Press.

Balassa, B. A. and Associates. 1971. *The Structure of Protection in Developing Countries.* Baltimore: Published for the World Bank and the Inter-American Development Bank by the Johns Hopkins Press.

Balassa, B. A. and McCarthy, D. 1984. *Adjustment Policies in Developing Countries, 1979-1983: An Update.* World Bank Staff Working Paper no. 675. Washington, D.C.: World Bank.

Balassa, B. A. and Williamson, J. 1987. *Adjusting to Success: Balance of Payments Policy in the East Asian NICs.* Policy Analyses in International Economics; no. 17. Washington, DC: Institute for International Economics.

Baldwin, R. E. 1966. *Economic Development and Growth.* New York: Wiley

——————. 1982. *The Inefficacy of Trade Policy.* Essays in International Finance, no. 150. Princeton, NJ: International Finance Section, Dept. of Economics, Princeton University

Baldwin, R. E. et al. 1965. *Trade, Growth and the Balance-of-Payments: Essays in Honor of Gottfried Haberler.* New York: Rand McNally.

Baldwin, R. E. et al. 1986. *Protectionism and Structural Adjustment.* Grusch: Verlag Ruegger.

Balogh, T. and Streeten, P. 1960. "Domestic versus Foreign Investment." *Oxford Bulletin of Economics and Statistics,* 22: 213-24.

Baran P. A. 1952. "On the Political Economy of Backwardness." *Manchester School,* January.

Barbone, L. and Rivera-Batiz, F. 1987. "Foreign Capital and the Contractionary impact of Currency Devaluation, with an Application to Jamaica." *Journal of Development Economics.* 26 (1).

Bardhan, P. K. 1965. "Equilibrium Growth in the International Economy." *Quarterly Journal of Economics,* 79: 455-64.

——————. 1970. *Economic Growth, Development, and Foreign Trade.* New York: Wiley.

——————. 1988. "Alternative Approaches to Development Economics: An Evaluation." In H. B. Chenery and T. N. Srinivasan eds. *The Handbook of Development Economics,* Vol. 1,

Barthes, R. 1974. *S/Z.* Trans. R. Miller. New York: Hill and Wang.

——————. 1977. *Image, Music, Text.* Trans. S. Heath. New York: Hill and Wang.

——————. 1982. *A Barthes Reader.* Ed. S. Sontag. New York: Hill and Wang.

Bauer, P. T. 1972. *Dissent on Development.* Cambridge MA: Harvard University Press.

——————. 1984. *Reality and Rhetoric: Studies in the Economics of Development.* Cambridge MA: Harvard University Press.

Bauer, P. T. and Yamey, B. S. 1957. *The Economics of Under-Developed Countries.* Digswell Place UK: Nisbet.

——————. 1961 (1951). "Economic Progress and Occupational Distribution." Reprinted in B. Okun and R. W. Richardson, eds. (1961) *Studies in Economic Development: A Book of Readings.* New York: Holt, Rinehart and Winston.

——————. 1968. *Markets, Market Control and Marketing Reform: Selected Papers.* London: Weidenfeld & Nicolson.

Bhagwati, J. N. 1958. "Immiserizing Growth: A Geometric Note." *Review of Economic Studies,* 25: 201-5.

——————. 1965. "On the Equivalence of Tariffs and Quotas." In Baldwin et al. *Trade, Growth and the Balance-of-Payments: Essays in Honor of Gottfried Haberler.* New York: Rand McNally.

——————. 1969. *Trade, Tariffs and Growth: Essays in International Economics.* London: Weidenfeld & Nicolson.

—————. 1978. *Anatomy and Consequences of Exchange Control Regimes.* Cambridge, MA: Ballinger Pub. Co.

—————. 1983. *The Theory of Commercial Policy: Essays in International Economic Theory, Volume I.* Ed. R. C. Feenstra. Cambridge, MA: MIT Press.

—————. 1985. *Essays in Development Economics.* Ed. G. Grossman. Cambridge, MA: MIT Press.

—————. 1988. *Protectionism.* Cambridge MA: MIT Press.

—————. 1991. *Political Economy and International Economics.* Ed. D. A. Irwin. Cambridge MA: MIT Press.

Bhagwati, J. N. ed. 1981. *International Trade: Selected Readings.* Cambridge MA: MIT Press.

—————. ed. 1982. *Import Competition and Response.* Chicago: University of Chicago Press.

Bhagwati, J. N. and Desai, P. 1970. *India: Planning for Industrialization: Industrialization and Trade Policies since 1951.* New York: Published for the Development Centre of the Organization for Economic Co-operation and Development by Oxford University Press.

Bhagwati, J. N. and Hudec, R. E. eds. 1996. *Fair Trade and Harmonization: Prerequisites for Free Trade?* Cambridge, MA: MIT Press.

Bhagwati, J. N.; Mundell, R. A.; Vanek, J.; and Jones, R. W. eds. 1971. *Trade, Balance of Payments and Growth: Papers in International Economics in Honor of Charles P. Kindleberger.* Amsterdam: North-Holland.

Bhagwati, J. N. and Ramaswami, V. K. 1963. "Domestic Distortions, Tariffs and the Theory of Optimum Subsidy." *Journal of Political Economy.* 71: 44-50.

Bhagwati, J. N. and Srinivasan, T. N. 1969. "Optimal Intervention to Achieve Non-Economic Objectives." *Review of Economic Studies,*

Billig, M. S. 1994. "The Death and Rebirth of Entrepreneurism on Negros Island, Philippines: A Critique of Cultural Theories of Enterprise." *Journal of Economic Issues,* 28: 659–78.

Blitzer, C. R.; Clark, P. B.; and Taylor, L. eds. 1975. *Economy-Wide Models and Development Planning.* London: Published for the World Bank by Oxford University Press.

Block, F. 1977. *The Origins of International Economic Disorder.* Berkeley CA: University of California Press.

Boettke, P. J. 1994. ed. *The Collapse of Development Planning.* New York: New York University Press.

Bosworth, B. P.; Dorbusch, R.; and Laban, R. eds. 1994. *The Chilean Economy: Policy Lessons and Challenges.* Washington DC: Brookings Institution.

Branson, W. H. 1986. "Stabilization, Stagflation, and Investment Incentives: The Case of Kenya 1979-80." In S. Edwards and L. Ahamad eds. *Economic Adjustment and Exchange Rates in Developing Countries.* Chicago: University of Chicago Press.

—————. 1989. *Macroeconomic Theory and Policy.* 3rd. ed. New York: Harper & Row.

Brecher, R. A. and Choudhri, E. U. 1982. "Immiserizing Investment from Abroad: The Singer-Prebisch Thesis Reconsidered." *Quarterly Journal of Economics,* 97: 181-90.

Brecher, R. A. and Díaz-Alejandro, C. F. "Tarrifs, Foreign Capital, and Immiserizing Growth." *Journal of International Economics,* 7: 317-22.

Brennan, G. and Buchanan, J. M. 1980. *The Power to Tax: Analytical Foundations of a Fiscal Constitution.* Cambridge UK: Cambridge University Press.

—————. 1981. *Monopoly in Money and Inflation: The case for a Constitution to Discipline Government.* London: Institute of Economic Affairs.

Bruno, M. 1979. "Stabilization and Stagflation in a Semi-Industrialized Economy." In R. Dornbusch and J. A. Frenkel eds. *International Economic Policy: Theory and Evidence.* Baltimore MD: Johns Hopkins.

Bruton, H. 1985. "The Search for Development Economics." *World Development,* 13 (10/11): 1099-1143.

Buchanan, J. M. 1960. *Fiscal Theory and Political Economy: Selected Essays.* Chapel Hill: University of North Carolina Press.

—————. 1969. *Cost and Choice: An Inquiry in Economic Theory.* Chicago: Markham Pub. Co.

—————. 1986. *Liberty, Market, and State: Political Economy in the 1980s.* New York: New York University Press.

—————. 1989. *Essays on Political Economy.* Honolulu: University of Hawaii Press.

Buchanan, J. M.; Tollison, R. D.; and Tullock, G. eds. 1980. *Toward a Theory of the Rent-Seeking Society.* Texas A & M University Economics Series; no. 4. College Station: Texas A & M University.

Buchanan, J. M. and Wagner, R. E. 1977. *Democracy in Deficit: The Political Legacy of Lord Keynes.* New York: Academic Press.

Buffie, E. F. 1984a. "Financial Repression, the New Structuralists, and Stabilization Policy in Semi-Industrialized Economies." *Journal of Development Economics.* 14: 305-22.

—————. 1984b. "The Macroeconomics of Trade Liberalization." *Journal of International Economics.* 17: 121-37.

—————. 1986a. "Devaluation and Imported Inputs: The Large Economy Case." *International Economic Review.* 27: 123-40.

—————. 1986b. "Devaluation, Investment and Growth in LDCs." *Journal of Development Economics.* 20: 2.

Burczak, T. A. 1994. *Subjectivism and the Limits of F. A. Hayek's Political Economy.* Ph.D. Thesis (Ph.D.), University of Massachusetts at Amherst.

Campos, R. de O. 1961. "Two Views on Inflation in Latin America." In A. O. Hirschman, ed. *Latin American Issues,* pp. 69-79. New York: The Twentieth Century Fund.

—————. 1963. "Economic Development and Inflation, with Special Reference to Latin America." Speech collected in Campos 1967, *Reflections on Latin American Development,* pp. 106-121. Austin: University of Texas Press.

Cardoso, E. A.; Barros, R.; and Urani, A. 1993. *Inflation and Unemployment as Determinants of Inequality in Brazil: The 1980s.* Discussion paper no. 298, Institute of Applied Economic Research, Brazil. Brasilia, DF: Instituto de Pesquisa Economica Aplicada, Servico Editorial.

Cardoso, E. A. and Helwege, A. 1992. *Latin America's Economy: Diversity, Trends, and Conflicts.* Cambridge MA: MIT Press.

Caves, R. E. 1965. "'Vent for Surplus' Models of Trade and Growth." In R. E. Baldwin et al. ed. *Trade Growth and Balance of Payments: Essays in Howor of Gottfried Haberler,* pp. 95-115. New York: Rand McNally.

Caves, R. E. and Johnson, H. G. 1968. *Readings in International Economics.* Homewood IL: Published for the American Economic Association by R. D. Irwin.

Caves, R. E.; Johnson, H. G.; and Kenen, P. B. 1965. "Preface (November 1964)." In R. E. Baldwin et al. *Trade, Growth, and Balance of Payments: Essays in Honor of Gottfried Haberler.* Chicago: Rand McNally.

Charusheela, S. 1994. *Procrustes' Bed: Ontological Pitfalls in Theories of Trade, Growth and Development.* Mimeo.

————. 1997. *Structuralism and Individualism in Economic Analysis: The 'Contractionary Devaluation Debate' in Development Economics.* Ph.D. Thesis, University of Massachusetts-Amherst.

————. 2003. "Interrogating the Walras-Saussure Connection." Paper presented at the *History of Economics Society* at the *Allied Social Sciences Association* meetings, Washington DC.

Chenery, H. B. 1955. "The Role of Industrialization in Development Programs." *The American Economic Review,* May 1955.

Chenery, H. B. ed. 1971. *Studies in Development Planning.* Cambridge, MA: Harvard University Press.

Chenery, H. B. et al. 1974. *Redistribution with Growth: Policies to Improve Income Distribution in Developing Countries in the Context of Economic Growth.* London: Published for the World Bank and the Institute of Development Studies, University of Sussex, by Oxford University Press.

Chenery, H. B. et al. 1979. *Structural Change and Development Policy.* New York: Published for the World Bank by Oxford University Press.

Chenery, H. B. et al. 1986. *Industrialization and Growth: A Comparative Study.* New York: Published for the World Bank by Oxford University Press.

Chenery, H. B. and Adelman, I. 1966. "Foreign Aid and Economic Development: The Case of Greece." *Review of Economic Statistics,* 48 (1): 1–19.

Chenery H. B. and Bruno, M. 1962. "Development Alternatives in an Open Economy: The Case of Israel." *Economic Journal,* 57: 79–103.

Chenery, H. B. and Srinivasan, T. N. eds. 1988-1995. *Handbook of Development Economics.* Amsterdam: North-Holland.

Chenery, H. B. and Strout, A. M. 1966. "Foreign Assistance and Economic Development." *American Economic Review,* 56: 149-79.

Chenery, H. B. and Syrquin, M. 1975. *Patterns of Development, 1950-1970.* London: Oxford University Press for the World Bank.

Cho, Y.-J. 1986. "Inefficiencies from Financial Liberalization in the Absence of Well-Functioning Equity Markets." *Journal of Money, Banking and Credit.* 18 (2): 191–99.

Cho, Y.-J. and Khatkhate, D. 1989. *Lessons of Financial Liberalization in Asia.* Washington D.C.: The World Bank.

Choksi, A. M. 1979. *State Intervention in the Industrialization of Developing Countries: Selected Issues.* World Bank Staff Papers, no. 341. Washington DC: World Bank.

Choksi, A. M.; Michaely, M.; and Papageorgiou, D. eds. 1991. *Liberalizing Foreign Trade*. Cambridge MA: B. Blackwell.

Choksi, A. M. and Papageorgiou, D. eds. 1986. *Economic Liberalization in Developing Countries*. New York: Basil Blackwell.

Chomsky, N. 1975. *Reflections on Language*. New York: Random House.

Clark, C. 1951. *The Conditions of Economic Progress*. 2d ed. London: Macmillan.

————. 1953. "Population Growth and Living Standards." *International Labor Review*, August 1953. Geneva: International Labour Office.

————. 1967. *Population Growth and Land Use*. New York: St. Martin's Press.

Cline, W. R. and Weintraub, S. eds. 1981. *Economic Stabilization in Developing Countries*. Washington DC: Brookings Institution.

Cockcroft, J. D.; Frank, A. G.; and Johnson, D. L. 1972. *Dependence and Underdevelopment: Latin America's Political Economy*. Garden City, NY: Anchor Books.

Connolly, M. and Taylor, D. 1984. "Testing the Monetary Approach to Devaluation in Developing Countries." *Journal of Political Economy*. 48 (4).

Cooper, R. N. 1971a. *Currency Devaluation in Developing Countries*. Essays in International Finance, No. 86. Princeton: International financial Section, Dept. of Economics, Princeton University.

————. 1971b. "Devaluation and Aggregate Demand in Aid-Receiving Countries." In J. Bhagwati et al. eds. *Trade, Balance of Payments and Growth*. New York: North-Holland.

Cooper, R. N., ed. 1969. *International Finance*. Harmondsworth: Penguin Modern Economics Readings.

Corbo, V.; Goldstein, M.; and Khan, M. S.; ed. 1987. *Growth-Oriented Adjustment Programs*. Washington, D.C. : International Monetary Fund, World Bank.

Corbo, V.; Krueger, A. O.; and Ossa, F. eds. 1985. *Export-Oriented Development Strategies: The Success of Five Newly Industrializing Countries*. Boulder, CO: Westview Press.

Corden, W. M. 1984. "The Normative Theory of International Trade." In R. W. Jones and P. B. Kenen eds. *The Handbook of International Economics, Vol. 1*. pp. 63-129. New York: North Holland.

Coward, R. and Ellis, J. 1977. *Language and Materialism: Developments in Semiology and the Theory of the Subject*. London: Routledge & Paul.

Cullenberg, S. 1989. *Technical Change, The Rate of Profit, and Competition: The Microfoundations of the Okishio Theorem*. Ph.D. Dissertation, University of Massachusetts, Amherst.

————. 1995. *The Falling Rate of Profit: Recasting the Marxian Debate*. London: Pluto.

Culler, J. D. 1986. *Ferdinand de Saussure*. Revised Edition. Ithaca, NY: Cornell University Press.

Danby, C. 1992. *Latin American Structuralism: An Annotated Bibliography*. Mimeo.

————. 1994. *The Structuralist-Monetarist Debate in Latin America*. Mimeo.

————. 2004. ""Contested States, Transnational Subjects: Toward a Post Keynesianism Without Modernity." In E. Zein-Elabdin and S. Charusheela eds. *Postcolonialism Meets Economics*. London: Routledge.

————. 2005 (Forthcoming). "Noyola's Institutional Approach to Inflation." *Journal of the History of Economic Thought*, March.

Davidson, P. 1972. *Money and the Real World*. New York: Wiley.

————. 1982. *International Money and the Real World*. New York: Wiley.

de George, R. T. and de George, F. M. ed. 1972. *The Structuralists: From Marx to Levi-Strauss*. Garden City, NY: Anchor Books.

de Marco, L. E. ed. 1972. *International Economics and Development: Essays in Honor of Raúl Prebisch*. New York: Academic Press.

de Soto, H. 1989. *The Other Path: The Invisible Revolution in the Third World*. Trans. J. Abbott. New York: Harper & Row.

Dell, S. 1982. "Stabilization: The Political Economy of Overkill." *World Development*. 10: 205-49.

Díaz-Alejandro, C. F. 1963. "A Note on the Impact of Devaluation and the Redistributive Effect." *Journal of Political Economy*. 71: 577-80.

————. 1966. *Exchange-Rate Devaluation in a Semi-Industrialized Country: The Experience of Argentina, 1955-1961*. Cambridge MA: MIT Press.

————. 1975. *Less Developed Countries and the Post-1971 International Financial System*. Essays in international finance; no. 108. Princeton, N.J.: International Finance Section, Dept. of Economics, Princeton University.

————. 1981. "Southern Cone Stabilization Plans." In W. Cline and S. Weintraub eds. *Economic Stabilization in Developing Countries*.

————. 1984a. "Latin American Debt: I Don't Think We are in Kansas Anymore." *Brookings Papers in Economic Activity 2*.

————. 1984b. *Good-Bye Financial Repression, Hello Financial Crash* . Notre Dame, Indiana: Helen Kellogg Institute for International Studies, University of Notre Dame, Working paper; #24.

Domar, E. 1946. "Capital Expansion, Rate of Growth, and Employment." *Econometrica*, 14: 137–47.

————. 1957. *Essays in the Theory of Economic Growth*. New York: Oxford University Press.

Donovan, D. J. 1981. "Real Responses Associated with Exchange Rate Action in Selected Upper Credit Tranche Stabilization Programs." *IMF Staff Papers*. 28: 698-727.

————. 1982. "Macroeconomic Performance and Adjustment under Fund-Supported Programs." *IMF Staff Papers*. 29: 171-203.

Dornbusch, R. 1980. *Open Economy Macroeconomics*. New York : Basic Books.

Dornbusch, R. and Edwards, S. eds. 1991. *The Macroeconomics of Populism in Latin America*. Chicago: University of Chicago Press

————. eds. 1995. *Reform, Recovery, and Growth: Latin America and The Middle East*. Chicago: University of Chicago Press.

Doroodian, K. 1993. "Macroeconomic Performance and Adjustment under Policies Commonly Supported by the International Monetary Fund." *Economic Development and Cultural Change*. 41: 849-64.

dos Santos, T. 1970. "Structure of Dependence." *American Economic Review*, 60 (2).

Edwards, S. 1983. "The Short Run Relation between Growth and Inflation in Latin America." *American Economic Review*. 73: 477-82.

—————. 1984. *The Order of Liberalization of The External Sector in Developing Countries.* Essays in International Finance; no. 156. Princeton, N.J. : International Finance Section, Dept. of Economics, Princeton University.

—————. 1986. "Are Devaluations Contractionary?" *Review of Economics and Statistics.* 68 (3): 501-8.

—————. 1988. "Terms of Trade, Tariffs and Labor Market Adjustment in Developing Countries." *World Bank Economic Review.* 2 (May): 165-85.

—————. 1989a. *Exchange Rate Misalignment in Developing Countries.* Baltimore: Published for the World Bank by the Johns Hopkins University Press.

—————. 1989b. *Real Exchange Rates, Devaluation, and Adjustment: Exchange Rate Policy in Developing Countries.* Cambridge, MA: MIT Press.

—————. 1989c. *On the Sequencing of Structural Reforms.* NBER Working Paper no. 3138. New York: National Bureau of Economic Research.

—————. 1993. "Openness, Trade Liberalization, and Growth in Developing Countries." *Journal of Economic Literature.* 31: 1358-93.

—————. 1994. "The Political Economy of Inflation and Stabilization in Developing Countries." *Economic Development and Cultural Change.* 42: 235-66.

—————. 1995. *Crisis and Reform in Latin America: From Despair to Hope.* Oxford; New York: Published for the World Bank by Oxford University Press.

Edwards, S. and Ahamed, L., eds. 1986. *Economic Adjustment and Exchange Rates in Developing Countries.* Chicago: University of Chicago Press.

Edwards, S. and Cox Edwards, A. 1987. *Monetarism and Liberalization: The Chilean Experiment.* Cambridge, MA: Ballinger Pub. Co.

Edwards, S. and Khan, M. S. 1985. "Interest Rate Determination in Developing Countries: A Conceptual Framework." *IMF Staff Papers.* 32: 377-403.

Edwards, S. and Larrain, F. ed. 1989. *Debt, Adjustment, and Recovery: Latin America's Prospects for Growth and Development.* Cambridge, MA : B. Blackwell.

Edwards, S. and Montiel, P. J. 1989. "Devaluation Crises and the Macroeconomic Consequences of Postponed Adjustment in Developing Countries." *IMF Staff Papers.* 36 (4): 875-905.

Edwards, S. and Santaella, J. A. 1993. "Devaluation Controversies in Developing Countries: Lessons from the Bretton Woods Era." In M. D. Bordo and B. Eichengreen eds. *A Retrospective on the Bretton Woods System.* Chicago: University of Chicago Press.

Emmanuel, A. 1972. *Unequal Exchange: A Study of the Imperialism of Trade.* Trans. B. Pearce. New York: Monthly Review Press.

Escobar, A. 1995. *Encountering Development: The Making and Unmaking of the Third World.* Princeton: Princeton University Press.

Feenstra, R. C.; Grossman, G. M.; and Irwin D. A. eds. 1996. *The Political Economy of Trade Policy: Papers in Honor of Jagdish Bhagwati.* Cambridge MA: MIT Press.

Fei, J. C. H. and Ranis, G. 1964. *Development of the Labor Surplus Economy: Theory and Policy.* Homewood IL: Irwin.

Felix, D. 1961. "An Alternative View of the 'Monetarist'-'Structuralist' Controversy." In A. O. Hirschman ed. *Latin American Issues*, pp. 81-93. New York: The Twentieth Century Fund.

—————. 1964. "Monetarists, Structuralists, and Import-Substituting Industrialization: A Critical Appraisal." pp. 370-400 in Baer and Kerstenetsky 1964.

Findlay, R. 1970. "Factor Proportions and Comparative Advantage in the Long Run." *Journal of Political Economy*, (February).

—————. 1973. *International Trade and Development Theory*. New York: Columbia University Press.

—————. 1986. "Growth and Development in Trade Models." In R. W. Jones and P. B. Kenen eds. *The Handbook of International Trade, Vol. 1*. pp. 185-236. New York: North Holland.

—————. 1995. *Factor Proportions, Trade, and Growth*. Cambridge MA: MIT Press.

Fitzgerald, E.V.K. 1990. "Kalecki on Financing Development: An Approach to the Macroeconomics of the Semi-Industrialized Economy." *Cambridge Journal of Economics* 14: 183-203.

Fleming, J. M. 1955. "External Economies and the Doctrine of Balanced Growth." *Economic Journal*, June 1955.

Foxley, A. 1983. *Latin American Experiments in Neoconservative Economics*. Berkeley: University of California Press.

—————. 1987. "Latin American Development after the Debt Crisis." *Journal of Development Economics*. 27: 201-225.

Frank, A. G. 1969. *Capitalism and Underdevelopment in Latin America: Historical Studies of Chile and Brazil*. New York: Monthly Review Press.

—————. 1970. *Latin America: Underdevelopment or Revolution*. New York: Monthly Review Press.

—————. 1972. *Lumpenbourgeoisie, Lumpendevelopment: Dependence, Class, and Politics in Latin America*. Trans. M. D. Berdecio. New York: Monthly Review Press.

—————. 1978. *World Accumulation, 1492-1789*. New York: Monthly Review Press.

—————. 1979. *Dependent Accumulation and Underdevelopment*. New York: Monthly Review Press.

—————. 1981. *Crisis in the Third World*. New York: Holmes & Meier Publishers.

—————. 1984. *Critique and Anti-Critique: Essays on Dependence and Reformism*. New York : Praeger.

Frenkel, J.A. and Johnson, H.G. 1977. "The Monetary Approach to the Balance of Payments: Essential Concepts and Historical Origins." in J.A. Frenkel and H.G. Johnson eds. *The Monetary Approach to the Balance of Payments*, pp. 21–45. Toronto: University of Toronto Press

Friedman, M. 1953. *Essays in Positive Economics*. Chicago: University of Chicago Press.

—————. 1959. *The Demand for Money: Some Theoretical and Empirical Results*. NBER Occasional Paper, no. 68. New York: National Bureau of Economic Research.

—————. 1963. *Inflation: Causes and Consequences*. Bombay: Asia Publishing House.

—————. 1968. "The Role of Monetary Policy." *American Economic Review*. 58: 1-17.

—————. 1969. *The Optimum Quantity of Money and Other Essays*. Chicago: Aldine Publishing Co.

—————. 1971. *A Theoretical Framework for Monetary Analysis*. NBER Occasional Paper, no. 112. New York: National Bureau of Economic Research.

—————. 1973. *Money and Economic Development*. New York: Praeger.

—————. 1977. "Nobel Lecture, Inflation and Unemployment." *Journal of Political Economy*

—————. 1982. *Capitalism and Freedom*. Chicago: University of Chicago Press.

Friedman, M. 1956. ed. *Studies in the Quantity Theory of Money*. Chicago: University of Chicago Press.

Friedman, M. and Roosa, R. V. 1967. *The Balance of Payments: Free versus Fixed Exchange Rates*. Washington DC: American Enterprise Institute for Public Policy Research.

Fry, M. J. 1988. *Money, Interest, and Banking in Economic Development*. Baltimore: Johns Hopkins University Press

Goldstein, M. and Montiel, P. J. 1986. "Evaluating Fund Stabilization Programs with Multicountry Data: Some Methodological Pitfalls." *IMF Staff Papers*. 33: 304- 44.

Grunwald, J. 1961. "The 'Structuralist' School on Price Stabilization and Economic Development: The Chilean Case." in A. O. Hirschman, ed. *Latin American Issues*. New York: The Twentieth Century Fund.

Guitian, M. 1976. "The Effects of Changes in the Exchange Rate on Output, Prices, and the Balance of Payments." *Journal of International Economics*. 6: 65-74.

Guitian, M. 1981. *Fund Conditionality: Evolution of Principles and Practices*. IMF Pamphlet series, no. 38. Washington DC: International Monetary Fund.

Gylfason, T. 1987. *Credit Policy and Economic Activity in Developing Countries with IMF Stabilization Programs*. Studies in International Finance, no. 60. Princeton: International Finance Section, Department of Economics, Princeton University.

Gylfason, T. and Radetzki, M. 1991. "Does Devaluation Make Sense in the Least Developed Countries?" *Economic Development and Cultural Change*. 40 (October): 1-25.

Gylfason, T. and Risager, O. 1984. "Does Devaluation Improve the Current Account?" *European Economic Review*. 25 (June): 37-64.

Gylfason, T. and Schmid, M. 1983. "Does Devaluation cause Stagflation?" *Canadian Journal of Economics*. 16 (4): 641-54.

Haberler, G. 1949. "The Market for Foreign Exchange and the Stability of the Balance of Payments: A Theoretical Analysis." Reprinted in R. N. Cooper ed., 1969, *International Finance*. Penguin Modern Economics Readings. Harmondsworth: Penguin.

Hahn, F. 1987. "Auctioneer." In J. Eatwell, M. Milgate, and P. Newmans, eds. *The New Palgrave Dictionary of Economics*, pp. 136-38.

Hamilton, C. 1988. *Contractionary Devaluation: A Review of the Literature.* Australian National Economics Faculty of Economics and Development Economics Research, School of Pacific Studies Research, and School of Social Science. Working Paper no. 158.

Hansen, J. A. 1983. "Contractionary Devaluation, Substitution in Production and Consumption, and the Role of the Labor Market." *Journal of International Economics.* Vol. 14.

————. 1971. *Growth in Open Economies.* New York: Springer-Verlag.

Harberger, A. 1963. "The Dynamics of Inflation in Chile." C. F. Christ et al, *Measurement in Economics,* pp. 219-250. Stanford: Stanford University Press.

————. 1964. "Some Notes on Inflation." pp. 319-351 in Baer and Kerstenetsky 1964.

Harrod, R. F. 1939. "An Essay in Dynamic Theory." *Economic Journal.* 49 (193): 14–33.

————. 1952. *Towards a Dynamic Economics.* London: MacMillan.

Hayek, F. A. von. 1944. *The Road to Serfdom.* Chicago: University of Chicago Press.

Heckscher, E. F. and Ohlin, B. 1991. *Heckscher-Ohlin Trade Theory.* Trans. H. Flam and M. J. Flanders. Cambridge MA: MIT Press.

Hicks, J. R. 1937. "Mr. Keynes and the 'Classics': A Suggested Interpretation." *Econometrica,* 5(2): 147–59.

Hirschman, A. O. 1949. "Devaluation and the Trade Balance: A Note." *Review of Economics and Statistics.* 31 (1): 50-53.

————. 1957. "Economic Policy in Underdeveloped countries." *Economic Development and Cultural Change,* July: 362-70.

————. 1958. *The Strategy of Economic Development.* New Haven: Yale University Press.

————. 1965. *Journeys Toward Progress.* Garden City: Anchor Books.

————. 1968. "The Political Economy of Import-Substitution Industrialization in Latin America." *Quarterly Journal of Economics.* 82: 1-32.

————. 1971. *A Bias for Hope: Essays on Development and Latin America.* New Haven: Yale University Press.

————. 1981. *Essays in Trespassing: Economics to Politics and Beyond.* Cambridge UK: Cambridge University Press.

————. 1992. *Rival Views of Market Society and Other Recent Essays.* Paperback edition with new preface. Cambridge MA: Harvard University Press.

Hopkins, T. K. and Wallerstein, I. M. 1980. *Processes of the World-System.* Beverly Hills, CA: Sage Publications.

Hopkins, T. K. and Wallerstein, I. M. and Black, R. L. 1982. *World-Systems Analysis: Theory and Methodology.* Beverly Hills, CA: Sage Publications.

Horwich, G. and Samuelson, P. A. eds. 1974. *Trade, Stability, and Macroeconomics: Essays in Honor of Lloyd A. Metzler.* New York: Academic Press.

Hume, D. 1752. "Of the Balance of Trade." Reprinted in R. N. Cooper, ed., 1969, *International Finance.* Penguin Modern Economics Readings.

International Monetary Fund. 1977. *The Monetary Approach to the Balance of Payments.* Washington DC: International Monetary Fund.

—————. 1981. *International Capital Markets: Recent Developments and Short Term Prospects.* IMF Occasional Paper no. 7. Washington DC: International Monetary Fund

—————. 1983a. *Interest Rate Policies in Developing Countries.* IMF Occasional Paper no. 22. Washington DC: International Monetary Fund

—————. 1983b. *Recent Multilateral Debt Restructuring with Official and Bank Creditors.* IMF Occasional Paper no. 25. Washington DC: International Monetary Fund

—————. 1984. *Exchange Rate Volatility and World Trade.* IMF Occasional Paper no. 28. Washington DC: International Monetary Fund

—————. 1985. *Recent Developments in External Debt Restructuring.* IMF Occasional Paper no. 40. Washington DC: International Monetary Fund

—————. 1986. *Fund-Supported Programs, Fiscal Policy, and Income Distribution.* IMF Occasional Paper no. 46. Washington DC: International Monetary Fund

—————. 1987. *Theoretical Aspects of the Design of Fund Supported Adjustment Programs.* IMF Occasional Paper no. 55. Washington DC: International Monetary Fund

Islam, S. 1984. "Devaluation, Stabilization Policies and the Developing Countries." *Journal of Development Economics.* Vol. 14.

Ito, T. and Krueger, A. O. eds. 1993. *Trade and Protectionism.* Chicago: University of Chicago Press.

Jameson, K. P. 1986. "Latin American Structuralism: A Methodological Perspective." *World Development,* 14 (2): 223-232.

Johnson, E. S. and Johnson, H. G. 1978. *The Shadow of Keynes: Understanding Keynes, Cambridge, and Keynesian Economics.* Chicago: University of Chicago Press.

Johnson, H. G. 1955. "Economic Expansion and International Trade." *Manchester School,* 23: 95-102.

—————. 1956. "The Transfer Problem and Exchange Rate Stability." *Journal of Political Economy.* 64 (3): 212-25.

—————. 1958. *International Trade and Economic Growth: Studies in Pure Theory.* Cambridge MA: Harvard University Press.

—————. 1959. "Towards a General Theory of the Balance of Payments." Reprinted in R. N. Cooper ed., 1969, *International Finance.* Penguin Modern Economics Readings.

—————. 1962. *Money, Trade and Economic Growth: Survey Lectures in Economic Theory.* Cambridge MA: Harvard University Press.

—————. 1965. "Optimal Trade Intervention in the Presence of Domestic Distortions." In R. E. Baldwin et al, ed. *Trade, Growth and the Balance-of-Payments: Essays in Honor of Gottfried Haberler,* pp. 3-34. New York: Rand McNally.

—————. 1967a. *Economic Policies Toward Less Developed Countries.* Washington DC: Brookings Institution.

—————. 1967b. *Essays in Monetary Economics.* London: Allen & Unwin.

—————. 1971a. *Aspects of the Theory of Tariffs.* London: Allen & Unwin.

——————. 1971b. *The Two-Sector Model of General Equilibrium.* Chicago: Aldine, Atherton.

——————. 1972. *Inflation and the Monetarist Controversy.* Amsterdam: North-Holland.

——————. 1976. "Elasticity, Absorption, Keynesian Multiplier, Keynesian Policy, and Monetary approaches to Devaluation: A Simple Geometric Exposition." *American Economic Review.* 66 (3).

——————. 1977a. "The Monetary Approach to Balance of Payments Theory and Policy: Explanation and Policy Implications." *Economica,* 44 (175): 217–29

——————. 1977b. *Money, Balance-of-Payments Theory, and the International Monetary Problem.* Essays in international finance no. 124. Princeton NJ: International Finance Section, Dept. of Economics, Princeton University.

Johnson, H. G. ed. 1971. *Trade Strategy for Rich and Poor Nations.* Toronto: University of Toronto Press.

Johnson, H. G. and Frenkel, J. A. eds. 1978. *The Economics of Exchange Rates: Selected Studies.* Reading MA: Addison-Wesley.

Jones, R. W. 1967. "International Capital Movements and the Theory of Tariffs and Trade." *Quarterly Journal of Economics,* 81: 1-38.

Jones, R. W. and Neary, J. P. 1984. "The Positive Theory of International Trade." In R. W. Jones and P. B. Kenen eds. *The Handbook of International Economics, Vols. 1-3.* pp. 1-62. Amsterdam: North Holland.

Jones, R. W. and Kenen, P. B. eds. 1984-1995. *The Handbook of International Economics, Vols. 1-3.* Amsterdam: North Holland.

Kaldor, N. 1959. "Economic Problems of Chile." In N. Kaldor (1969), *Essays in Economic Policy,* Volume II, pp. 233-298. London: Duckworth. (Originally published in *El Trimestre Económico,* 21:4, October-December 1965.) Study prepared for ECLA, July-September 1956.

——————. 1964. "Foreign Trade and the Balance of Payments," and "Stabilizing the Terms of Trade in Underdeveloped Countries." In N. Kaldor, *Essays on Economic Policy Vol. 2,* pp. 23-60 and 112-30. New York: W. W. Norton.

Kalecki, M. 1954. "El problema del financiamiento del desarrollo económico." *El Trimestre Económico* 21:4 (October-December) pp. 381-401. Based on lectures delivered in Mexico City in August 1953. English version of the same paper: "The Problem of Financing Economic Development" *Indian Economic Review* No. 3 (February 1955) pp. 1-22. Collected in M. Kalecki (1976). *Essays on Developing Economies,* pp. 41-63. Atlantic Highlands NJ: Humanities Press.

——————. 1965. "The Difference between Crucial Economic Problems of Developed and Underdeveloped Non-Socialist Economies." Address given in Mexico City, June 1965. Collected in Kalecki (1976), *Essays on Developing Economies,* pp. 20-27. Atlantic Highlands NJ: Humanities Press.

——————. 1968. *Theory of Economic Dynamics.* New York: Monthly Review Press.

Kamas, L. 1992. "Devaluation, National Output, and the Trade Balance: Some Evidence from Columbia." *Weltwirtschaftliches Archives.* 128: 425-44.

Kamin, S. B. 1988. *Devaluation, External Balance, and Macroeconomic Performance: A Look at the Numbers.* Princeton Studies in International

Finance no. 62. Princeton: International Finance Section, Dept. of Economics, Princeton University.

Katzner, D. W. 1988. *Walrasian Microeconomics: An Introduction to the Economic Theory of Market Behavior.* Reading, MA: Addison-Wesley.

Keynes, J. M. 1965. [1936]. *The General Theory of Employment, Interest, and Money.* New York: Harcourt, Brace, Jovanovich.

Khan, M. S. 1990a. "The Macroeconomic Effects of Fund-Supported Adjustment Programs." *IMF Staff Papers.* 37 (2): 195-231.

——. 1990b. "Evaluating the Effects of IMF-Supported Adjustment Programs: A Survey." In K. Phylaktis and M. Pradham eds. *International Finance and the Less Developed Countries.* New York: St. Martin's Press.

Khan, M. S. and Knight, M. D. 1981. "Stabilization Programs in Developing Countries: A Formal Framework." *IMF Staff Papers.* 28 (March): 1-53.

Khan, M. S. and Lizondo J. S. 1987. "Devaluation, Fiscal Deficits, and the Real Exchange Rate." *World Bank Economic Review.* 1: 357-74.

Khan, M. S. and Montiel, P. J. 1987. "Real Exchange Rate Dynamics in a Small Primary-Exporter Country." *IMF Staff Papers* 34 (December): 687-710.

——. 1989. "Growth-Oriented Adjustment Programs: A Conceptual Framework." *IMF Staff Papers.* 36 (2): 279-306.

Khan, M. S.; Montiel, P. J.; and Haque, N. U.; ed. 1991. *Macroeconomic Models for Adjustment in Developing Countries.* Washington, D.C.: International Monetary Fund.

Khan, M. S. and Zahler, R. 1982. *Macroeconomic Effects of Changes in Barriers to Trade and Capital Flows.* Estudios e informes de la CEPAL ; 20. Santiago de Chile: ECLAC, United Nations.

Kibritçioglu, A. 2004. "On the Smithian Origins of 'New' Trade and Growth Theories." Unpublished paper available at http://dialup.ankara.edu.tr/~kibritci/wp1_smith.html. Accessed March 17, 2004.

Killick, T. ed. 1984. *The Quest for Economic Stabilization: The IMF and the Third World.* New York: St. Martin's Press.

Killick, T.; Malik, M.; and Manuel, M. 1992. "What Can We Know about the Effects of IMF Programs?" *World Economy.* 15 (September): 599-632.

Kindleberger, C. P. 1965a. *Balance-of-Payments Deficits and the International Market for Liquidity.* Essays in International Finance, no. 46. Princeton NJ: International Finance Section, Dept. of Economics, Princeton University.

——. 1965b. *International Short Term Capital Movements.* New York: Kelley.

——. 1987. *International Capital Movements: Based on the Marshall lectures given at the University of Cambridge, 1985.* Cambridge UK: Cambridge University Press.

Kirkpatrick, C.H. and Nixson, F.I. 1976. "The Origins of Inflation in Less Developed Countries: A Selective Review." In M. Parkin and G. Zis, ed., *Inflation in Open Economies.* Toronto: Toronto University Press.

Krueger, A. O. 1974. "The Political Economy of the Rent-Seeking Society." *American Economic Review,* 64: 291-303.

——. 1975. *The Benefits and Costs of Import Substitution in India: A Microeconomic Study.* Minneapolis: University of Minnesota Press.

⸻. 1977. *Growth, Distortions, and Patterns of Trade among Many Countries*. Princeton Studies in International Finance; no. 40. Princeton, N.J.: International Finance Section, Dept. of Economics, Princeton University.

⸻. 1978. *Liberalization Attempts and Consequences*. Cambridge MA: Published for the National Bureau of Economic Research by Ballinger Publishing Co.

⸻. 1979. *The Developmental Role of the Foreign Sector and Aid*. Cambridge: Harvard University Press.

⸻. 1983. *Exchange-Rate Determination*. New York: Cambridge University Press.

⸻. 1986. "How to Liberalize a Small, Open Economy." In M. Connolly and J. McDermott eds. *The Economics of the Caribbean Basin*. New York: Praeger.

⸻. 1993. *Political Economy of Policy Reform in Developing Countries*. Cambridge, MA: MIT Press.

⸻. 1995. *Trade Policies and Developing Nations*. Washington, D.C.: Brookings Institution.

Krueger, A. O. ed. 1988. *Development with Trade: LDCs and the International Economy*. San Francisco, CA: ICS Press.

Krueger, A. O. ed. 1996. *The Political Economy of Trade Protection*. Chicago: University of Chicago Press.

Krueger, A. O. et al. 1981. *Trade and Employment in Developing Countries*. Chicago: University of Chicago Press.

Krueger, A. O. and Bates, R. H. eds. 1993. *Political and Economic Interactions in Economic Policy Reform: Evidence from Eight Countries*. Cambridge, MA: Blackwell.

Krueger, A. O. and Jones, R. W. eds. 1990. *The Political Economy of International Trade*. New York: B. Blackwell.

Krugman, P. ed. 1986. *Strategic Trade Policy and the New International Economics*. Cambridge MA: MIT Press.

Krugman, P. and Taylor, L. 1978. "Contractionary Effects of Devaluation." *Journal of Economic Issues*. 8: 445-56.

Kuznets, S. S. 1961. (1950). "International Differences in Income Levels." Reprinted in B. Okun and R. W. Richardson, 1961, *Studies in Economic Development: A Book of Readings*. New York: Holt, Rinehart and Winston

⸻. 1965. *Economic Growth and Structure: Selected Essays*. New York: Norton.

⸻. 1966. *Modern Economic Growth: Rate, Structure, and Spread*. New Haven: Yale University Press.

⸻. 1971. *Economic Growth of Nations: Total Output and Production Structure*. Cambridge MA: Belknap Press of Harvard University Press.

⸻. 1973. *Population, Capital, and Growth: Selected Essays*. New York: Norton.

Lacan, J. 1988. *Ecrits techniques de Freud*. Trans. J. Forrester. New York: W.W. Norton.

Lal, D. 1985. *The Poverty of 'Development Economics.'* Cambridge: Harvard University Press.

—————. 1986. "Comment." In A. M. Choksi and D. Papageorgiou eds. *Economic Liberalization in Developing Countries,* pp.217–218. New York: Basil Blackwell

—————. 1989. "A Simple Framework for Analyzing Various Real Aspects of Stabilization and Structural Adjustment Policy." *Journal of Development Studies.* 25: 291-313.

Lane, M. 1970. ed. *Introduction to Structuralism.* New York: Basic Books.

Laursen, S. and Metzler, L. A. 1950. "Flexible Exchange Rates and the Theory of Employment." *Review of Economics and Statistics.* 32: 251-99.

Leijonhufvud, A. 1966. *On Keynesian Economics and the Economics of Keynes.* Oxford UK: Oxford University Press.

Leontief, W. W. 1966. *Input-Output Economics.* New York: Oxford University Press.

Leontieff, W. W. ed. 1977. *Structure, System, and Economic Policy: Proceedings of Section F of the British Association for the Advancement of Science, held at the University of Lancaster 1-8 September 1976.* Cambridge UK: Cambridge University Press.

Lévi-Strauss, C. 1966. *The Savage Mind.* Chicago: University of Chicago Press.

—————. 1967. *The Scope of Anthropology.* Trans. S. O. Paul and R. A. Paul. London: J. Cape.

—————. 1973. *Tristes tropiques.* Trans. J. Weightman and D. Weightman. London: J. Cape.

—————. 1979. [1969]. *The Raw and the Cooked.* Trans. J. Weightman and D. Weightman. New York: Octagon Books.

—————. 1981. *The Naked Man.* Trans. J. Weightman and D. Weightman. London: J. Cape.

—————. 1983. [1976]. *Structural Anthropology.* Trans. M. Layton. Chicago: University of Chicago Press.

—————. 1995. *The Story of Lynx.* Trans. C. Tihanyi. Chicago: University of Chicago Press.

Lewis, W. A. 1954. "Economic Development with Unlimited Supplies of Labor ." *Manchester School of Economic and Social Studies.* 22 (2): 139- 91.

—————. 1955. *The Theory of Economic Growth.* London: Allen & Unwin.

—————. 1966. *Development Planning: The Essentials of Economic Policy.* London: Allen & Unwin.

Liles, B. L. 1971. *An Introductory Transformational Grammar.* Englewood Cliffs, NJ: Prentice-Hall.

Lipsey, R. G. and Lancaster, K. 1956. "The General Theory of the Second Best." *Review of Economic Studies,* 22 (2): 139-91.

Little, I. M. D. 1982. *Economic Development: Theory, Policy, and International Relations.* New York: Basic Books.

Little, I. M. D. et al. 1993. *Boom, Crisis, and Adjustment: The Macroeconomic Experience of Developing Countries.* New York: Published for the World Bank by Oxford University Press.

Lizondo, S. J. and Montiel, P. J. 1989. "Contractionary Devaluation in Developing Countries: An Analytical Overview." *IMF Staff Papers.* 36 (1): 182-227.

Locke, J. 1980. [1690.] *Second Treatise of Government.* Ed. C. B. Macpherson. Indianapolis IN: Hackett.

Marx, K. 1977. *Capital: A Critique of Political Economy.* Trans. B. Fowkes (Vols. 1 & 3), and D. Fernbach (Vol. 2). New York: Vintage Books.

McCloskey, D. N. 1994. *Knowledge and Persuasion in Economics.* New York: Cambridge University Press.

McKinnon, R. I. 1973. *Money and Capital in Economic Development.* Washington: Brookings Institution.

————. 1984. *An International Standard for Monetary Stabilization.* Washington DC : Institute for International Economics.

————. 1991. *The Order of Economic Liberalization: Financial Control in the Transition to a Market Economy.* Baltimore: Johns Hopkins University Press.

McKinnon, R. I. ed. 1976. *Money and Finance in Economic Growth and Development: Essays in Honor of Edward S. Shaw.* New York: M. Dekker.

McKinnon, R. I. and Mathieson, D. 1981. *How to Manage a Repressed Economy.* Essays in International Finance, no. 145. Princeton, NJ: International Finance Section, Dept. of Economics, Princeton University.

Meier, G. M. 1968. *The International Economics of Development.* New York: Harper & Row.

Meier, G. M. and Baldwin, R. E. 1957. *Economic Development: Theory, History, Policy.* New York: John Wiley and Sons.

Meier, G. M. and Seers, D. eds. 1984. *Pioneers in Development.* New York: Published for the World Bank by Oxford University Press.

Meller, P. and Solimano, A. 1987. "A Simple Macro Model for a Small Economy Facing a Binding External Constraint." *Journal of Development Economics.* 26 (June): 25-35.

Minsky, H. P. 1982. *Can "It" Happen Again? Essays on Instability and Finance.* Armonk, NY: M.E. Sharpe.

————. 1986. *Stabilizing an Unstable Economy.* New Haven: Yale University Press.

Muller, J. P. and Richardson, W. J. 1982. *Lacan and Language: A Reader's Guide to Ecrits.* New York: International Universities Press.

Myint, H. 1952. "An Interpretation of Economic Backwardness." *Oxford Economic Papers,* June 1952.

————. 1958. "The 'Classical' Theory of International Trade and the Underdeveloped Countries." *Economic Journal,* 68: 317-37.

————. 1967. *The Economics of Developing Countries.* London: Hutchinson.

Myrdal, G. 1968. *Asian Drama,* Vols. 1-3. New York: Pantheon.

————. 1970. *The Challenge of World Poverty: A World Anti-Poverty Program in Outline.* New York: Pantheon Books.

Neill, R. 2004. "The Staple Theory of Canadian Economic history." Unpublished paper, available at http://www.upei.ca/~rneill/web_papers/staple_theo.html. Accessed March 17, 2004.

Nelson, R. R.; Schultz, T. P.; and Slighton, R. L. 1971. *Structural Change in a Developing Economy: Colombia's Problems and Prospects.* Princeton: Princeton University Press.

Nunenkamp, P. and Schweickert, R. 1990. "Adjustment Policies and Economic Growth in Developing Countries: Is Devaluation Contractionary?" *Weltwirtschaftliches Archiv.* 126: 474-93.

Nurkse, R. 1954. "The Problem of International Investment Today in the Light of Nineteenth-Century Experience." *Economic Journal,* 64: 744-58.
—————. 1955. *Problems of Capital Formation in Underdeveloped Countries.* 3rd ed. New York: Oxford University Press.
Okun, B. and Richardson, R. W. eds. 1961. *Studies in Economic Development: A Book of Readings.* New York: Holt, Rinehart and Winston.
Olivera, J. H.G. 1964. "On Structural Inflation and Latin American Structuralism." *Oxford Economic Papers* 16 (3): 321-332.
Oniki, H. and Uzawa, H. 1965. "Patterns of Trade and Investment in a Dynamic Model of International Trade." *Review of Economic Studies,* 32: 15-38.
Paaw, D. S. and Fei, J. C. 1973. *The Transition in Open Dualistic Economies: Theories and South East Asian Experience.* New Haven: Yale University Press.
Palma, G. 1978. "The Origins of Dependency." *World Development* 6: 881-924.
Piaget, J. 1971. [1968]. *Structuralism.* Trans. C. Maschler. New York: Basic Books.
Prebisch, R. 1962 [1949–1950]. "The Economic Development of Latin America and its Principal Problems." *Economic Bulletin for Latin America* 7 (1): 1-22.
—————. 1959. "Commercial Policies in the Underdeveloped Countries." *American Economic Review,* 44: 251-73.
—————. 1961. "Economic Development or Monetary Stability: The False Dilemma." *Economic Bulletin for Latin America* 6 (1): 1-25.
—————. 1971. *Transformacion y desarrollo, la gran tarea de America Latina.* (English version of his report to the Inter-American Development Bank). New York: Praeger.
—————. 1984. "Five Stages in My Thinking on Development." In G M. Meier and D. Seers, eds., *Pioneers in Development.* pp. 79-90. Oxford: Oxford University Press.
Ranis, G. and Schultz, T. P. eds. 1988. *The State of Development Economics: Progress and Perspectives.* New York: Basil Blackwell.
Resnick, S. A. and Wolff, R. D. 1987a. *Economics: Marxian versus Neoclassical.* Baltimore: Johns Hopkins University Press.
—————. 1987b. *Knowledge and Class: A Marxian Critique of Political Economy.* Chicago: University of Chicago Press.
—————. 1989. *Radical Economics: A Tradition of Theoretical Differences.* Working Paper 1989-5, Department of Economics, University of Massachusetts, Amherst.
Ricardo, D. 1977. *The Principles of Political Economy and Taxation.* London: Dent and Sons.
Rosentein-Rodan, P. N. 1943. "Problems of Industrialization of Eastern and South Eastern Europe." *Economic Journal,* June-September.
—————. 1967. "The Philosophy of International Investment in the Second Half of the Twentieth Century." In J. H. Adler, ed. *Capital Movements and Economic Development.* London: Macmillan.
Rosenstein-Rodan, P. N. ed. 1964. *Capital Formation and Economic Development.* Cambridge MA: MIT Press.
Rostow, W. W. 1952. *The Process of Economic Growth.* New York: Norton.
—————. 1971. *The Stages of Economic Growth: A Non-Communist Manifesto.* 2nd ed. Cambridge: Cambridge University Press.

————. 1975. *How It All Began: Origins of the Modern Economy.* New York: McGraw-Hill.

————. 1987. *Rich Countries and Poor Countries: Reflections on the Past, Lessons for the Future.* Boulder: Westview Press.

Rostow, W. W. ed. 1964. *The Economics of Take-Off into Sustained Growth: Proceedings of a Conference held by the International Economic Association.* New York: St Martin's Press.

Rousseau, J.-J. 1987. *Selections.* Indianapolis: Hackett Publishing Co.

Ruccio, D. F. 1991. "When Failure becomes Success: Class and the Debate over Stabilization and Adjustment." *World Development.* 19: 1315-1334.

Sachs, J. D. ed. 1989a. *Developing Country Debt and Economic Performance: The International Financial System.* Chicago: Published for the National Bureau of Economic Research by the University of Chicago Press.

Sachs, J. ed. 1989b. *Developing Country Debt and the World Economy.* Chicago: University of Chicago Press.

Said, E. W. 1978. *Orientalism.* New York: Pantheon Books.

Samuelson, P. A. 1939. "The Gains from International Trade." *Canadian Journal of Economics and Political Science.*

————. 1980. *Economics.* 11th ed. New York: McGraw-Hill.

Saussure, F. de. 1966. *Course in Structural Linguistics.* Ed. C. Bally and A. Sechehaye. Trans. W. Baskin. New York: McGraw-Hill.

Schultz, T. W. 1964. *Transforming Traditional Agriculture.* New Haven: Yale University Press.

Schumpeter, J. A. 1934. *The Theory of Economic Development: An Inquiry into Profits, Capital, Credit, Interest, and the Business Cycle.* Cambridge MA: Harvard University Press.

————. 1947. *Capitalism, Socialism, and Democracy.* 2nd ed. New York: Harper.

Seers, D. 1962a. "Inflation and Growth: A Summary of Experience in Latin America." *Economic Bulletin for Latin America* 7 (1): 23-51.

————. 1962b. "A Theory of Inflation and Growth in Under-Developed Economies Based on the Experience of Latin America." With Appendix: "A Note on the Structuralist School" *Oxford Economic Papers,* 14 (2): 174-195.

————. 1964. "Inflation and Growth: The Heart of the Controversy." In Baer and Kerstenetsky 1964, pp. 89-103.

Sen, A. K. 1981. *Poverty and Famines: An Essay on Entitlement and Deprivation.* New York: Oxford University Press.

————. 1984. *Resources, Values, and Development.* Cambridge MA: Harvard University Press.

————. 1987. *On Ethics and Economics.* New York: B. Blackwell.

————. 1992. *Inequality Reexamined.* Cambridge MA: Harvard University Press.

Shaikh, A. 1979. "Foreign Trade and the Law of Value." Parts 1 and 2. *Science and Society,* Fall pp. 281-302, and Winter pp. 27-57.

Shaw, E. S. 1973. *Financial Deepening in Economic Development.* New York: Oxford University Press.

Sheehey, E. J. 1986. "Unanticipated Inflation, Devaluation, and Output in Latin America." *World Development.* 14: 665-71.

Singer, H. W. 1950. "The Distribution of Gains between Investing and Borrowing Countries." *American Economic Review,* 40: 473-85.

Singer, H. W. 1964. *International Development: Growth and Change.* New York: McGraw-Hill.

——————. 1975. *The Strategy of International Development: Essays in the Economics of Backwardness.* Ed. A. Cairncross and M. Puri. London: Macmillan.

Smith, A. 1955. *An Inquiry into the Nature and Causes of the Wealth of Nations.* Great books of the Western World, v. 39. Chicago: Encyclopaedia Britannica.

Solimano, A. 1986. "Contractionary Devaluation in the Southern Cone: The Case of Chile." *Journal of Development Economics.* 23 (September): 135-51.

Solow, R. 1953. "A Note on the Price Level and Interest Rate in a Growth Model." *Review of Economic Studies,* 21 (1): 74–79.

——————. 1956. "A Contribution to the Theory of Economic Growth." *Quarterly Journal of Economics,* 70 (1): 65-94.

——————. 1970. *Growth Theory: An Exposition.* Oxford UK: Clarendon.

Sraffa, P. 1960. *Production of Commodities by Means of Commodities: Prelude to a Critique of Economic Theory.* Cambridge UK: Cambridge University Press.

Stiglitz, J. E. 1970. "Factor Price Equalization in a Dynamic Economy." *Journal of Political Economy,* 78: 456-88.

Stiglitz, J. E. and Weiss, A. 1981. "Credit Rationing in Markets with Imperfect Information." *American Economic Review,* 71: 393-410.

Stikker, D. 1968. The *Role of Private Enterprise in Investment and Promotion of Exports in Developing Countries.* New York: United Nations.

Stolper, W. and Samuelson, P. 1941. "Protection and Real Wages." *Review of Economic Studies,* 9: 58-73.

Streeten, P. 1972. [1969.] "New Approaches to Private Investment in Less Developed Countries." In J. H. Dunning, ed. *International Investment.* Harmondsworth, UK: Penguin.

Sturrock, J. 1986. *Structuralism.* London: Paladin.

Sturrock, J. ed. 1979. *Structuralism and Since: From Levi Strauss to Derrida.* Oxford: Oxford University Press.

Sunkel, O. 1958. "La inflación chilena: un enfoque heterodoxo." *El Trimestre Económico* 25:4 (October- December) pp. 570-599. Translated as "Inflation in Chile: An Unorthodox Approach." *International Economic Papers* 10 (1960) pp. 107-131.

——————. 1989. "Structuralism, Dependency, and Institutionalism: An Exploration of Common Ground and Disparities." *Journal of Economic Issues,* 23 (2).

Swan, T. W. 1956. "Economic Growth and Capital Accumulation." *Economic Record,* 32: 334-61.

Sweezy, P. M. 1972. *Modern Capitalism and Other Essays.* New York: Monthly Review.

Taylor, L. 1979. *Macro Models for Economic Development.* New York: McGraw-Hill.

——————. 1981. "IS-LM in the Tropics: Diagrammatics of the New Structuralist Macro Critique." In W. Cline and S. Weintraub eds. *Economic Stabilization in Developing Countries.*

—————. 1983. *Structuralist Macroeconomics: Applicable Models for the Third World*. New York: Basic Books.

—————. 1988. *Varieties of Stabilization Experience: Towards Sensible Macroeconomics in the Third World*. Oxford: Clarendon Press.

—————. 1989. *Stabilization and Growth in Developing Countries: A Structuralist Approach*. New York: Harwood Academic Publishers.

—————. 1991. *Income Distribution, Inflation, and Growth: Lectures on Structuralist Macroeconomic Theory*. Cambridge MA: MIT Press.

—————. 1993. "A Three Gap Analysis of Foreign Resource Flows and Developing Country Growth." In L. Taylor ed. *The Rocky Road to Reform: Adjustment, Income Distribution, and Growth in the Developing World*. pp. 9-38. Cambridge MA: MIT Press

Taylor, L. ed. 1990. *Socially Relevant Policy Analysis: Structuralist Computable General Equilibrium Models for the Developing World*. Cambridge MA: MIT Press.

Taylor, L. ed. 1993. *The Rocky Road to Reform: Adjustment, Income Distribution, and Growth in the Developing World*. Cambridge MA: MIT Press.

Taylor, L. et al. 1980. *Models of Growth and Distribution for Brazil*. New York: Published for the World Bank by Oxford University Press.

Taylor, L. and Shapiro, H. 1992. "The State and Industrial Strategy," in C. Wilber and K. Jameson eds. *The Political Economy of Development and Underdevelopment,* 5th edition. New York: McGraw-Hill.

Taylor, L.; Syrquin, M.; and Westphal, L. E. 1984. *Economic Structure and Performance: Essays in Honor of Hollis B. Chenery*. Orlando: Academic Press.

Todaro, M. P. 1989. *Economic Development in the Third World*. 4th ed. New York: Longman.

Thorp, R. 1971. "Inflation and the Financing of Economic Development" In K. Griffin, ed. *Financing Development in Latin America*, pp. 182-224. London: Macmillan.

Toye, J. F. J. 1987. *Dilemmas of Development: Reflections on the Counter-Revolution in Development Theory and Policy*. New York: Blackwell.

—————. 1995. *Structural Adjustment and Employment Policy: Issues and Experience*. Geneva: International Labour Office.

Triffin, R. 1964. "The Myths and Realities of the So-Called Gold Standard." Reprinted in R. N. Cooper, ed., 1969, *International Finance*. Penguin Modern Economics Readings.

Uzawa, H. 1961. "On a Two-Sector Model of Economic Growth." *Review of Economic Studies,* 29: 40-47.

Van Wijnbergen, S. 1982. "Stagflationary Effects of Monetary Stabilization Policies." *Journal of Development Economics,* 10 (April): 133–69.

—————. 1983. "Credit Policy, Inflation and Growth in a Financially Repressed Economy." *Journal of Development Economics,* 13 (August): 45–65

—————. 1986. "Exchange Rate Management and Stabilization Policies in Developing Countries." *Journal of Development Economics.* 23: 2.

Vaneck, J. 1971. "Economic Growth and International Trade in Pure Theory." *Quarterly Journal of Economics,* 65: 377-90.

Vickers, D. 1978. *Financial Markets in the Capitalist Process.* Philadelphia: University of Pennsylvania Press.

————. 1985. *Money, Banking, and the Macroeconomy.* Englewood Cliffs NJ: Prentice-Hall.

————. 1987. *Money Capital in the Theory of the Firm: A Preliminary Analysis.* Cambridge UK: Cambridge University Press.

Viner, J. 1963. (1953). *The Economics of Development: Lectures Delivered at the National University of Brazil.* Reprinted in A. N. Agarwala and S. P Singh eds. *The Economics of Underdevelopment.* New York: Oxford University Press.

Wachter, S. M. 1976. *Latin American Inflation: The Structuralist-Monetarist Debate.* Lexington: D.C. Heath.

Wallerstein, I. M. 1976. *Capitalist Agriculture and the Origins of the European World-Economy in the Sixteenth Century. (The Modern World System, 1.)* New York: Academic Press.

————. 1979. *The Capitalist World-Economy: Essays.* Cambridge: Cambridge University Press.

————. 1980. *Mercantilism and the Consolidation of the European World-Economy, 1600-1750. (The Modern World System, 2.)* New York: Academic Press.

————. 1983. *Historical Capitalism.* London: Verso.

————. 1989. *The Second Era of Great Expansion of the Capitalist World-Economy, 1730-1840s. (The Modern World System, 3.)* San Diego: Academic Press.

Weintraub, S. 1965. *The Foreign-Exchange Gap of the Developing Countries.* Essays in International Finance, no. 48. Princeton: International Finance Section, Dept. of Economics, Princeton University.

————. 1978. *Keynes, Keynesians, and Monetarists.* Philadelphia: University of Pennsylvania Press.

World Bank. 1991. *World Development Report.* New York: Oxford University Press.

————. 1993. *The East Asian Miracle: Economic Growth and Public Policy.* New York: Oxford University Press.

Zein-Elabdin, E. and Charusheela, S. eds. 2004. *Postcolonialism Meets Economics.* London: Routledge.

Index

For Product Safety Concerns and Information please contact our EU
representative GPSR@taylorandfrancis.com Taylor & Francis Verlag GmbH,
Kaufingerstraße 24, 80331 München, Germany

Printed and bound by CPI Group (UK) Ltd, Croydon, CR0 4YY

11/04/2025

01843977-0004